NON SANZ DROICT.

William Shakespeare

The Tragedy of OTHELLO
The Moor of Venice

With New Dramatic
Criticism and an
Updated Bibliography

Edited by Alvin Kernan

The Signet Classic Shakespeare
GENERAL EDITOR: SYLVAN BARNET

A SIGNET CLASSIC

SIGNET CLASSIC
Published by the Penguin Group
Penguin Books USA Inc., 375 Hudson Street,
New York, New York 10014, U.S.A.
Penguin Books Ltd, 27 Wrights Lane,
London W8 5TZ, England
Penguin Books Australia Ltd, Ringwood,
Victoria, Australia
Penguin Books Canada Ltd, 10 Alcorn Avenue,
Toronto, Ontario, Canada M4V 3B2
Penguin Books (N.Z.) Ltd, 182–190 Wairau Road,
Auckland 10, New Zealand

Penguin Books Ltd, Registered Offices:
Harmondsworth, Middlesex, England

Published by Signet Classic, an imprint of Dutton Signet,
a division of Penguin Books USA Inc.

38 37 36 35 34 33 32

Library of Congress Catalog Card Number: 86-60162

Printed in the United States of America

Contents

Shakespeare: Prefatory Remarks

Between the record of his baptism in Stratford on 26 April 1564 and the record of his burial in Stratford on 25 April 1616, some forty documents name Shakespeare, and many others name his parents, his children, and his grandchildren. More facts are known about William Shakespeare than about any other playwright of the period except Ben Jonson. The facts should, however, be distinguished from the legends. The latter, inevitably more engaging and better known, tell us that the Stratford boy killed a calf in high style, poached deer and rabbits, and was forced to flee to London, where he held horses outside a playhouse. These traditions are only traditions; they may be true, but no evidence supports them, and it is well to stick to the facts.

Mary Arden, the dramatist's mother, was the daughter of a substantial landowner; about 1557 she married John Shakespeare, who was a glovemaker and trader in various farm commodities. In 1557 John Shakespeare was a member of the Council (the governing body of Stratford), in 1558 a constable of the borough, in 1561 one of the two town chamberlains, in 1565 an alderman (entitling him to the appelation "Mr."), in 1568 high bailiff—the town's highest political office, equivalent to mayor. After 1577, for an unknown reason he drops out of local politics. The birthday of William Shakespeare, the eldest son of this locally prominent man, is unrecorded; but the Stratford parish register records that the infant was baptized on 26 April 1564. (It is quite possible that he was born on 23 April, but this date has probably been assigned by tradition because it is the date on which, fifty-two years later, he died.) The attendance records of the Stratford grammar school of the period are not extant, but it is reasonable to assume that the son of a local official attended the school and received substantial training in Latin. The masters of the school from Shakespeare's seventh to fifteenth years held Oxford degrees; the Elizabethan curriculum excluded mathematics and the natural sciences but taught a good deal of Latin rhetoric, logic, and literature. On 27 November 1582 a marriage license was issued to Shakespeare and Anne Hathaway, eight years his senior. The couple had a child in May, 1583. Perhaps the marriage was necessary, but perhaps the couple had earlier engaged in a formal "troth-plight," which would render their children legitimate even if no further ceremony were performed. In 1585 Anne Hathaway bore Shakespeare twins.

That Shakespeare was born is excellent; that he married and had children is pleasant; but that we know nothing about his departure from Stratford to London, or about the beginning of his theatrical career, is lamentable and must be admitted. We would gladly sacrifice details about his children's baptism for details about his earliest days on the stage. Perhaps the poaching episode is true (but it is first reported almost a century after Shakespeare's death), or perhaps he first left Stratford to be a schoolteacher, as another tradition holds; perhaps he was moved by

Such wind as scatters young men through the world,
To seek their fortunes further than at home
Where small experience grows.

In 1592, thanks to the cantankerousness of Robert Greene, a rival playwright and a pamphleteer, we have our first reference, a snarling one, to Shakespeare as an actor and playwright. Greene warns those of his own educated friends who wrote for the theater against an actor who has presumed to turn playwright:

There is an upstart crow, beautified with our feathers, that with his *tiger's heart wrapped in a player's hide* supposes he is as well able to bombast out a blank verse as the best of you, and being an absolute Johannes-factotum is in his own conceit the only Shake-scene in a country.

The reference to the player, as well as the allusion to Aesop's crow (who strutted in borrowed plumage, as an actor struts in fine words not his own), makes it clear that by this date Shakespeare had both acted and written. That Shakespeare is meant is indicated not only by "Shake-scene" but by the parody of a line from one of Shakespeare's plays, *3 Henry VI*: "O, tiger's heart wrapped in a woman's hide." If Shakespeare in 1592 was prominent enough to be attacked by an envious dramatist, he probably had served an apprenticeship in the theater for at least a few years.

In any case, by 1592 Shakespeare had acted and written, and there are a number of subsequent references to him as an actor: documents indicate that in 1598 he is a "principal comedian," in 1603 a "principal tragedian," in 1608 he is one of the "men players." The profession of actor was not for a gentleman, and it occasionally drew the scorn of university men who resented writing speeches for persons less educated than themselves, but it was respectable enough: players, if prosperous, were in effect members of the bourgeoisie, and there is nothing to suggest that Stratford considered William Shakespeare less than a solid citizen. When, in 1596, the Shakespeares were granted a coat of arms, the grant was made to Shakespeare's father, but probably William Shakespeare (who next year bought the second-largest house in town) had arranged the matter on his own behalf. In subsequent transactions he is occasionally styled a gentleman.

Although in 1593 and 1594 Shakespeare published two narrative poems dedicated to the Earl of Southampton, *Venus and Adonis* and *The Rape of Lucrece*, and may well have written most or all of his sonnets in the middle nineties, Shakespeare's literary activity seems to have been almost entirely devoted to the theater. (It may be significant that the two narrative poems were written in years when the plague closed the theaters for several months.) In 1594 he was a charter member of a theatrical company called the Chamberlain's Men (which in 1603 changed its name to the King's Men); until he retired to Stratford (about 1611, apparently), he was with this remarkably stable company. From 1599 this company acted primarily at the Globe Theatre, in which Shakespeare held a one-tenth interest. Other Elizabethan dramatists are known to have acted, but no other is known also to have been entitled to a share in the profits of the playhouse.

Shakespeare's first eight published plays did not have his name on them, but this is not remarkable; the most popular play of the sixteenth century, Thomas Kyd's *The Spanish Tragedy*, went through many editions without naming Kyd, and Kyd's authorship is known only because a book on the profession of acting happens to quote (and attribute to Kyd) some lines on the interest of Roman emperors in the drama. What is remarkable is that after 1598 Shakespeare's name commonly appears on printed plays—some of which are not his. Another indication of his popularity comes from Francis Meres, author of *Palladis Tamia: Wit's Treasury* (1598): in this anthology of snippets accompanied by an essay on literature, many playwrights are mentioned, but Shakespeare's name occurs more often than any other, and Shakespeare is the only playwright whose plays are listed.

From his acting, playwriting, and share in a theater, Shakespeare seems to have made considerable money. He put it to work, making substantial investments in Stratford real estate. When he made his will (less than a month before he died), he sought to leave his property intact to his descendants. Of small bequests to relatives and to friends (including three actors, Richard Burbage, John Heminges, and Henry Condell), that to his wife of the second-best bed has provoked the most comment; perhaps it was the bed the couple had slept in, the best being reserved for visitors. In any case, had Shakespeare not

excepted it, the bed would have gone (with the rest of his
household possessions) to his daughter and her husband.
On 25 April 1616 he was buried within the chancel of the
church at Stratford. An unattractive monument to his
memory, placed on a wall near the grave, says he died
on 23 April. Over the grave itself are the lines, perhaps by
Shakespeare, that (more than his literary fame) have kept
his bones undisturbed in the crowded burial ground where
old bones were often dislodged to make way for new:

> Good friend, for Jesus' sake forbear
> To dig the dust enclosèd here.
> Blessed be the man that spares these stones
> And cursed be he that moves my bones.

Thirty-seven plays, as well as some nondramatic poems,
are held to constitute the Shakespeare canon. The dates
of composition of most of the works are highly uncertain,
but there is often evidence of a *terminus a quo* (starting
point) and/or a *terminus ad quem* (terminal point) that
provides a framework for intelligent guessing. For example,
Richard II cannot be earlier than 1595, the publication
date of some material to which it is indebted; *The Merchant of Venice* cannot be later than 1598, the year Francis
Meres mentioned it. Sometimes arguments for a date hang
on an alleged topical allusion, such as the lines about the
unseasonable weather in *A Midsummer Night's Dream,*
II.i.81–117, but such an allusion (if indeed it is an allusion)
can be variously interpreted, and in any case there is always
the possibility that a topical allusion was inserted during
a revision, years after the composition of a play. Dates are
often attributed on the basis of style, and although conjectures about style usually rest on other conjectures,
sooner or later one must rely on one's literary sense. There
is no real proof, for example, that *Othello* is not as early
as *Romeo and Juliet,* but one feels *Othello* is later, and
because the first record of its performance is 1604, one is
glad enough to set its composition at that date and not
push it back into Shakespeare's early years. The following
chronology, then, is as much indebted to informed guess-

work and sensitivity as it is to fact. The dates, necessarily imprecise, indicate something like a scholarly consensus.

PLAYS

1588–93	*The Comedy of Errors*
1588–94	*Love's Labor's Lost*
1590–91	*2 Henry VI*
1590–91	*3 Henry VI*
1591–92	*1 Henry VI*
1592–93	*Richard III*
1592–94	*Titus Andronicus*
1593–94	*The Taming of the Shrew*
1593–95	*The Two Gentlemen of Verona*
1594–96	*Romeo and Juliet*
1595	*Richard II*
1594–96	*A Midsummer Night's Dream*
1596–97	*King John*
1596–97	*The Merchant of Venice*
1597	*1 Henry IV*
1597–98	*2 Henry IV*
1598–1600	*Much Ado About Nothing*
1598–99	*Henry V*
1599	*Julius Caesar*
1599–1600	*As You Like It*
1599–1600	*Twelfth Night*
1600–01	*Hamlet*
1597–1601	*The Merry Wives of Windsor*
1601–02	*Troilus and Cressida*
1602–04	*All's Well That Ends Well*
1603–04	*Othello*
1604	*Measure for Measure*
1605–06	*King Lear*
1605–06	*Macbeth*
1606–07	*Antony and Cleopatra*
1605–08	*Timon of Athens*
1607–09	*Coriolanus*
1608–09	*Pericles*

1609–10	*Cymbeline*
1610–11	*The Winter's Tale*
1611–12	*The Tempest*
1612–13	*Henry VIII*

POEMS

1592	*Venus and Adonis*
1593–94	*The Rape of Lucrece*
1593–1600	*Sonnets*
1600–01	*The Phoenix and the Turtle*

Shakespeare's Theater

In Shakespeare's infancy, Elizabethan actors performed wherever they could—in great halls, at court, in the courtyards of inns. The innyards must have made rather unsatisfactory theaters: on some days they were unavailable because carters bringing goods to London used them as depots; when available, they had to be rented from the innkeeper; perhaps most important, London inns were subject to the Common Council of London, which was not well disposed toward theatricals. In 1574 the Common Council required that plays and playing places in London be licensed. It asserted that

> sundry great disorders and inconveniences have been found to ensue to this city by the inordinate haunting of great multitudes of people, specially youth, to plays, interludes, and shows, namely occasion of frays and quarrels, evil practices of incontinency in great inns having chambers and secret places adjoining to their open stages and galleries,

and ordered that innkeepers who wished licenses to hold performances put up a bond and make contributions to the poor.

The requirement that plays and innyard theaters be licensed, along with the other drawbacks of playing at inns, probably drove James Burbage (a carpenter-turned-actor) to rent in 1576 a plot of land northeast of the city walls and to build here—on property outside the jurisdiction of the city—England's first permanent construction designed for plays. He called it simply the Theatre. About all that is known of its construction is that it was wood. It soon had imitators, the most famous being the Globe (1599), built across the Thames (again outside the city's jurisdiction), out of timbers of the Theatre, which had been dismantled when Burbage's lease ran out.

There are three important sources of information about the structure of Elizabethan playhouses—drawings, a contract, and stage directions in plays. Of drawings, only the so-called De Witt drawing (*c.* 1596) of the Swan—really a friend's copy of De Witt's drawing—is of much significance. It shows a building of three tiers, with a stage jutting from a wall into the yard or center of the building. The tiers are roofed, and part of the stage is covered by a roof that projects from the rear and is supported at its front on two posts, but the groundlings, who paid a penny to stand in front of the stage, were exposed to the sky. (Performances in such a playhouse were held only in the daytime; artificial illumination was not used.) At the rear of the stage are two doors; above the stage is a gallery. The second major source of information, the contract for the Fortune, specifies that although the Globe is to be the model, the Fortune is to be square, eighty feet outside and fifty-five inside. The stage is to be forty-three feet broad, and is to extend into the middle of the yard (i.e., it is twenty-seven and a half feet deep). For patrons willing to pay more than the general admission charged of the groundlings, there were to be three galleries provided with seats. From the third chief source, stage directions, one learns that entrance to the stage was by doors, presumably spaced widely apart at the rear ("Enter one citizen at one door, and another at the other"), and that in addition to the platform stage there was occasionally some sort of curtained booth or alcove allowing for "discovery" scenes, and some sort of playing space "aloft" or "above" to represent (for example) the top of a city's walls or a room above the street. Doubtless each theater had its own peculiarities, but perhaps we can talk about a "typical" Elizabethan theater if we realize that no theater need exactly have fit the description, just as no father is the typical father with 3.7 children. This hypothetical theater is wooden, round or polygonal (in *Henry V* Shakespeare calls it a "wooden *O*"), capable of holding some eight hundred spectators standing in the yard around the projecting elevated stage and some fifteen hundred additional spectators seated in the three roofed galleries. The stage, protected by a "shadow" or "heavens" or roof, is entered by two doors; behind the doors is the "tiring house" (attiring house, i.e., dressing room), and above the doors is some sort of gallery that may sometimes hold spectators but that can be used (for example) as the bedroom from which Romeo—according to a stage direction in one text—"goeth down." Some evidence suggests that a throne can be lowered onto the platform stage, perhaps from the "shadow"; certainly characters can descend from the stage through a trap or traps into the cellar or "hell." Sometimes this space beneath the platform accommodates a sound-effects man or musician (in *Antony and Cleopatra* "music of the hautboys is under the stage") or an actor (in *Hamlet* the "Ghost cries under the stage"). Most characters simply walk on and off, but because there is no curtain in front of the platform, corpses will have to be carried off (Hamlet must lug Polonius' guts into the neighbor room) or will have to fall at the rear, where the curtain on the alcove or booth can be drawn to conceal them.

Such may have been the so-called "public theater." Another kind of theater, called the "private theater" because its much greater admission charge limited its audience to the wealthy or the prodigal, must be briefly mentioned. The private theater was basically a large room, entirely roofed, and therefore artificially illuminated, with a stage at one end. In 1576 one such theater was established in Blackfriars, a Dominican priory in London that had been suppressed in 1538 and confiscated by the Crown and thus was not under the city's jurisdiction. All the actors in the Blackfriars theater were boys about eight to thirteen years old (in the public theaters similar boys played female parts, but a boy Lady Macbeth played to a man Macbeth). This private theater had a precarious existence, and ceased operations in 1584. In 1596 James Burbage, who had already made theatrical history by building the Theatre, began to construct a second Blackfriars theater. He died in 1597, and for several years this second Blackfriars theater was used by a troupe of boys, but in 1608 two of Burbage's sons and five other actors (including Shakespeare) became joint operators of the theater, using it in the winter when the open-air Globe was unsuitable. Perhaps such a smaller theater, roofed, artificially illuminated, and with a tradition of a courtly audience, exerted an influence on Shakespeare's late plays.

Performances in the private theaters may well have had intermissions during which music was played, but in the public theaters the action was probably uninterrupted, flowing from scene to scene almost without a break. Actors would enter, speak, exit, and others would immediately enter and establish (if necessary) the new locale by a few properties and by words and gestures. Here are some samples of Shakespeare's scene painting:

> This is Illyria, lady.
>
> Well, this is the Forest of Arden.
>
> This castle hath a pleasant seat; the air
> Nimbly and sweetly recommends itself
> Unto our gentle senses.

On the other hand, it is a mistake to conceive of the Elizabethan stage as bare. Although Shakespeare's Chorus in *Henry V* calls the stage an "unworthy scaffold" and urges the spectators to "eke out our performance with your mind," there was considerable spectacle. The last act of *Macbeth*, for example, has five stage directions calling for "drum and colors," and another sort of appeal

to the eye is indicated by the stage direction "Enter Macduff, with Macbeth's head." Some scenery and properties
may have been substantial; doubtless a throne was used,
and in one play of the period we encounter this direction:
"Hector takes up a great piece of rock and casts at Ajax,
who tears up a young tree by the roots and assails Hector."
The matter is of some importance, and will be glanced at
again in the next section.

The Texts of Shakespeare

Though eighteen of his plays were published during his
lifetime, Shakespeare seems never to have supervised their
publication. There is nothing unusual here; when a playwright sold a play to a theatrical company, he surrendered
his ownership of it. Normally a company would not publish the play, because to publish it meant to allow competi-
tors to acquire the piece. Some plays, however, did get
published: apparently treacherous actors sometimes pieced
together a play for a publisher, sometimes a company in
need of money sold a play, and sometimes a company
allowed a play to be published that no longer drew audiences. That Shakespeare did not concern himself with
publication, then, is scarcely remarkable; of his contem-
poraries only Ben Jonson carefully supervised the
publication of his own plays. In 1623, seven years after
Shakespeare's death, John Heminges and Henry Condell
(two senior members of Shakespeare's company, who had
performed with him for about twenty years) collected his
plays—published and unpublished—into a large volume,
commonly called the First Folio. (A folio is a volume con-
sisting of sheets that have been folded once, each sheet
thus making two leaves, or four pages. The eighteen plays
published during Shakespeare's lifetime had been issued
one play per volume in small books called quartos. Each
sheet in a quarto has been folded twice, making four
leaves, or eight pages.) The First Folio contains thirty-six
plays; a thirty-seventh, *Pericles*, though not in the Folio

is regarded as canonical. Heminges and Condell suggest in
an address "To the great variety of readers" that the
republished plays are presented in better form than in the
quartos: "Before you were abused with diverse stolen and
surreptitious copies, maimed and deformed by the frauds
and stealths of injurious impostors that exposed them;
even those, are now offered to your view cured and perfect of their limbs, and all the rest absolute in their
numbers, as he [i.e., Shakespeare] conceived them."

Whoever was assigned to prepare the texts for publication in the First Folio seems to have taken his job seriously
and yet not to have performed it with uniform care. The
sources of the texts seem to have been, in general, good
unpublished copies or the best published copies. The first
play in the collection, *The Tempest,* is divided into acts
and scenes, has unusually full stage directions and descrip-
tions of spectacle, and concludes with a list of the characters, but the editor was not able (or willing) to present
all of the succeeding texts so fully dressed. Later texts
occasionally show signs of carelessness: in one scene of
Much Ado About Nothing the names of actors, instead of
characters, appear as speech prefixes (presumably evidence that the printer's copy for this play was a prompt
copy); proofreading throughout the Folio is spotty and
apparently was done without reference to the printer's
copy; the pagination of *Hamlet* jumps from 156 to 257.

A modern editor of Shakespeare must first select his
copy; no problem if the play exists only in the Folio, but
a considerable problem if the relationship between a
quarto and the Folio—or an early quarto and a later one
—is unclear. When an editor has chosen what seems to him
to be the most authoritative text or texts for his copy, he
has not done with making decisions. First of all, he must
reckon with Elizabethan spelling. If he is not producing a
facsimile, he probably modernizes it, but ought he to preserve the old form of words that apparently were pronounced quite unlike their modern forms—"lanthorn,"
"alabaster"? If he preserves these forms, is he really pre-
serving Shakespeare's forms or perhaps those of a compositor in the printing house? What is one to do when one

finds "lanthorn" and "lantern" in adjacent lines? (The editors of this series in general, but not invariably, assume that words should be spelled in their modern forms.) Elizabethan punctuation, too, presents problems. For example, in the First Folio, the only text for the play, Macbeth rejects his wife's idea that he can wash the blood from his hand:

> no: this my Hand will rather
> The multitudinous Seas incarnardine,
> Making the Greene one, Red.

Obviously an editor will remove the superfluous capitals, and he will probably alter the spelling to "incarnadine," but will he leave the comma before "red," letting Macbeth speak of the sea as "the green one," or will he (like most modern editors) remove the comma and thus have Macbeth say that his hand will make the ocean *uniformly* red?

An editor will sometimes have to change more than spelling or punctuation. Macbeth says to his wife:

> I dare do all that may become a man,
> Who dares no more, is none.

For two centuries editors have agreed that the second line is unsatisfactory, and have emended "no" to "do": "Who dares do more is none." But when in the same play Ross says that fearful persons

> floate vpon a wilde and violent Sea
> Each way, and moue,

need "move" be emended to "none," as it often is, on the hunch that the compositor misread the manuscript? The editors of the Signet Classic Shakespeare have restrained themselves from making abundant emendations. In their minds they hear Dr. Johnson on the dangers of emending: "I have adopted the Roman sentiment, that it is more honorable to save a citizen than to kill an enemy." Some departures (in addition to spelling, punctuation, and lineation) from the copy text have of course been made, but the original readings are listed in a note following the play, so that the reader can evaluate them for himself.

The editors of the Signet Classic Shakespeare, following tradition, have added line numbers and in many cases act and scene divisions as well as indications of locale at the beginning of scenes. The Folio divided most of the plays into acts and some into scenes. Early eighteenth-century editors increased the divisions. These divisions, which provide a convenient way of referring to passages in the plays, have been retained, but when not in the text chosen as the basis for the Signet Classic text they are enclosed in square brackets [ ] to indicate that they are editorial additions. Similarly, although no play of Shakespeare's published during his lifetime was equipped with indications of locale at the heads of scene divisions, locales have here been added in square brackets for the convenience of the reader, who lacks the information afforded to spectators by costumes, properties, and gestures. The spectator can tell at a glance he is in the throne room, but without an editorial indication the reader may be puzzled for a while. It should be mentioned, incidentally, that there are a few authentic stage directions—perhaps Shakespeare's, perhaps a prompter's—that suggest locales: for example, "Enter Brutus in his orchard," and "They go up into the Senate house." It is hoped that the bracketed additions provide the reader with the sort of help provided in these two authentic directions, but it is equally hoped that the reader will remember that the stage was not loaded with scenery.

No editor during the course of his work can fail to recollect some words Heminges and Condell prefixed to the Folio:

It had been a thing, we confess, worthy to have been wished, that the author himself had lived to have set forth and overseen his own writings. But since it hath been ordained otherwise, and he by death departed from that right, we pray you do not envy his friends the office of their care and pain to have collected and published them.

Nor can an editor, after he has done his best, forget Heminges' and Condell's final words: "And so we leave you to other of his friends, whom if you need can be your guides. If you need them not, you can lead yourselves, and others. And such readers we wish him."

SYLVAN BARNET
Tufts University

Introduction

When Shakespeare wrote *Othello,* about 1604, his knowledge of human nature and his ability to dramatize it in language and action were at their height. The play offers, even in its minor characters, a number of unusually full and profound studies of humanity: Brabantio, the sophisticated, civilized Venetian senator, unable to comprehend that his delicate daughter could love and marry a Moor, speaking excitedly of black magic and spells to account for what his mind cannot understand; Cassio, the gentleman-soldier, polished in manners and gracious in bearing, wildly drunk and revealing a deeply rooted pride in his ramblings about senior officers being saved before their juniors; Emilia, the sensible and conventional waiting woman, making small talk about love and suddenly remarking that though she believes adultery to be wrong, still if the price were high enough she would sell—and so, she believes, would most women. The vision of human nature which the play offers is one of ancient terrors and primal drives—fear of the unknown, pride, greed, lust— underlying smooth, civilized surfaces—the noble senator, the competent and well-mannered lieutenant, the conventional gentlewoman.

The contrast between surface manner and inner nature is even more pronounced in two of the major characters. "Honest Iago" conceals beneath his exterior of the plain soldier and blunt, practical man of the world a diabolism so intense as to defy rational explanation—it must be taken like lust or pride as simply a given part of human nature, an anti-life spirit which seeks the destruction of everything outside the self. Othello appears in the opening acts as the very personification of self-control, of the man with so secure a sense of his own worth that nothing can ruffle the consequent calmness of mind and manner. But the man who has roamed the wild and savage world unmoved by its terrors, who has not changed countenance when the cannon killed his brother standing beside him, this man is still capable of believing his wife a whore on the slightest of evidence and committing murders to revenge himself. In Desdemona alone do the heart and the hand go together: she is what she seems to be. Ironically, she alone is accused of pretending to be what she is not. Her very openness and honesty make her suspect in a world where few men are what they appear, and her chastity is inevitably brought into question in a world where every other major character is in some degree touched with sexual corruption.

Most criticism of *Othello* has concerned itself with exploring the depths of these characters and tracing the intricate, mysterious operations of their minds. I should like, however, to leave this work to the individual reader and to the critical essays printed at the back of this volume in order to discuss, briefly, what might be called the "gross mechanics" of the play, the larger patterns in which events and characters are arranged. These patterns are the context within which the individual characters are defined, just as the pattern of a sentence is the context which defines the exact meaning of the individual words within it.

Othello is probably the most neatly, the most formally constructed of Shakespeare's plays. Every character is, for example, balanced by another similar or contrasting character. Desdemona is balanced by her opposite, Iago; love and concern for others at one end of the scale, hatred and concern for self at the other. The true and loyal soldier Cassio balances the false and traitorous soldier Iago. These balances and contrasts throw into relief the essential qualities of the characters. Desdemona's love, for example, shows up a good deal more clearly in contrast to Iago's hate, and vice versa. The values of contrast are increased and the full range of human nature displayed by extending

these simple contrasts into developing series. The essential purity of Desdemona stands in contrast to the more
"practical" view of chastity held by Emilia, and her view
in turn is illuminated by the workaday view of sensuality
held by the courtesan Bianca, who treats love, ordinarily,
as a commodity. Or, to take another example, Iago's success in fooling Othello is but the culmination of a series of
such betrayals that includes the duping of Roderigo, Brabantio, and Cassio. Each duping is the explanatory image
of the other, for in every case Iago's method and end are
the same: he plays on and teases to life some hitherto
controlled and concealed dark passion in his victim. In
each case he seeks in some way the same end, the symbolic
murder of Desdemona, the destruction in some form of
the life principle of which she is the major embodiment.

These various contrasts and parallelisms ultimately
blend into a larger, more general pattern that is the central movement of the play. We can begin to see this pattern
in the "symbolic geography" of the play. Every play, or
work of art, creates its own particular image of space and
time, its own symbolic world. The outer limits of the world
of *Othello* are defined by the Turks—the infidels, the unbelievers, the "general enemy" as the play calls them—
who, just over the horizon, sail back and forth trying to
confuse and trick the Christians in order to invade their
dominions and destroy them. Out beyond the horizon,
reported but unseen, are also those "anters vast and deserts
idle" of which Othello speaks. Out there is a land of
"rough quarries, rocks, and hills whose heads touch
heaven" inhabited by "cannibals that each other eat" and
monstrous forms of men "whose heads grow beneath their
shoulders." On the edges of this land is the raging ocean
with its "high seas, and howling winds," its "guttered rocks
and congregated sands" hidden beneath the waters to "enclog the guiltless keel."

Within the circle formed by barbarism, monstrosity,
sterility, and the brute power of nature lie the two
Christian strongholds of Venice and Cyprus. Renaissance
Venice was known for its wealth acquired by trade, its
political cunning, and its courtesans; but Shakespeare,

while reminding us of the tradition of the "supersubtle Venetian," makes Venice over into a form of *The City*, the ageless image of government, of reason, of law, and of social concord. Here, when Brabantio's strong passions and irrational fears threaten to create riot and injustice, his grievances are examined by a court of law, judged by reason, and the verdict enforced by civic power. Here, the clear mind of the Senate probes the actions of the Turks, penetrates through their pretenses to their true purposes, makes sense of the frantic and fearful contradictory messages which pour in from the fleet, and arranges the necessary defense. Act I, Scene iii—the Senate scene—focuses on the magnificent speeches of Othello and Desdemona as they declare their love and explain it, but the lovers are surrounded, guarded, by the assembled, ranked governors of Venice, who control passions that otherwise would have led to a bloody street brawl and bring justice out of what otherwise would have been riot. The solemn presence and ordering power of the Senate would be most powerfully realized in a stage production, where the senators would appear in their rich robes, with all their symbols of office, seated in ranks around several excited individuals expressing such primal passions as pride of race, fear of dark powers, and violent love. In a play where so much of the language is magnificent, rich, and of heroic proportions, simpler statements come to seem more forceful; and the meaning of *The City* is perhaps nowhere more completely realized than in Brabantio's brief, secure answer to the first fearful cries of theft and talk of copulating animals that Iago and Roderigo send up from the darkness below his window:

> What tell'st thou me of robbing? This is Venice;
> My house is not a grange.   (I.i.102–03)

Here then are the major reference points on a map of the world of *Othello*: out at the far edge are the Turks, barbarism, disorder, and amoral destructive powers; closer and more familiar is Venice, *The City*, order, law, and reason. Cyprus, standing on the frontier between barbarism and *The City*, is not the secure fortress of civilization that Venice is. It is rather an outpost, weakly defended and far out in the raging ocean, close to the "general enemy" and the immediate object of his attack. It is a "town of war yet wild" where the "people's hearts [are] brimful of fear." Here passions are more explosive and closer to the surface than in Venice, and here, instead of the ancient order and established government of *The City*, there is only one man to control violence and defend civilization—the Moor Othello, himself of savage origins and a converted Christian.

The movement of the play is from Venice to Cyprus, from *The City* to the outpost, from organized society to a condition much closer to raw nature, and from collective life to the life of the solitary individual. This movement is a characteristic pattern in Shakespeare's plays, both comedies and tragedies: in *A Midsummer Night's Dream* the lovers and players go from the civilized, daylight world of Athens to the irrational, magical wood outside Athens and the primal powers of life represented by the elves and fairies; Lear moves from his palace and secure identity to the savage world of the heath where all values and all identities come into question; and everyone in *The Tempest* is shipwrecked at some time on Prospero's magic island, where life seen from a new perspective assumes strange and fantastic shapes. At the other end of this journey there is always some kind of return to *The City*, to the palace, and to old relationships, but the nature of this return differs widely in Shakespeare's plays. In *Othello* the movement at the end of the play is back toward Venice, the Turk defeated; but Desdemona, Othello, Emilia, and Roderigo do not return. Their deaths are the price paid for the return.

This passage from Venice to Cyprus to fight the Turk and encounter the forces of barbarism is the geographical form of an action that occurs on the social and psychological levels as well. That is, there are social and mental conditions that correspond to Venice and Cyprus, and there are forces at work in society and in man that correspond to the Turks, the raging seas, and "cannibals that each other eat."

The exposure to danger, the breakdown and the ultimate reestablishment of society—the parallel on the social level to the action on the geographical level—is quickly traced. We have already noted that the Venetian Senate embodies order, reason, justice, and concord, the binding forces that hold *The City* together. In Venice the ancient laws and the established customs of society work to control violent men and violent passions to ensure the safety and well-being of the individual and the group. But there are anarchic forces at work in the city, which threaten traditional social forms and relationships, and all these forces center in Iago. His discontent with his own rank and his determination to displace Cassio endanger the orderly military hierarchy in which the junior serves his senior. He endangers marriage, the traditional form for ordering male and female relationships, by his own unfounded suspicions of his wife and by his efforts to destroy Othello's marriage by fanning to life the darker, anarchic passions of Brabantio and Roderigo. He tries to subvert the operation of law and justice by first stirring up Brabantio to gather his followers and seek revenge in the streets; and then when the two warlike forces are met, Iago begins a quarrel with Roderigo in hopes of starting a brawl. The nature of the antisocial forces that Iago represents are focused in the imagery of his advice to Roderigo on how to call out to her father the news of Desdemona's marriage. Call, he says,

> with like timorous [frightening] accent and dire yell
> As when, by night and negligence, the fire
> Is spied in populous cities.   (I.i.72–74)

Fire, panic, darkness, neglect of duty—these are the natural and human forces that destroy great cities and turn their citizens to mobs.

In Venice, Iago's attempts to create civic chaos are frustrated by Othello's calm management of himself and the orderly legal proceedings of the Senate. In Cyprus,

however, society is less secure—even as the island is more
exposed to the Turks—and Othello alone is responsible
for finding truth and maintaining order. Here Iago's poison
begins to work, and he succeeds at once in manufacturing
the riot that he failed to create in Venice. Seen on stage,
the fight on the watch between Cassio and Montano is
chaos come again: two drunken officers, charged with the
defense of the town, trying to kill each other like savage
animals, a bedlam of voices and shouts, broken, disordered
furniture, and above all this the discordant clamor of the
"dreadful" alarm bell—used to signal attacks and fire.
This success is but the prologue for other more serious
disruptions of society and of the various human relationships that it fosters. The General is set against his officer,
husband against wife, Christian against Christian, servant
against master. Justice becomes a travesty of itself as
Othello—using legal terms such as "It is the *cause*"—
assumes the offices of accuser, judge, jury, and executioner
of his wife. Manners disappear as the Moor strikes his
wife publicly and treats her maid as a procuress. The
brightly lighted Senate chamber is now replaced with a
dark Cyprus street where Venetians cut one another down
and men are murdered from behind. This anarchy finally
gives way in the last scene, when Desdemona's faith is
proven, to a restoration of order and an execution of justice on the two major criminals.

What we have followed so far is a movement expressed
in geographical and social symbols from Venice to a
Cyprus exposed to attack, from *The City* to barbarism,
from Christendom to the domain of the Turks, from order
to riot, from justice to wild revenge and murder, from
truth to falsehood. It now remains to see just what this
movement means on the level of the individual in the
heart and mind of man. Of the three major characters,
Desdemona, Othello, and Iago, the first and the last do
not change their natures or their attitudes toward life during the course of the play. These two are polar opposites,
the antitheses of each other. To speak in the most general
terms, Desdemona expresses in her language and actions
an innocent, unselfish love and concern for others. Othello

catches her very essence when he speaks of her miraculous love, which transcended their differences in age, color, beauty, and culture:

> She loved me for the dangers I had passed,
> And I loved her that she did pity them. (I.iii.166–67)

This love in its various forms finds expression not only in her absolute commitment of herself to Othello, but in her gentleness, her kindness to others, her innocent trust in all men, her pleas for Cassio's restoration to Othello's favor; and it endures even past death at her husband's hands, for she comes back to life for a moment to answer Emilia's question, "who hath done this deed?" with the unbelievable words,

> Nobody—I myself. Farewell.
> Commend me to my kind lord. O, farewell!
>   (V.ii.123–24)

Iago is her opposite in every way. Where she is open and guileless, he is never what he seems to be; where she thinks the best of everyone, he thinks the worst, usually turning to imagery of animals and physical functions to express his low opinion of human nature; where she seeks to serve and love others, he uses others to further his own dark aims and satisfy his hatred of mankind; where she is emotional and idealistic, he is icily logical and cynical. Desdemona and Iago are much more complicated than this, but perhaps enough has been said to suggest the nature of these two moral poles of the play. One is a life force that strives for order, community, growth, and light. The other is an anti-life force that seeks anarchy, death, and darkness. One is the foundation of all that men have built in the world, including *The City;* the other leads back toward ancient chaos and barbarism.

Othello, like most men, is a combination of the forces of love and hate, which are isolated in impossibly pure states in Desdemona and Iago. His psychic voyage from

Venice to Cyprus is a passage of the soul and the will from
the values of one of these characters to those of the other.
This passage is charted by his acceptance and rejection of
one or the other. He begins by refusing to have Iago as his
lieutenant, choosing the more "theoretical" though less
experienced Cassio. He marries Desdemona. Though he
is not aware that he does so, he expresses the full meaning
of this choice when he speaks of her in such suggestive
terms as "my soul's joy" and refers to her even as he is
about to kill her, as "Promethean heat," the vital fire
that gives life to the world. Similarly, he comes to know
that all that is valuable in life depends on her love, and in
the magnificent speech beginning, "O now, forever/ Farewell the tranquil mind" (III.iii.344–45), he details the
emptiness of all human activity if Desdemona be proved
false. But Iago, taking advantage of latent "Iagolike" feelings and thoughts in Othello, persuades him that Desdemona
is only common clay. Othello then gives himself over to
Iago at the end of III.iii, where they kneel together to plan
the revenge, and Othello says, "Now art thou my lieutenant." To which Iago responds with blood-chilling simplicity, "I am your own forever." The full meaning of this
choice is expressed, again unconsciously, by Othello when
he says of Desdemona,

> Perdition catch my soul
> But I do love thee! and when I love thee not,
> Chaos is come again. (III.iii.90–92)

The murder of Desdemona acts out the final destruction
in Othello himself of all the ordering powers of love,
of trust, of the bond between human beings.

Desdemona and Iago then represent two states of mind,
two understandings of life, and Othello's movement from
one to the other is the movement on the level of character and psychology from Venice to Cyprus, from *The
City* to anarchy. His return to *The City* and the defeat of
the Turk is effected, at the expense of his own life, when
he learns *what* he has killed and executes himself as the

only fitting judgment on his act. His willingness to speak of what he has done—in contrast to Iago's sullen silence—is a willingness to recognize the meaning of Desdemona's faith and chastity, to acknowledge that innocence and love do exist, and that therefore *The City* can stand, though his life is required to validate the truth and justice on which it is built.

Othello offers a variety of interrelated symbols that locate and define in historical, natural, social, moral, and human terms those qualities of being and universal forces that are forever at war in the universe and between which tragic man is always in movement. On one side there are Turks, cannibals, barbarism, monstrous deformities of nature, the brute force of the sea, riot, mobs, darkness, Iago, hatred, lust, concern for the self only, and cynicism. On the other side there are Venice, *The City*, law, senates, amity, hierarchy, Desdemona, love, concern for others, and innocent trust. As the characters of the play act and speak, they bring together, by means of parallelism and metaphor, the various forms of the different ways of life. There is, for example, a meaningful similarity in the underhanded way Iago works and the ruse by which the Turks try to fool the Venetians into thinking they are bound for Rhodes when their object is Cyprus. Or, there is again a flash of identification when we hear that the reefs and shoals that threaten ships are "ensteeped," that is, hidden under the surface of the sea, as Iago is hidden under the surface of his "honesty." But Shakespeare binds the various levels of being more closely together by the use of imagery that compares things on one level of action with things on another. For example, when Iago swears that his low judgment of all female virtue "is true, or else I am a Turk" (II.i.113), logic demands, since one woman, Desdemona, *is* true and chaste, that we account him "a Turk." He is thus identified with the unbelievers, the Ottoman Turks, and that Asiatic power, which for centuries threatened Christendom, is shown to have its social and psychological equivalent in Iago's particular attitude toward life. Similarly, when Othello sees the drunken brawl on the watchtower, he exclaims,

> Are we turned Turks, and to ourselves do that
> Which heaven hath forbid the Ottomites? (II.iii.169–70)

At the very time when the historical enemy has been defeated, his fleet providentially routed by the great storm, his characteristics—drunken loss of control, brawling over honor, disorder—begin to conquer the island only so recently and fortuitously saved. The conquest continues, and the defender of the island, Othello, convinced of Desdemona's guilt, compares his determination to revenge himself to "the Pontic Sea, / Whose icy current and compulsive course / Nev'r keeps retiring ebb" (III.iii.450–52). The comparison tells us that in his rage and hatred he has become one with the savage seas and the brute, amoral powers of nature that are displayed in the storm scene at the beginning of Act II. But most important is Othello's identification of himself at the end of the play as the "base Judean" who "threw a pearl away richer than all his tribe." The more familiar Quarto reading is "base Indian," but both words point toward the barbarian who fails to recognize value and beauty when he possesses it—the primitive savage who picks up a pearl and throws it away not knowing its worth; or the Jews (Judas may be specifically meant) who denied and crucified another great figure of love, thinking they were dealing with only a troublesome rabble-rouser. A few lines further on Othello proceeds to the final and absolute identification of himself with the infidel. He speaks of a "malignant and a turbaned Turk" who "beat a Venetian and traduced the state," and he then acknowledges that he is that Turk by stabbing himself, even as he once stabbed the other unbeliever. So he ends as both the Turk and the destroyer of the Turk, the infidel and the defender of the faith.

When Iago's schemes are at last exposed, Othello, finding it impossible for a moment to believe that a *man* could have contrived such evil, stares at Iago's feet and then says sadly, "but that's a fable." What he hopes to find when he looks down are the cloven hoofs of the devil, and had they been there he would have been an actor in a morality play, tempted beyond his strength, like many a man before him, by a supernatural power outside himself. In some ways I have schematized *Othello* as just such a morality play, offering an allegorical journey between heaven and hell on a stage filled with purely symbolic figures. This is the kind of abstraction of art toward which criticism inevitably moves, and in this case the allegorical framework is very solidly there. But Othello does not see the cloven hoofs when he looks down; he sees a pair of human feet at the end of a very human body; and he is forced to realize that far from living in some simplified, "fabulous" world where evil is a metaphysical power raiding human life from without, he dwells where evil is somehow inextricably woven with good into man himself. On his stage the good angel does not return to heaven when defeated, but is murdered, and her body remains on the bed, "cold, cold." He lives where good intentions, past services, psychic weaknesses, and an inability to see through evil cannot excuse an act, as they might in some simpler world where more perfect justice existed. In short, Othello is forced to recognize that he lives in a tragic world, and he pays the price for having been great enough to inhabit it.

Here is the essence of Shakespeare's art, an ability to create immediate, full, and total life as men actually live and experience it; and yet at the same time to arrange this reality so that it gives substance to and derives shape from a formal vision of all life that comprehends and reaches back from man and nature through society and history to cosmic powers that operate through all time and space. His plays are both allegorical and realistic at once; his characters both recognizable men and at the same time devils, demigods, and forces in nature. I have discussed only the more allegorical elements in *Othello*, the skeleton of ideas and formal patterns within which the characters must necessarily be understood. But it is equally true that the exact qualities of the abstract moral values and ideas, their full reality, exist only in the characters. It is necessary to know that Desdemona represents one particular human value, love or charity, in order to avoid making such mistakes as searching for some tragic flaw in her which would justify her death. But at the same time, if we would know what love and charity *are* in all their fullness, then our definition can only be the actions, the language, the emotions of the character Desdemona. She is Shakespeare's word for love. If we wish to know not just the obvious fact that men choose evil over good, but *why* they do so, then we must look both analytically and feelingly at all the evidence that the world offers for believing that Desdemona is false and at all the biases in Othello's mind that predispose him to believe such evidence. Othello's passage from Venice to Cyprus, from absolute love for Desdemona to extinguishing the light in her bedchamber, and to the execution of himself, these are Shakespeare's words for tragic man.

ALVIN KERNAN

The Tragedy of
OTHELLO

The Moor of Venice

The Names of the Actors

Othello, the Moor
Brabantio, father to Desdemona
Cassio, an honorable lieutenant
Iago, a villain
Roderigo, a gulled gentleman
Duke of Venice
Senators
Montano, Governor of Cyprus
Gentlemen of Cyprus
Lodovico and Gratiano, two noble Venetians
Sailors
Clown
Desdemona, wife to Othello
Emilia, wife to Iago
Bianca, a courtesan
[Messenger, Herald, Officers, Gentlemen,
   Musicians, Attendants
      Scene: Venice and Cyprus]

The Tragedy of Othello

ACT I

Scene I. [*Venice. A street.*]

Enter Roderigo and Iago.

Roderigo. Tush! Never tell me? I take it much un-
    kindly
  That thou, Iago, who hast had my purse
  As if the strings were thine, shouldst know of this.

Iago. 'Sblood,° [1] but you'll not hear me! If ever I did
    dream
  Of such a matter, abhor me.

Roderigo.   Thou told'st me   *5*
  Thou didst hold him in thy hate.

Iago.   Despise me
  If I do not. Three great ones of the city,
  In personal suit to make me his lieutenant,
  Off-capped° to him; and, by the faith of man,
  I know my price; I am worth no worse a place.   *10*
  But he, as loving his own pride and purposes,
  Evades them with a bombast circumstance,°

---

[1] The degree sign (°) indicates a footnote, which is keyed to the text by
the line number. Text references are printed in *italic* type; the annota-
tion follows in roman type. I.i.⁴ *'Sblood* by God's blood   ⁹ *Off-capped*
doffed their caps—as a mark of respect   ¹² *bombast circumstance*
stuffed, roundabout speech

Horribly stuffed with epithets of war;
Nonsuits° my mediators. For, "Certes," says he,
"I have already chose my officer." And what was
15   he?
Forsooth, a great arithmetician,°
One Michael Cassio, a Florentine,
(A fellow almost damned in a fair wife)°
That never set a squadron in the field,
20   Nor the division of a battle knows
More than a spinster; unless the bookish theoric,
Wherein the tonguèd° consuls can propose
As masterly as he. Mere prattle without practice
Is all his soldiership. But he, sir, had th' election;
25   And I, of whom his eyes had seen the proof
At Rhodes, at Cyprus, and on other grounds
Christian and heathen, must be belee'd and calmed
By debitor and creditor. This counter-caster,°
He, in good time, must his lieutenant be,
And I—God bless the mark!—his Moorship's an-
30   cient.°

Roderigo. By heaven, I rather would have been his
hangman.

Iago. Why, there's no remedy. 'Tis the curse of service:
Preferment goes by letter and affection,°
And not by old gradation,° where each second
35   Stood heir to th' first. Now, sir, be judge yourself,
Whether I in any just term am affined°
To love the Moor.

Roderigo.   I would not follow him then.

---

14 *Nonsuits* rejects **16** *arithmetician* theorist (rather than practical)
18 *A . . . wife* (a much-disputed passage, which is probably best taken as
a general sneer at Cassio as a dandy and a ladies' man. But in the story
from which Shakespeare took his plot the counterpart of Cassio is
married, and it may be that at the beginning of the play Shakespeare
had decided to keep him married but later changed his mind)
22 *tonguèd* eloquent **28** *counter-caster* i.e., a bookkeeper who *casts*
(reckons up) figures on a *counter* (abacus) **30** *ancient* standard-bearer;
an underofficer **33** *letter and affection* recommendations (from men
of power) and personal preference **34** *old gradation* seniority
36 *affined* bound

Iago. O, sir, content you.
    I follow him to serve my turn upon him.
    We cannot all be masters, nor all masters   40
    Cannot be truly followed. You shall mark
    Many a duteous and knee-crooking° knave
    That, doting on his own obsequious bondage,
    Wears out his time, much like his master's ass,
    For naught but provender; and when he's old,
       cashiered.   45
    Whip me such honest knaves! Others there are
    Who, trimmed in forms and visages of duty,
    Keep yet their hearts attending on themselves,
    And, throwing but shows of service on their lords,
    Do well thrive by them, and when they have lined
       their coats,   50
    Do themselves homage. These fellows have some
       soul;
    And such a one do I profess myself. For, sir,
    It is as sure as you are Roderigo,
    Were I the Moor, I would not be Iago.
    In following him, I follow but myself.   55
    Heaven is my judge, not I for love and duty,
    But seeming so, for my peculiar° end;
    For when my outward action doth demonstrate
    The native° act and figure of my heart
    In complement extern,° 'tis not long after   60
    But I will wear my heart upon my sleeve
    For daws to peck at; I am not what I am.

Roderigo. What a full fortune does the thick-lips owe°
    If he can carry't thus!

Iago.   Call up her father,
    Rouse him. Make after him, poison his delight,   65
    Proclaim him in the streets, incense her kinsmen,
    And though he in a fertile climate dwell,
    Plague him with flies; though that his joy be joy,

---

⁴² *knee-crooking* bowing   ⁵⁷ *peculiar* personal   ⁵⁹ *native* natural, innate
⁶⁰ *complement extern* outward appearances   ⁶³ *owe* own

Yet throw such chances of vexation on't
70   As it may lose some color.

Roderigo. Here is her father's house. I'll call aloud.

Iago. Do, with like timorous° accent and dire yell
As when, by night and negligence, the fire
Is spied in populous cities.

Roderigo. What, ho, Brabantio! Signior Brabantio,
75   ho!

Iago. Awake! What, ho, Brabantio! Thieves! Thieves!
Look to your house, your daughter, and your bags!
Thieves! Thieves!

Brabantio above° [at a window].

Brabantio. What is the reason of this terrible summons?
80   What is the matter there?

Roderigo. Signior, is all your family within?

Iago. Are your doors locked?

Brabantio.   Why, wherefore ask you
this?

Iago. Zounds, sir, y'are robbed! For shame. Put on
your gown!
Your heart is burst, you have lost half your soul.
85   Even now, now, very now, an old black ram
Is tupping your white ewe. Arise, arise!
Awake the snorting citizens with the bell,
Or else the devil will make a grandsire of you.
Arise, I say!

Brabantio.   What, have you lost your wits?

Roderigo. Most reverend signior, do you know my
90   voice?

Brabantio. Not I. What are you?

---

⁷² *timorous* frightening   ⁷⁸ s.d. *above* (i.e., on the small upper stage
above and to the rear of the main platform stage, which resembled the
projecting upper story of an Elizabethan house)

Roderigo. My name is Roderigo.

Brabantio.   The worser welcome!
I have charged thee not to haunt about my doors.
In honest plainness thou hast heard me say
My daughter is not for thee; and now, in madness,   *95*
Being full of supper and distemp'ring draughts,°
Upon malicious knavery dost thou come
To start° my quiet.

Roderigo. Sir, sir, sir——

Brabantio.   But thou must needs be sure
My spirits and my place° have in their power   *100*
To make this bitter to thee.

Roderigo.   Patience, good sir.

Brabantio. What tell'st thou me of robbing? This is
    Venice;
My house is not a grange.°

Roderigo.   Most grave Brabantio,
In simple and pure soul I come to you.

Iago. Zounds, sir, you are one of those that will not   *105*
serve God if the devil bid you. Because we come
to do you service and you think we are ruffians,
you'll have your daughter covered with a Barbary°
horse, you'll have your nephews° neigh to you,
you'll have coursers for cousins,° and gennets for   *110*
germans.°

Brabantio. What profane wretch art thou?

Iago. I am one, sir, that comes to tell you your daughter
and the Moor are making the beast with two backs.

Brabantio. Thou art a villain.

Iago.   You are—a senator.   *115*

Brabantio. This thou shalt answer. I know thee,
    Roderigo.

Roderigo. Sir, I will answer anything. But I beseech
    you,
If't be your pleasure and most wise consent,
As partly I find it is, that your fair daughter,
120 At this odd-even° and dull watch o' th' night,
Transported, with no worse nor better guard
But with a knave of common hire, a gondolier,
To the gross clasps of a lascivious Moor—
If this be known to you, and your allowance,
125 We then have done you bold and saucy wrongs;
But if you know not this, my manners tell me
We have your wrong rebuke. Do not believe
That from the sense of all civility°
I thus would play and trifle with your reverence.
130 Your daughter, if you have not given her leave,
I say again, hath made a gross revolt,
Tying her duty, beauty, wit, and fortunes
In an extravagant° and wheeling stranger
Of here and everywhere. Straight satisfy yourself.
135 If she be in her chamber, or your house,
Let loose on me the justice of the state
For thus deluding you.

Brabantio.   Strike on the tinder, ho!
Give me a taper! Call up all my people!
This accident° is not unlike my dream.
140 Belief of it oppresses me already.
Light, I say! Light!   *Exit* [*above*].

Iago.   Farewell, for I must leave you.
It seems not meet, nor wholesome to my place,
To be produced—as, if I stay, I shall—
Against the Moor. For I do know the State,
145 However this may gall him with some check,°
Cannot with safety cast° him; for he's embarked
With such loud reason to the Cyprus wars,

---

¹²⁰ *odd-even* between night and morning   ¹²⁸ *sense of all civility* feeling of what is proper   ¹³³ *extravagant* vagrant, wandering (Othello is not Venetian and thus may be considered a wandering soldier of fortune)   ¹³⁹ *accident* happening   ¹⁴⁵ *check* restraint   ¹⁴⁶ *cast* dismiss

Which even now stands in act,° that for their souls
Another of his fathom° they have none
To lead their business; in which regard, 150
Though I do hate him as I do hell-pains,
Yet, for necessity of present life,
I must show out a flag and sign of love,
Which is indeed but sign. That you shall surely find
 him,
Lead to the Sagittary° the raisèd search; 155
And there will I be with him. So farewell. *Exit.*

*Enter Brabantio [in his nightgown], with Servants
                    and torches.*

Brabantio. It is too true an evil. Gone she is;
 And what's to come of my despisèd time
 Is naught but bitterness. Now, Roderigo,
 Where didst thou see her?—O unhappy girl!— 160
 With the Moor, say'st thou?—Who would be a
  father?—
 How didst thou know 'twas she?—O, she deceives
  me
 Past thought!—What said she to you? Get moe°
  tapers!
 Raise all my kindred!—Are they married, think
  you?

Roderigo. Truly I think they are. 165

Brabantio. O heaven! How got she out? O treason of
  the blood!
 Fathers, from hence trust not your daughters' minds
 By what you see them act.° Is there not charms
 By which the property° of youth and maidhood
 May be abused? Have you not read, Roderigo, 170
 Of some such thing?

Roderigo.   Yes, sir, I have indeed.

Brabantio. Call up my brother.—O, would you had
  had her!—

---

¹⁴⁸ *stands in act* takes place ¹⁴⁹ *fathom* ability ¹⁵⁵ *Sagittary* (probably
the name of an inn) ¹⁶³ *moe* more ¹⁶⁸ *act* do ¹⁶⁹ *property* true
nature

Some one way, some another.—Do you know
Where we may apprehend her and the Moor?

175 *Roderigo.* I think I can discover him, if you please
To get good guard and go along with me.

Brabantio. Pray you lead on. At every house I'll call;
I may command at most.—Get weapons, ho!
And raise some special officers of might.—
180 On, good Roderigo; I will deserve your pains.°

Exeunt.

Scene II. [*A street.*]

Enter Othello, Iago, Attendants with torches.

Iago. Though in the trade of war I have slain men,
Yet do I hold it very stuff° o' th' conscience
To do no contrived murder. I lack iniquity
Sometime to do me service. Nine or ten times
I had thought t' have yerked° him here, under the
5   ribs.

Othello. 'Tis better as it is.

Iago.   Nay, but he prated,
And spoke such scurvy and provoking terms
Against your honor, that with the little godliness
I have
I did full hard forbear him. But I pray you, sir,
10   Are you fast married? Be assured of this,
That the magnifico° is much beloved,
And hath in his effect a voice potential
As double as the Duke's.° He will divorce you,
Or put upon you what restraint or grievance

180 *deserve your pains* be worthy of (and reward) your efforts
I.ii.² *stuff* essence ⁵ *yerked* stabbed ¹¹ *magnifico* nobleman ¹²⁻¹³ *hath
. . . Duke's* i.e., can be as effective as the Duke

    The law, with all his might to enforce it on,   *15*
    Will give him cable.°

Othello.   Let him do his spite.
    My services which I have done the Signiory°
    Shall out-tongue his complaints. 'Tis yet to know° —
    Which when I know that boasting is an honor
    I shall promulgate—I fetch my life and being   *20*
    From men of royal siege;° and my demerits°
    May speak unbonneted to as proud a fortune
    As this that I have reached.° For know, Iago,
    But that I love the gentle Desdemona,
    I would not my unhousèd° free condition   *25*
    Put into circumscription and confine
    For the seas' worth. But look, what lights come
       yond?

       Enter Cassio, with [Officers and] torches.

Iago. Those are the raisèd father and his friends.
    You were best go in.

Othello.   Not I. I must be found.
    My parts, my title, and my perfect soul°   *30*
    Shall manifest me rightly. Is it they?

Iago. By Janus, I think no.

Othello. The servants of the Duke? And my lieutenant?
    The goodness of the night upon you, friends.
    What is the news?

Cassio.   The Duke does greet you, general;   *35*
    And he requires your haste-posthaste appearance
    Even on the instant.

Othello.   What is the matter, think you?

Cassio. Something from Cyprus, as I may divine.
    It is a business of some heat. The galleys

---

16 *cable* range, scope   17 *Signiory* the rulers of Venice   18 *yet to know* unknown as yet   21 *siege* rank   21 *demerits* deserts   22–23 *May . . . reached,* i.e., are the equal of the family I have married into   25 *unhousèd* unconfined   30 *perfect soul* clear, unflawed conscience

40   Have sent a dozen sequent° messengers
        This very night at one another's heels,
        And many of the consuls, raised and met,
        Are at the Duke's already. You have been hotly
            called for.
        When, being not at your lodging to be found,
45   The Senate hath sent about three several° quests
        To search you out.

Othello.   'Tis well I am found by you.
        I will but spend a word here in the house,
        And go with you.   [*Exit.*]

Cassio.   Ancient, what makes he here?
Iago. Faith, he tonight hath boarded a land carack.°
50   If it prove lawful prize, he's made forever.

Cassio. I do not understand.

Iago.   He's married.

Cassio.   To who?
                    [*Enter Othello.*]

Iago. Marry,° to—Come, captain, will you go?

Othello.   Have with you.

Cassio. Here comes another troop to seek for you.

        Enter Brabantio, Roderigo, with Officers and torches.

Iago. It is Brabantio. General, be advised.
        He comes to bad intent.

55 Othello.   Holla! Stand there!

Roderigo. Signior, it is the Moor.

Brabantio.   Down with him, thief!
                        [*They draw swords.*]

Iago. You, Roderigo? Come, sir, I am for you.

Othello. Keep up your bright swords, for the dew will
        rust them.

---

40 *sequent* successive   45 *several* separate   49 *carack* treasure ship
52 *Marry* By Mary (an interjection)

Good signior, you shall more command with years
Than with your weapons.   60

Brabantio. O thou foul thief, where hast thou stowed
     my daughter?
Damned as thou art, thou hast enchanted her!
For I'll refer me to all things of sense,°
If she in chains of magic were not bound,
Whether a maid so tender, fair, and happy,   65
So opposite to marriage that she shunned
The wealthy, curlèd darlings of our nation,
Would ever have, t' incur a general mock,°
Run from her guardage to the sooty bosom
Of such a thing as thou—to fear, not to delight.   70
Judge me the world if 'tis not gross in sense°
That thou hast practiced ° on her with foul charms,
Abused her delicate youth with drugs or minerals
That weaken motion.° I'll have't disputed on;
'Tis probable, and palpable to thinking.   75
I therefore apprehend and do attach° thee
For an abuser of the world, a practicer
Of arts inhibited and out of warrant.°
Lay hold upon him. If he do resist,
Subdue him at his peril.

Othello.   Hold your hands,   80
Both you of my inclining and the rest.
Were it my cue to fight, I should have known it
Without a prompter. Whither will you that I go
To answer this your charge?

Brabantio.   To prison, till fit time
Of law and course of direct session   85
Call thee to answer.

Othello.   What if I do obey?
How may the Duke be therewith satisfied,
Whose messengers are here about my side

---

[63] *refer . . . sense* i.e., base (my argument) on all ordinary understanding of nature   [68] *general mock* public shame   [71] *gross in sense* obvious   [72] *practiced* used tricks   [74] *motion* thought, i.e., reason [76] *attach* arrest   [78] *inhibited . . . warrant* prohibited and illegal (black magic)

immediate

    Upon some present° business of the state
    To bring me to him?

90 *Officer.*   'Tis true, most worthy signior.
    The Duke's in council, and your noble self
    I am sure is sent for.

    Brabantio.   How? The Duke in council?
    In this time of the night? Bring him away.
    Mine's not an idle cause. The Duke himself,
95 Or any of my brothers° of the state,
    Cannot but feel this wrong as 'twere their own;
    For if such actions may have passage free,
    Bondslaves and pagans shall our statesmen be.
                                 Exeunt.

Scene III. [*A council chamber.*]

*Enter Duke, Senators, and Officers [set at a table,
with lights and Attendants].*

Duke. There's no composition° in this news
    That gives them credit.°

First Senator.   Indeed, they are disproportioned.
    My letters say a hundred and seven galleys.

Duke. And mine a hundred forty.

Second Senator.   And mine two hundred.
5 But though they jump° not on a just accompt° —
    As in these cases where the aim° reports
    'Tis oft with difference—yet do they all confirm
    A Turkish fleet, and bearing up to Cyprus.

Duke. Nay, it is possible enough to judgment.°
10 I do not so secure me in the error,

89 *present* immediate 95 *brothers* i.e., the other senators I.iii.¹ *compo-sition* agreement ² *gives them credit* makes them believable 5 *jump* agree 5 *just accompt* exact counting 6 *aim* approximation 9 *to judg-ment* when carefully considered

But the main article I do approve
In fearful sense.°

Sailor. (*Within*) What, ho! What, ho! What, ho!

Enter Sailor.

Officer. A messenger from the galleys.

Duke.   Now? What's the business?

Sailor. The Turkish preparation makes for Rhodes.
So was I bid report here to the State   15
By Signior Angelo.

Duke. How say you by this change?

First Senator.   This cannot be
By no assay of reason. 'Tis a pageant°
To keep us in false gaze.° When we consider
Th' importancy of Cyprus to the Turk,   20
And let ourselves again but understand
That, as it more concerns the Turk than Rhodes,
So may he with more facile question° bear it,
For that it stands not in such warlike brace,°
But altogether lacks th' abilities   25
That Rhodes is dressed in. If we make thought of
   this, ·
We must not think the Turk is so unskillful
To leave that latest which concerns him first,
Neglecting an attempt of ease and gain
To wake and wage a danger profitless.   30

Duke. Nay, in all confidence he's not for Rhodes.

Officer. Here is more news.

Enter a Messenger.

Messenger. The Ottomites, reverend and gracious,
Steering with due course toward the isle of Rhodes,
Have there injointed them with an after° fleet.   35

10-12 *I do . . . sense* i.e., just because the numbers disagree in the reports,
I do not doubt that the principal information (that the Turkish fleet is
out) is fearfully true   18 *pageant* show, pretense   19 *in false gaze* looking the wrong way   23 *facile question* easy struggle   24 *warlike brace*
"military posture"   35 *after* following

First Senator. Ay, so I thought. How many, as you
 guess?

Messenger. Of thirty sail; and now they do restem
 Their backward course, bearing with frank ap-
  pearance
 Their purposes toward Cyprus. Signior Montano,
40 Your trusty and most valiant servitor,
 With his free duty° recommends° you thus,
 And prays you to believe him.

Duke. 'Tis certain then for Cyprus.
 Marcus Luccicos, is not he in town?

45 *First Senator.* He's now in Florence.

Duke. Write from us to him; post-posthaste dispatch.

First Senator. Here comes Brabantio and the valiant
 Moor.

  Enter Brabantio, Othello, Cassio, Iago, Roderigo,
    and Officers.

Duke. Valiant Othello, we must straight° employ you
 Against the general° enemy Ottoman.
 [*To Brabantio*] I did not see you. Welcome, gentle
50 signior.
 We lacked your counsel and your help tonight.

Brabantio. So did I yours. Good your grace, pardon
 me.
 Neither my place, nor aught I heard of business,
 Hath raised me from my bed; nor doth the general
  care
55 Take hold on me; for my particular grief
 Is of so floodgate and o'erbearing nature
 That it engluts and swallows other sorrows,
 And it is still itself.

Duke.   Why, what's the matter?

Brabantio. My daughter! O, my daughter!

41 *free duty* unlimited respect   41 *recommends* informs   48 *straight* at
once   49 *general* universal

Senators.   Dead?

Brabantio.   Ay, to me.
  She is abused, stol'n from me, and corrupted   60
  By spells and medicines bought of mountebanks;
  For nature so prepost'rously to err,
  Being not deficient, blind, or lame of sense,
  Sans° witchcraft could not.

Duke. Whoe'er he be that in this foul proceeding   65
  Hath thus beguiled your daughter of herself,
  And you of her, the bloody book of law
  You shall yourself read in the bitter letter
  After your own sense; yea, though our proper° son
  Stood in your action.°

Brabantio.   Humbly I thank your Grace.   70
  Here is the man—this Moor, whom now, it seems,
  Your special mandate for the state affairs
  Hath hither brought.

All.   We are very sorry for't.

Duke. [*To Othello*] What in your own part can you
  say to this?

Brabantio. Nothing, but this is so.   75

Othello. Most potent, grave, and reverend signiors,
  My very noble and approved° good masters,
  That I have ta'en away this old man's daughter,
  It is most true; true I have married her.
  The very head and front° of my offending   80
  Hath this extent, no more. Rude am I in my speech,
  And little blessed with the soft phrase of peace,
  For since these arms of mine had seven years' pith°
  Till now some nine moons wasted,° they have used
  Their dearest° action in the tented field;   85
  And little of this great world can I speak

More than pertains to feats of broils and battle;
And therefore little shall I grace my cause
In speaking for myself. Yet, by your gracious
     patience,
90 I will a round° unvarnished tale deliver
Of my whole course of love—what drugs, what
     charms,
What conjuration, and what mighty magic,
For such proceeding I am charged withal,
I won his daughter—

Brabantio.   A maiden never bold,
95 Of spirit so still and quiet that her motion
Blushed at herself;° and she, in spite of nature,
Of years, of country, credit, everything,
To fall in love with what she feared to look on!
It is a judgment maimed and most imperfect
100 That will confess perfection so could err
Against all rules of nature, and must be driven
To find out practices of cunning hell
Why this should be. I therefore vouch again
That with some mixtures pow'rful o'er the blood,
105 Or with some dram, conjured to this effect,
He wrought upon her.

Duke.   To vouch this is no proof,
Without more wider and more overt test
Than these thin habits° and poor likelihoods
Of modern° seeming do prefer against him.

110 *First Senator.* But, Othello, speak.
Did you by indirect and forcèd courses
Subdue and poison this young maid's affections?
Or came it by request, and such fair question°
As soul to soul affordeth?

Othello.   I do beseech you,
115 Send for the lady to the Sagittary

---

⁹⁰ *round* blunt   ⁹⁵⁻⁹⁶ *her motion/Blushed at herself* i.e., she was so
modest that she blushed at every thought (and movement)   ¹⁰⁸ *habits*
clothing   ¹⁰⁹ *modern* trivial   ¹¹³ *question* discussion

And let her speak of me before her father.
If you do find me foul in her report,
The trust, the office, I do hold of you
Not only take away, but let your sentence
Even fall upon my life.

Duke.   Fetch Desdemona hither.   120

Othello. Ancient, conduct them; you best know the
 place.
     [Exit Iago, with two or three Attendants.]

And till she come, as truly as to heaven
I do confess the vices of my blood,
So justly to your grave ears I'll present
How I did thrive in this fair lady's love,   125
And she in mine.

Duke.   Say it, Othello.

Othello. Her father loved me; oft invited me;
Still° questioned me the story of my life
From year to year, the battle, sieges, fortune
That I have passed.   130
I ran it through, even from my boyish days
To th' very moment that he bade me tell it.
Wherein I spoke of most disastrous chances,
Of moving accidents by flood and field,
Of hairbreadth scapes i' th' imminent° deadly
 breach,   135
Of being taken by the insolent foe
And sold to slavery, of my redemption thence
And portance° in my travel's history,
Wherein of anters° vast and deserts idle,°
Rough quarries, rocks, and hills whose heads touch
 heaven,   140
It was my hint to speak. Such was my process.
And of the Cannibals that each other eat,
The Anthropophagi,° and men whose heads

---

128 *Still* regularly 135 *imminent* threatening 138 *portance* manner of
acting 139 *anters* caves 139 *idle* empty, sterile 143 *Anthropophagi*
man-eaters

      Grew beneath their shoulders. These things to hear

145   Would Desdemona seriously incline;
      But still the house affairs would draw her thence;
      Which ever as she could with haste dispatch,
      She'd come again, and with a greedy ear
      Devour up my discourse. Which I observing,

150   Took once a pliant hour, and found good means
      To draw from her a prayer of earnest heart
      That I would all my pilgrimage dilate,°
      Whereof by parcels she had something heard,
      But not intentively.° I did consent,

155   And often did beguile her of her tears
      When I did speak of some distressful stroke
      That my youth suffered. My story being done,
      She gave me for my pains a world of kisses.
      She swore in faith 'twas strange, 'twas passing°
         strange;

160   'Twas pitiful, 'twas wondrous pitiful.
      She wished she had not heard it; yet she wished
      That heaven had made her such a man. She thanked
         me,
      And bade me, if I had a friend that loved her,
      I should but teach him how to tell my story,

165   And that would woo her. Upon this hint I spake.
      She loved me for the dangers I had passed,
      And I loved her that she did pity them.
      This only is the witchcraft I have used.
      Here comes the lady. Let her witness it.

             Enter Desdemona, Iago, Attendants.

170 *Duke.* I think this tale would win my daughter too.
      Good Brabantio, take up this mangled matter at the
        best.°
      Men do their broken weapons rather use
      Than their bare hands.

---

152 *dilate* relate in full   154 *intentively* at length and in sequence
159 *passing* surpassing   171 *Take . . . best* i.e., make the best of this disaster

Brabantio.   I pray you hear her speak.
   If she confess that she was half the wooer,
   Destruction on my head if my bad blame   *175*
   Light on the man. Come hither, gentle mistress.
   Do you perceive in all this noble company
   Where most you owe obedience?

Desdemona.   My noble father,
   I do perceive here a divided duty.
   To you I am bound for life and education;   *180*
   My life and education both do learn me
   How to respect you. You are the lord of duty,
   I am hitherto your daughter. But here's my husband,
   And so much duty as my mother showed
   To you, preferring you before her father,   *185*
   So much I challenge° that I may profess
   Due to the Moor my lord.

Brabantio.   God be with you. I have done.
   Please it your Grace, on to the state affairs.
   I had rather to adopt a child than get° it.
   Come hither, Moor.   *190*
   I here do give thee that with all my heart
   Which, but thou hast already, with all my heart
   I would keep from thee. For your sake,° jewel,
   I am glad at soul I have no other child,
   For thy escape would teach me tyranny,   *195*
   To hang clogs on them. I have done, my lord.

Duke. Let me speak like yourself and lay a sentence°
   Which, as a grise° or step, may help these lovers.
   When remedies are past, the griefs are ended
   By seeing the worst, which late on hopes depended.°   *200*
   To mourn a mischief that is past and gone
   Is the next° way to draw new mischief on.
   What cannot be preserved when fortune takes,

---

¹⁸⁶ *challenge* claim as right   ¹⁸⁹ *get* beget   ¹⁹³ *For your sake* because of you   ¹⁹⁷ *lay a sentence* provide a maxim   ¹⁹⁸ *grise* step   ²⁰⁰ *late on hopes depended* was supported by hope (of a better outcome) until lately   ²⁰² *next* closest, surest

Patience her injury a mock'ry makes.
The robbed that smiles, steals something from the
205   thief;
He robs himself that spends a bootless° grief.

Brabantio. So let the Turk of Cyprus us beguile:
We lose it not so long as we can smile.
He bears the sentence well that nothing bears
210   But the free comfort which from thence he hears;
But he bears both the sentence and the sorrow
That to pay grief must of poor patience borrow.
These sentences, to sugar, or to gall,
Being strong on both sides, are equivocal.
215   But words are words. I never yet did hear
That the bruisèd heart was piercèd° through the ear.
I humbly beseech you, proceed to th' affairs of state.

Duke. The Turk with a most mighty preparation makes
for Cyprus. Othello, the fortitude° of the place is
220   best known to you; and though we have there a
substitute° of most allowed sufficiency,° yet opinion, a more sovereign mistress of effects, throws a
more safer voice on you.° You must therefore be
content to slubber° the gloss of your new fortunes
225   with this more stubborn and boisterous° expedition.

Othello. The tyrant Custom, most grave senators,
Hath made the flinty and steel couch of war
My thrice-driven° bed of down. I do agnize°
A natural and prompt alacrity
230   I find in hardness and do undertake
This present wars against the Ottomites.

---

206 *bootless* valueless   216 *piercèd* (some editors emend to *pieced*, i.e.,
"healed." But *pierced* makes good sense: Brabantio is saying in effect
that his heart cannot be further hurt [pierced] by the indignity of the
useless, conventional advice the Duke offers him. *Pierced* can also
mean, however, "lanced" in the medical sense, and would then mean
"treated")   219 *fortitude* fortification   221 *substitute* viceroy   221 *most
allowed sufficiency* generally acknowledged capability   221-23 *opinion
. . . you* i.e., the general opinion, which finally controls affairs, is that
you would be the best man in this situation   224 *slubber* besmear
225 *stubborn and boisterous* rough and violent   228 *thrice-driven* i.e.,
softest   228 *agnize* know in myself

Most humbly, therefore, bending to your state,
I crave fit disposition for my wife,
Due reference of place, and exhibition,°
With such accommodation and besort   235
As levels with° her breeding.

Duke.   Why, at her father's.

Brabantio. I will not have it so.

Othello.   Nor I.

Desdemona.   Nor would I there reside,
To put my father in impatient thoughts
By being in his eye. Most gracious Duke,
To my unfolding° lend your prosperous° ear,   240
And let me find a charter° in your voice,
T' assist my simpleness.

Duke.   What would you, Desdemona?

Desdemona. That I love the Moor to live with him,
My downright violence, and storm of fortunes,
May trumpet to the world. My heart's subdued   245
Even to the very quality of my lord.°
I saw Othello's visage in his mind,
And to his honors and his valiant parts
Did I my soul and fortunes consecrate.
So that, dear lords, if I be left behind,   250
A moth of peace, and he go to the war,
The rites° for why I love him are bereft me,
And I a heavy interim shall support
By his dear absence. Let me go with him.

Othello. Let her have your voice.°   255
Vouch with me, heaven, I therefore beg it not
To please the palate of my appetite,
Nor to comply with heat° —the young affects°

---

²³⁴ *exhibition* grant of funds   ²³⁶ *levels with* is suitable to   ²⁴⁰ *unfolding* explanation   ²⁴⁰ *prosperous* favoring   ²⁴¹ *charter* permission
²⁴⁵⁻⁴⁶ *My . . . lord* i.e., I have become one in nature and being with the man I married (therefore, I too would go to the wars like a soldier)
²⁵² *rites* (may refer either to the marriage rites or to the rites, formalities, of war)   ²⁵⁵ *voice* consent   ²⁵⁸ *heat* lust   ²⁵⁸ *affects* passions

In me defunct—and proper satisfaction;°
260　But to be free and bounteous to her mind;
And heaven defend° your good souls that you think
I will your serious and great business scant
When she is with me. No, when light-winged toys
Of feathered Cupid seel° with wanton° dullness
265　My speculative and officed instrument,°
That my disports corrupt and taint my business,
Let housewives make a skillet of my helm,
And all indign° and base adversities
Make head° against my estimation!°—

270 *Duke.* Be it as you shall privately determine,
Either for her stay or going. Th' affair cries haste,
And speed must answer it.

First Senator.　　　　　　　You must away tonight.

Othello. With all my heart.

Duke. At nine i' th' morning here we'll meet again
275　Othello, leave some officer behind,
And he shall our commission bring to you,
And such things else of quality and respect
As doth import you.

Othello.　　　　　So please your grace, my ancient;
A man he is of honesty and trust.
280　To his conveyance I assign my wife,
With what else needful your good grace shall think
To be sent after me.

Duke.　　　　　Let it be so.
Good night to every one. [*To Brabantio*] And, noble
　　signior,
If virtue no delighted° beauty lack,
285　Your son-in-law is far more fair than black.

First Senator. Adieu, brave Moor. Use Desdemona
　　well.

259 *proper satisfaction* i.e., consummation of the marriage   261 *defend*
forbid   264 *seel* sew up   264 *wanton* lascivious   265 *speculative . . .
instrument* i.e., sight (and, by extension, the mind)   268 *indign* unworthy   269 *Make head* form an army, i.e., attack   269 *estimation*
reputation   284 *delighted* delightful

Brabantio. Look to her, Moor, if thou hast eyes to see:
  She has deceived her father, and may thee.
           [Exeunt Duke, Senators, Officers, &c.]

Othello. My life upon her faith! Honest Iago,
  My Desdemona must I leave to thee.   *290*
  I prithee let thy wife attend on her,
  And bring them after in the best advantage.°
  Come, Desdemona. I have but an hour
  Of love, of wordly matter, and direction
  To spend with thee. We must obey the time.   *295*
           Exit [Moor with Desdemona].

Roderigo. Iago?

Iago. What say'st thou, noble heart?

Roderigo. What will I do, think'st thou?

Iago. Why, go to bed and sleep.

Roderigo. I will incontinently° drown myself.   *300*

Iago. If thou dost, I shall never love thee after. Why,
  thou silly gentleman?

Roderigo. It is silliness to live when to live is torment;
  and then have we a prescription to die when death is
  our physician.   *305*

Iago. O villainous! I have looked upon the world for
  four times seven years, and since I could distinguish
  betwixt a benefit and an injury, I never found man
  that knew how to love himself. Ere I would say I
  would drown myself for the love of a guinea hen, *310*
  I would change my humanity with a baboon.

Roderigo. What should I do? I confess it is my shame
  to be so fond, but it is not in my virtue° to amend it.

Iago. Virtue? A fig! 'Tis in ourselves that we are thus,
  or thus. Our bodies are our gardens, to the which *315*
  our wills are gardeners; so that if we will plant
  nettles or sow lettuce, set hyssop and weed up thyme,

---

²⁹² *advantage* opportunity   ³⁰⁰ *incontinently* at once   ³¹³ *virtue* strength
(Roderigo is saying that his nature controls him)

supply it with one gender of herbs or distract° it
with many—either to have it sterile with idleness or
820 manured with industry—why, the power and corri-
gible° authority of this lies in our wills. If the balance of our lives had not one scale of reason to poise
another of sensuality, the blood and baseness of
our natures would conduct us to most prepost'rous
825 conclusions.° But we have reason to cool our raging
motions, our carnal stings or unbitted° lusts,
whereof I take this that you call love to be a sect
or scion.°

Roderigo. It cannot be.

830 *Iago.* It is merely a lust of the blood and a permission of
the will. Come, be a man! Drown thyself? Drown
cats and blind puppies! I have professed me thy
friend, and I confess me knit to thy deserving with
cables of perdurable toughness. I could never better
835 stead° thee than now. Put money in thy purse.
Follow thou the wars; defeat thy favor° with an
usurped° beard. I say, put money in thy purse.
It cannot be long that Desdemona should continue
her love to the Moor. Put money in thy purse. Nor
840 he his to her. It was a violent commencement in
her and thou shalt see an answerable° sequestra-
tion—put but money in thy purse. These Moors
are changeable in their wills—fill thy purse with
money. The food that to him now is as luscious as
845 locusts° shall be to him shortly as bitter as coloquintida.° She must change for youth; when she is
sated with his body, she will find the errors of her
choice. Therefore, put money in thy purse. If thou
wilt needs damn thyself, do it a more delicate way
850 than drowning. Make all the money thou canst. If

318 *distract* vary   320-21 *corrigible* corrective   325 *conclusions* ends
326 *unbitted* i.e., uncontrolled   327-28 *sect or scion* offshoot   335 *stead*
serve   336 *defeat thy favor* disguise your face   337 *usurped* assumed
341 *answerable* similar   345 *locusts* (a sweet fruit)   345-46 *coloquintida*
(a purgative derived from a bitter apple)

sanctimony° and a frail vow betwixt an erring°
barbarian and supersubtle Venetian be not too hard
for my wits, and all the tribe of hell, thou shalt enjoy
her. Therefore, make money. A pox of drowning
thyself, it is clean out of the way. Seek thou rather   *355*
to be hanged in compassing° thy joy than to be
drowned and go without her.

Roderigo. Wilt thou be fast to my hopes, if I depend
　　on the issue?

Iago. Thou art sure of me. Go, make money. I have   *360*
　　told thee often, and I retell thee again and again, I
　　hate the Moor. My cause is hearted;° thine hath no
　　less reason. Let us be conjunctive° in our revenge
　　against him. If thou canst cuckold him, thou dost
　　thyself a pleasure, me a sport. There are many   *365*
　　events in the womb of time, which will be delivered.
　　Traverse, go, provide thy money! We will have more
　　of this tomorrow. Adieu.

Roderigo. Where shall we meet i' th' morning?

Iago. At my lodging.   *370*

Roderigo. I'll be with thee betimes.

Iago. Go to, farewell. Do you hear, Roderigo?

Roderigo. I'll sell all my land.   　　　　　*Exit.*

Iago. Thus do I ever make my fool my purse;
　　For I mine own gained knowledge° should profane   *375*
　　If I would time expend with such snipe
　　But for my sport and profit. I hate the Moor,
　　And it is thought abroad that 'twixt my sheets
　　H'as done my office. I know not if't be true,
　　But I, for mere suspicion in that kind,   *380*
　　Will do, as if for surety.° He holds me well;
　　The better shall my purpose work on him.

---

[351] *sanctimony* sacred bond (of marriage)　[351] *erring* wandering
[356] *compassing* encompassing, achieving　[362] *hearted* deep-seated in the
heart　[363] *conjunctive* joined　[375] *gained knowledge* i.e., practical,
worldly wisdom　[381] *surety* certainty

Cassio's a proper° man. Let me see now:
To get his place, and to plume up my will°
385 In double knavery. How? How? Let's see.
After some time, to abuse Othello's ears
That he is too familiar with his wife.
He hath a person and a smooth dispose°
To be suspected—framed° to make women false.
390 The Moor is of a free and open nature
That thinks men honest that but seem to be so;
And will as tenderly be led by th' nose
As asses are.
I have't! It is engendered! Hell and night
393 Must bring this monstrous birth to the world's light.
                           [*Exit.*]

---

383 *proper* handsome   384 *plume up my will* (many explanations have been offered for this crucial line, which in Q1 reads "make up my will." The general sense is something like "to make more proud and gratify my ego")   388 *dispose* manner   389 *framed* designed

ACT II

Scene I. [*Cyprus.*]

Enter Montano and two Gentlemen, [one above].°

Montano. What from the cape can you discern at sea?

First Gentleman. Nothing at all, it is a high-wrought
flood.
I cannot 'twixt the heaven and the main
Descry a sail.

Montano. Methinks the wind hath spoke aloud at land;   5
A fuller blast ne'er shook our battlements.
If it hath ruffianed so upon the sea,
What ribs of oak, when mountains melt on them,
Can hold the mortise? What shall we hear of this?

Second Gentleman. A segregation° of the Turkish
fleet.   10
For do but stand upon the foaming shore,
The chidden billow seems to pelt the clouds;
The wind-shaked surge, with high and monstrous
main,°
Seems to cast water on the burning Bear
And quench the guards of th' ever-fixèd pole.°   15

II.i. s.d. (the Folio arrangement of this scene requires that the First
Gentleman stand above—on the upper stage—and act as a lookout re-
porting sights which cannot be seen by Montano standing below on the
main stage)   10 *segregation* separation   13 *main* (both "ocean" and
"strength")   14–15 *Seems . . . pole* (the constellation Ursa Minor contains two stars which are the *guards*, or companions, of the *pole*, or
North Star)

I never did like molestation view
On the enchafèd flood.

Montano.   If that the Turkish fleet
Be not ensheltered and embayed, they are drowned;
It is impossible to bear it out.

Enter a [third] Gentleman.

20 *Third Gentleman.* News, lads! Our wars are done.
The desperate tempest hath so banged the Turks
That their designment halts. A noble ship of Venice
Hath seen a grievous wrack and sufferance°
On most part of their fleet.

Montano. How? Is this true?

25 *Third Gentleman.*   The ship is here put in,
A Veronesa; Michael Cassio,
Lieutenant to the warlike Moor Othello,
Is come on shore; the Moor himself at sea,
And is in full commission here for Cyprus.

30 *Montano.* I am glad on't. 'Tis a worthy governor.

Third Gentleman. But this same Cassio, though he
    speak of comfort
Touching the Turkish loss, yet he looks sadly
And prays the Moor be safe, for they were parted
With foul and violent tempest.

Montano.   Pray heavens he be;
35 For I have served him, and the man commands
Like a full soldier. Let's to the seaside, ho!
As well to see the vessel that's come in
As to throw out our eyes for brave Othello,
Even till we make the main and th' aerial blue
An indistinct regard.°

40 *Third Gentleman.*   Come, let's do so;
For every minute is expectancy
Of more arrivancie.°

---

23 *sufferance* damage   39-40 *the main . . . regard* i.e., the sea and sky
become indistinguishable   42 *arrivancie* arrivals

Enter Cassio.

Cassio. Thanks, you the valiant of the warlike isle,
　That so approve° the Moor. O, let the heavens
　Give him defense against the elements,   45
　For I have lost him on a dangerous sea.

Montano. Is he well shipped?

Cassio. His bark is stoutly timbered, and his pilot
　Of very expert and approved allowance;°
　Therefore my hopes, not surfeited to death,°   50
　Stand in bold cure.°　(*Within*) A sail, a sail, a sail!

Cassio. What noise?

First Gentleman. The town is empty; on the brow o'
　th' sea
　Stand ranks of people, and they cry, "A sail!"

Cassio. My hopes do shape him for the governor.   55

                                               [*A shot.*]

Second Gentleman. They do discharge their shot of
　courtesy:
　Our friends at least.

Cassio.　　　　　　　　I pray you, sir, go forth
　And give us truth who 'tis that is arrived.

Second Gentleman. I shall.　　　　　　　　*Exit.*

Montano. But, good lieutenant, is your general wived?   60

Cassio. Most fortunately. He hath achieved a maid
　That paragons° description and wild fame;°
　One that excels the quirks of blazoning pens,°
　And in th' essential vesture of creation°
　Does tire the ingener.°

---

⁴⁴ *approve* ("honor" or, perhaps, "are as warlike and valiant as your
governor")　⁴⁹ *approved allowance* known and tested　⁵⁰ *not surfeited
to death* i.e., not so great as to be in danger　⁵¹ *Stand in bold cure* i.e.,
are likely to be restored　⁶² *paragons* exceeds　⁶² *wild fame* extravagant report　⁶³ *quirks of blazoning pens* ingenuities of praising pens
⁶⁴ *essential vesture of creation* i.e., essential human nature as given by
the Creator　⁶⁵ *tire the ingener* (a difficult line which probably means
something like "outdo the human ability to imagine and picture")

Enter [Second] Gentleman.

65   How now? Who has put in?

Second Gentleman. 'Tis one Iago, ancient to the
    general.

Cassio. H'as had most favorable and happy speed:
    Tempests themselves, high seas, and howling winds,
    The guttered° rocks and congregated° sands,
70 Traitors ensteeped° to enclog the guiltless keel,
    As having sense° of beauty, do omit
    Their mortal° natures, letting go safely by
    The divine Desdemona.

Montano.   What is she?

Cassio. She that I spake of, our great captain's captain,
75 Left in the conduct of the bold Iago,
    Whose footing° here anticipates our thoughts
    A se'nnight's° speed. Great Jove, Othello guard,
    And swell his sail with thine own pow'rful breath,
    That he may bless this bay with his tall° ship,
80 Make love's quick pants in Desdemona's arms,
    Give renewed fire to our extinguished spirits.

Enter Desdemona, Iago, Roderigo, and Emilia.

    O, behold! The riches of the ship is come on shore!
    You men of Cyprus, let her have your knees.
                              [*Kneeling.*]
    Hail to thee, lady! and the grace of heaven,
85 Before, behind thee, and on every hand,
    Enwheel thee round.

Desdemona.   I thank you, valiant Cassio.
    What tidings can you tell of my lord?

Cassio. He is not yet arrived, nor know I aught
    But that he's well and will be shortly here.

90 *Desdemona.* O but I fear. How lost you company?

---

⁶⁹ *guttered* jagged ⁶⁹ *congregated* gathered ⁷⁰ *ensteeped* submerged
⁷¹ *sense* awareness ⁷² *mortal* deadly ⁷⁶ *footing* landing ⁷⁷ *se'nnight's*
week's ⁷⁹ *tall* brave

Cassio. The great contention of sea and skies
    Parted our fellowship. (*Within*) A sail, a sail!
    [*A shot.*]
                        But hark. A sail!

Second Gentleman. They give this greeting to the
    citadel;
    This likewise is a friend.

Cassio.   See for the news.   95
                      [*Exit Gentleman.*]
    Good ancient, you are welcome. [*To Emilia*] Wel-
    come, mistress.
    Let it not gall your patience, good Iago,
    That I extend° my manners. 'Tis my breeding°
    That gives me this bold show of courtesy. [*Kisses
    Emilia.*]

Iago. Sir, would she give you so much of her lips   100
    As of her tongue she oft bestows on me,
    You would have enough.

Desdemona.   Alas, she has no speech.

Iago. In faith, too much.
    I find it still when I have leave to sleep.°
    Marry, before your ladyship,° I grant,   105
    She puts her tongue a little in her heart
    And chides with thinking.

Emilia.   You have little cause to say so.

Iago. Come on, come on! You are pictures° out of
    door,
    Bells in your parlors, wildcats in your kitchens,
    Saints in your injuries,° devils being offended,   110

---

⁹⁸ *extend* stretch   ⁹⁸ *breeding* careful training in manners (Cassio is
considerably more the polished gentleman than Iago, and aware of it)
¹⁰⁴ *still . . . sleep* i.e., even when she allows me to sleep she continues
to scold   ¹⁰⁵ *before your ladyship* in your presence   ¹⁰⁸ *pictures* models
(of virtue)   ¹¹⁰ *in your injuries* when you injure others

Players in your housewifery,° and housewives in
your beds.

Desdemona. O, fie upon thee, slanderer!

Iago. Nay, it is true, or else I am a Turk:
You rise to play, and go to bed to work.

Emilia. You shall not write my praise.

115 *Iago.*   No, let me not.

Desdemona. What wouldst write of me, if thou shouldst
praise me?

Iago. O gentle lady, do not put me to't,
For I am nothing if not critical.

Desdemona. Come on, assay. There's one gone to the
harbor?

Iago. Ay, madam.

120 *Desdemona.* [*Aside*] I am not merry; but I do beguile
The thing I am by seeming otherwise.—
Come, how wouldst thou praise me?

Iago. I am about it; but indeed my invention
Comes from my pate as birdlime° does from
frieze° —
125 It plucks out brains and all. But my Muse labors,
And thus she is delivered:
If she be fair° and wise: fairness and wit,
The one's for use, the other useth it.

Desdemona. Well praised. How if she be black° and
witty?

130 *Iago.* If she be black, and thereto have a wit,
She'll find a white that shall her blackness fit.

Desdemona. Worse and worse!

---

111 *housewifery* (this word can mean "careful, economical household
management," and Iago would then be accusing women of only pretending to be good housekeepers, while in bed they are either [1] economical of their favors, or more likely [2] serious and dedicated workers)
124 *birdlime* a sticky substance put on branches to catch birds
124 *frieze* rough cloth   127 *fair* light-complexioned   129 *black* brunette

Emilia. How if fair and foolish?

Iago. She never yet was foolish that was fair,
  For even her folly helped her to an heir.   *135*

Desdemona. These are old fond° paradoxes to make
  fools laugh i' th' alehouse. What miserable praise
  hast thou for her that's foul and foolish?

Iago. There's none so foul, and foolish thereunto,
  But does foul pranks which fair and wise ones do.   *140*

Desdemona. O heavy ignorance. Thou praisest the
  worst best. But what praise couldst thou bestow on
  a deserving woman indeed—one that in the authority of her merit did justly put on the vouch of very
  malice itself?°   *145*

Iago. She that was ever fair, and never proud;
  Had tongue at will, and yet was never loud;
  Never lacked gold, and yet went never gay;
  Fled from her wish, and yet said "Now I may";
  She that being angered, her revenge being nigh,
  Bade her wrong stay, and her displeasure fly;   *150*
  She that in wisdom never was so frail
  To change the cod's head for the salmon's tail;°
  She that could think, and nev'r disclose her mind;
  See suitors following, and not look behind:
  She was a wight° (if ever such wights were)—   *155*

Desdemona. To do what?

Iago. To suckle fools and chronicle small beer.°

Desdemona. O most lame and impotent conclusion.
  Do not learn of him, Emilia, though he be thy hus-   *160*
  band. How say you, Cassio? Is he not a most profane
  and liberal° counselor?

---

¹³⁶ *fond* foolish   ¹⁴³⁻⁴⁵ *one . . . itself* i.e., a woman so honest and
deserving that even malice would be forced to approve of her   ¹⁵³ *To
. . . tail* i.e., to exchange something valuable for something useless
¹⁵⁶ *wight* person   ¹⁵⁸ *chronicle small beer* i.e., keep household accounts
(the most trivial of occupations in Iago's opinion)   ¹⁶² *liberal* licentious

Cassio. He speaks home,° madam. You may relish
  him more in° the soldier than in the scholar. [*Takes
  Desdemona's hand.*]

165 *Iago.* [*Aside*] He takes her by the palm. Ay, well said,
  whisper! With as little a web as this will I ensnare
  as great a fly as Cassio. Ay, smile upon her, do! I
  will gyve° thee in thine own courtship.—You say
  true; 'tis so, indeed!—If such tricks as these strip
170 you out of your lieutenantry, it had been better you
  had not kissed your three fingers so oft—which now
  again you are most apt to play the sir° in. Very
  good! Well kissed! An excellent curtsy!° 'Tis so,
  indeed. Yet again your fingers to your lips? Would
175 they were clyster pipes° for your sake! [*Trumpets
  within.*] The Moor! I know his trumpet.°

Cassio. 'Tis truly so.

Desdemona. Let's meet him and receive him.

Cassio. Lo, where he comes.

Enter Othello and Attendants.

Othello. O my fair warrior!

180 *Desdemona.*   My dear Othello.

Othello. It gives me wonder great as my content
  To see you here before me. O my soul's joy!
  If after every tempest come such calms,
  May the winds blow till they have wakened death.
185 And let the laboring bark climb hills of seas
  Olympus-high, and duck again as low
  As hell's from heaven. If it were now to die,
  'Twere now to be most happy; for I fear
  My soul hath her content so absolute
190 That not another comfort like to this
  Succeeds in unknown fate.

---

168 *speaks home* thrusts deeply with his speech   163-64 *relish him more
in* enjoy him more as   168 *gyve* bind   172 *the sir* the fashionable gentleman   173 *curtsy* courtesy, i.e., bow   175 *clyster pipes* enema tubes
176 *his trumpet* (great men had their own distinctive calls)

Desdemona.   The heavens forbid ③
But that our loves and comforts should increase
Even as our days do grow. *when days had passed.*

Othello.   Amen to that, sweet powers!
I cannot speak enough of this content;
It stops me here [*touches his heart*]; it is too much
    of joy.
And this, and this, the greatest discords be   195

                              [*They kiss.*]

That e'er our hearts shall make!

Iago.   [*Aside*] O, you are well tuned now!
But I'll set down the pegs° that make this music,
As honest as I am.

Othello.   Come, let us to the castle.
News, friends! Our wars are done; the Turks are
    drowned.   200
How does my old acquaintance of this isle?
Honey, you shall be well desired in Cyprus;
I have found great love amongst them. O my sweet,
I prattle out of fashion, and I dote
In mine own comforts. I prithee, good Iago,   205
Go to the bay and disembark my coffers.
Bring thou the master to the citadel;
He is a good one, and his worthiness
Does challenge° much respect. Come, Desdemona,
Once more well met at Cyprus.   210
*Exit Othello and Desdemona [and all but Iago and
                                    Roderigo].*

Iago. [*To an Attendant*] Do thou meet me presently
at the harbor. [*To Roderigo*] Come hither. If thou
be'st valiant (as they say base men being in love
have then a nobility in their natures more than is
native to them), list me. The lieutenant tonight   215
watches on the court of guard.° First, I must tell thee
this: Desdemona is directly in love with him.

Roderigo. With him? Why, 'tis not possible.

198 *set down the pegs* loosen the strings (to produce discord)   209 *challenge* require, exact   216 *court of guard* guardhouse

Iago. Lay thy finger thus [*puts his finger to his lips*],
220 and let thy soul be instructed. Mark me with what
violence she first loved the Moor but for bragging
and telling her fantastical lies. To love him still for
prating? Let not thy discreet heart think it. Her
eye must be fed. And what delight shall she have to
225 look on the devil? When the blood is made dull with
the act of sport, there should be a game° to inflame
it and to give satiety a fresh appetite, loveliness in
favor,° sympathy in years,° manners, and beauties;
all which the Moor is defective in. Now for want of
230 these required conveniences,° her delicate tenderness will find itself abused, begin to heave the
gorge,° disrelish and abhor the Moor. Very nature
will instruct her in it and compel her to some second
choice. Now, sir, this granted—as it is a most preg-
235 nant° and unforced position—who stands so emi-
nent in the degree of this fortune as Cassio does?
A knave very voluble; no further conscionable°
than in putting on the mere form of civil and hu-
mane° seeming for the better compass of his salt°
240 and most hidden loose° affection. Why, none! Why,
none! A slipper° and subtle knave, a finder of
occasion, that has an eye can stamp and counterfeit
advantages, though true advantage never present
itself. A devilish knave. Besides, the knave is hand-
245 some, young, and hath all those requisites in him
that folly and green minds look after. A pestilent
complete knave, and the woman hath found him
already.

Roderigo. I cannot believe that in her; she's full of
250 most blessed condition.

Iago. Blessed fig's-end! The wine she drinks is made of
grapes. If she had been blessed, she would never

226 *game* sport (with the added sense of "gamey," "rank")   228 *favor*
countenance, appearance   228 *sympathy in years* sameness of age
230 *conveniences* advantages   231-32 *heave the gorge* vomit   234-35 *preg-
nant* likely   237 *no further conscionable* having no more conscience
238-39 *humane* polite   239 *salt* lecherous   240 *loose* immoral   241 *slip-
per* slippery

have loved the Moor. Blessed pudding! Didst thou
not see her paddle with the palm of his hand? Didst
not mark that?   255

Roderigo. Yes, that I did; but that was but courtesy.

Iago. Lechery, by this hand! [*Extends his index finger.*]
An index° and obsure prologue to the history of
lust and foul thoughts. They met so near with their
lips that their breaths embraced together. Villainous   260
thoughts, Roderigo. When these mutualities so
marshal the way, hard at hand comes the master and
main exercise, th' incorporate° conclusion: Pish!
But, sir, be you ruled by me. I have brought you
from Venice. Watch you tonight; for the command,   265
I'll lay't upon you. Cassio knows you not. I'll not be
far from you. Do you find some occasion to anger
Cassio, either by speaking too loud, or tainting°
his discipline, or from what other course you please
which the time shall more favorably minister.   270

Roderigo. Well.

Iago. Sir, he's rash and very sudden in choler,° and
haply may strike at you. Provoke him that he may;
for even out of that will I cause these of Cyprus to
mutiny, whose qualification shall come into no true   275
taste° again but by the displanting of Cassio. So
shall you have a shorter journey to your desires by
the means I shall then have to prefer them; and the
impediment most profitably removed without the
which there were no expectation of our prosperity.   280

Roderigo. I will do this if you can bring it to any
opportunity.

Iago. I warrant thee. Meet me by and by at the citadel.
I must fetch his necessaries ashore. Farewell.

Roderigo. Adieu.   *Exit.*   285

Iago. That Cassio loves her, I do well believe 't;

²⁵⁸ *index* pointer ²⁶³ *incorporate* carnal ²⁶⁸ *tainting* discrediting
²⁷² *choler* anger ²⁷⁵⁻⁷⁶ *qualification . . . taste* i.e., appeasement will not
be brought about (wine was "qualified" by adding water)

That she loves him, 'tis apt and of great credit.
The Moor, howbeit that I endure him not,
Is of a constant, loving, noble nature,
290 And I dare think he'll prove to Desdemona
A most dear° husband. Now I do love her too;
Not out of absolute° lust, though peradventure°
I stand accountant for as great a sin,
But partly led to diet° my revenge,
295 For that I do suspect the lusty Moor
Hath leaped into my seat; the thought whereof
Doth, like a poisonous mineral, gnaw my inwards;
And nothing can or shall content my soul
Till I am evened with him, wife for wife.
300 Or failing so, yet that I put the Moor
At least into a jealousy so strong
That judgment cannot cure. Which thing to do,
If this poor trash of Venice, whom I trace°
For his quick hunting, stand the putting on,
305 I'll have our Michael Cassio on the hip,
Abuse him to the Moor in the right garb°
(For I fear Cassio with my nightcap too),
Make the Moor thank me, love me, and reward me
For making him egregiously an ass
310 And practicing upon° his peace and quiet,
Even to madness. 'Tis here, but yet confused:
Knavery's plain face is never seen till used.   *Exit.*

---

²⁹¹ *dear* expensive   ²⁹² *out of absolute* absolutely out of   ²⁹² *peradventure* perchance   ²⁹⁴ *diet* feed   ³⁰³ *trace* (most editors emend to "trash," meaning to hang weights on a dog to slow his hunting; but "trace" clearly means something like "put on the trace" or "set on the track")   ³⁰⁶ *right garb* i.e., "proper fashion"   ³¹⁰ *practicing upon* scheming to destroy

Scene II. [*A street.*]

Enter Othello's Herald, with a proclamation.

Herald. It is Othello's pleasure, our noble and valiant
general, that upon certain tidings now arrived im-
porting the mere perdition° of the Turkish fleet,
every man put himself into triumph. Some to dance,
some to make bonfires, each man to what sport and   5
revels his addition° leads him. For, besides these
beneficial news, it is the celebration of his nuptial.
So much was his pleasure should be proclaimed.
All offices° are open, and there is full liberty of
feasting from this present hour of five till the bell   10
have told eleven. Bless the isle of Cyprus and our
noble general Othello!
                                                    Exit.

Scene III. [*The citadel of Cyprus.*]

Enter Othello, Desdemona, Cassio, and Attendants.

Othello. Good Michael, look you to the guard tonight.
  Let's teach ourselves that honorable stop,
  Not to outsport discretion.

Cassio. Iago hath direction what to do;
  But notwithstanding, with my personal eye   5
  Will I look to't.

Othello.   Iago is most honest.
  Michael, good night. Tomorrow with your earliest
  Let me have speech with you. [*To Desdemona*]
      Come, my dear love,

II.ii.⁸ *mere perdition* absolute destruction ⁶ *addition* rank ⁹ *offices*
kitchens and storerooms of food

The purchase made, the fruits are to ensue,
10   That profit's yet to come 'tween me and you.
      Good night.

              Exit [Othello with Desdemona and Attendants].

                    Enter Iago.

Cassio. Welcome, Iago. We must to the watch.

Iago. Not this hour, lieutenant; 'tis not yet ten o' th'
      clock. Our general cast° us thus early for the love
15   of his Desdemona; who let us not therefore blame.
      He hath not yet made wanton the night with her, and
      she is sport for Jove.

Cassio. She's a most exquisite lady.

Iago. And, I'll warrant her, full of game.

20 *Cassio.* Indeed, she's a most fresh and delicate creature.

Iago. What an eye she has! Methinks it sounds a parley
      to provocation.

Cassio. An inviting eye; and yet methinks right modest.

Iago. And when she speaks, is it not an alarum° to
25   love?

Cassio. She is indeed perfection.

Iago. Well, happiness to their sheets! Come, lieutenant,
      I have a stoup° of wine, and here without are a
      brace of Cyprus gallants that would fain have a
30   measure to the health of black Othello.

Cassio. Not tonight, good Iago. I have very poor and
      unhappy brains for drinking; I could well wish
      courtesy would invent some other custom of enter-
      tainment.

35 *Iago.* O, they are our friends. But one cup! I'll drink
      for you.

Cassio. I have drunk but one cup tonight, and that was
      craftily qualified° too; and behold what innovation

II.iii.¹⁴ *cast* dismissed   ²⁴ *alarum* the call to action, "general quarters"
²⁸ *stoup* two-quart tankard   ³⁸ *qualified* diluted

it makes here. I am unfortunate in the infirmity and
dare not task my weakness with any more.   40

Iago. What, man! 'Tis a night of revels, the gallants
desire it.

Cassio. Where are they?

Iago. Here, at the door. I pray you call them in.

Cassio. I'll do't, but it dislikes me.   *Exit.* 45

Iago. If I can fasten but one cup upon him
With that which he hath drunk tonight already,
He'll be as full of quarrel and offense
As my young mistress' dog. Now, my sick fool
    Roderigo,
Whom love hath turned almost the wrong side out, 50
To Desdemona hath tonight caroused
Potations pottle-deep;° and he's to watch.
Three else° of Cyprus, noble swelling spirits,
That hold their honors in a wary distance,°
The very elements of this warlike isle, 55
Have I tonight flustered with flowing cups,
And they watch too. Now, 'mongst this flock of
    drunkards
Am I to put our Cassio in some action
That may offend the isle. But here they come.

    Enter Cassio, Montano, and Gentlemen.

If consequence do but approve my dream, 60
My boat sails freely, both with wind and stream.

Cassio. 'Fore God, they have given me a rouse° already.

Montano. Good faith, a little one; not past a pint, as
I am a soldier.

Iago. Some wine, ho! 65
    [*Sings*] And let me the canakin clink, clink;
          And let me the canakin clink.

---

[52] *pottle-deep* to the bottom of the cup [53] *else* others [54] *hold . . .
distance* are scrupulous in maintaining their honor [62] *rouse* drink

A soldier's a man;

O man's life's but a span,

Why then, let a soldier drink.

70

Some wine, boys!

Cassio. 'Fore God, an excellent song!

Iago. I learned it in England, where indeed they are
most potent in potting. Your Dane, your German,

75   and your swag-bellied° Hollander—Drink, ho!—
are nothing to your English.

Cassio. Is your Englishman so exquisite° in his drink-
ing?

Iago. Why, he drinks you with facility your Dane dead

80   drunk; he sweats not to overthrow your Almain; he
gives your Hollander a vomit ere the next pottle can
be filled.

Cassio. To the health of our general!

Montano. I am for it, lieutenant, and I'll do you justice.

85 *Iago.* O sweet England!

[*Sings*] King Stephen was and a worthy peer;

His breeches cost him but a crown;

He held them sixpence all too dear,

With that he called the tailor lown.°

90   He was a wight of high renown,

And thou art but of low degree:

'Tis pride that pulls the country down;

And take thine auld cloak about thee.

Some wine, ho!

95 *Cassio.* 'Fore God, this is a more exquisite song than
the other.

Iago. Will you hear't again?

Cassio. No, for I hold him to be unworthy of his place
that does those things. Well, God's above all; and

100   there be souls must be saved, and there be souls
must not be saved.

---

⁷⁵ *swag-bellied* hanging   ⁷⁷ *exquisite* superb   ⁸⁹ *lown* lout

Iago. It's true, good lieutenant.

Cassio. For mine own part—no offense to the general,
nor any man of quality—I hope to be saved.

Iago. And so do I too, lieutenant.   105

Cassio. Ay, but, by your leave, not before me. The lieutenant is to be saved before the ancient. Let's have
no more of this; let's to our affairs.—God forgive us
our sins!—Gentlemen, let's look to our business.
Do not think, gentlemen, I am drunk. This is my   110
ancient; this is my right hand, and this is my left.
I am not drunk now. I can stand well enough, and
I speak well enough.

Gentlemen. Excellent well!

Cassio. Why, very well then. You must not think then 115
that I am drunk.   *Exit.*

Montano. To th' platform, masters. Come, let's set
the watch.

Iago. You see this fellow that is gone before.
He's a soldier fit to stand by Caesar
And give direction; and do but see his vice.   120
'Tis to his virtue a just equinox,°
The one as long as th' other. 'Tis pity of him.
I fear the trust Othello puts him in,
On some odd time of his infirmity,
Will shake this island.

Montano.   But is he often thus?   125

Iago. 'Tis evermore his prologue to his sleep:
He'll watch the horologe a double set°
If drink rock not his cradle.

Montano.   It were well
The general were put in mind of it.
Perhaps he sees it not, or his good nature   130
Prizes the virtue that appears in Cassio
And looks not on his evils. Is not this true?

---

121 *just equinox* exact balance (of dark and light)   127 *watch . . . set*
stay awake twice around the clock

Enter Roderigo.

Iago. [*Aside*] How now, Roderigo?
  I pray you after the lieutenant, go! [*Exit Roderigo.*]

135 *Montano.* And 'tis great pity that the noble Moor
      Should hazard such a place as his own second
      With one of an ingraft° infirmity.
      It were an honest action to say so
      To the Moor.

Iago.   Not I, for this fair island!
140   I do love Cassio well and would do much
      To cure him of this evil.   (Help! Help! *Within.*)
                    But hark? What noise?

Enter Cassio, pursuing Roderigo.

Cassio. Zounds, you rogue! You rascal!

Montano. What's the matter, lieutenant?

Cassio. A knave teach me my duty? I'll beat the knave
145   into a twiggen° bottle.

Roderigo. Beat me?

Cassio. Dost thou prate, rogue?   [*Strikes him.*]

Montano. Nay, good lieutenant! I pray you, sir, hold
      your hand.

                    [*Stays him.*]

150 *Cassio.* Let me go, sir, or I'll knock you o'er the
      mazzard.°

Montano. Come, come, you're drunk!

Cassio. Drunk?   [*They fight.*]

Iago. [*Aside to Roderigo*] Away, I say! Go out and
155   cry a mutiny!

                    [*Exit Roderigo.*]

      Nay, good lieutenant. God's will, gentlemen!
      Help, ho! Lieutenant. Sir. Montano.
      Help, masters! Here's a goodly watch indeed!
                    [*A bell rung.*]

---

¹³⁷ *ingraft* ingrained   ¹⁴⁵ *twiggen* wicker-covered   ¹⁵¹ *mazzard* head

Who's that which rings the bell? Diablo, ho!
The town will rise. God's will, lieutenant,   *160*
You'll be ashamed forever.

Enter Othello and Attendants.

Othello.   What is the matter here?

Montano. Zounds, I bleed still. I am hurt to the death.
He dies.   [*He and Cassio fight again.*]

Othello. Hold for your lives!

Iago. Hold, ho! Lieutenant. Sir. Montano. Gentlemen!   *165*
Have you forgot all place of sense and duty?
Hold! The general speaks to you. Hold, for shame!

Othello. Why, how now, ho? From whence ariseth this?
Are we turned Turks, and to ourselves do that
Which heaven hath forbid the Ottomites?°   *170*
For Christian shame put by this barbarous brawl!
He that stirs next to carve for his own rage
Holds his soul light;° he dies upon his motion.
Silence that dreadful bell! It frights the isle
From her propriety.° What is the matter, masters?   *175*
Honest Iago, that looks dead with grieving,
Speak. Who began this? On thy love, I charge thee.

Iago. I do not know. Friends all, but now, even now,
In quarter° and in terms like bride and groom
Devesting them for bed; and then, but now—   *180*
As if some planet had unwitted men—
Swords out, and tilting one at other's breasts
In opposition bloody. I cannot speak
Any beginning to this peevish odds,°
And would in action glorious I had lost   *185*
Those legs that brought me to a part of it!

Othello. How comes it, Michael, you are thus forgot?

Cassio. I pray you pardon me; I cannot speak.

Othello. Worthy Montano, you were wont to be civil;
The gravity and stillness of your youth   *190*

---

[170] *heaven . . . Ottomites* i.e., by sending the storm which dispersed
the Turks   [173] *Holds his soul light* values his soul lightly   [175] *propriety*
proper order   [179] *In quarter* on duty   [184] *odds* quarrel

The world hath noted, and your name is great
In mouths of wisest censure.° What's the matter
That you unlace° your reputation thus
And spend your rich opinion° for the name
195   Of a night-brawler? Give me answer to it.

Montano. Worthy Othello, I am hurt to danger.
Your officer, Iago, can inform you,
While I spare speech, which something now offends°
   me,
Of all that I do know; nor know I aught
200   By me that's said or done amiss this night,
Unless self-charity be sometimes a vice,
And to defend ourselves it be a sin
When violence assails us.

Othello.   Now, by heaven,
My blood begins my safer guides to rule,
205   And passion, having my best judgment collied,°
Assays to lead the way. If I once stir
Or do but lift this arm, the best of you
Shall sink in my rebuke. Give me to know
How this foul rout began, who set it on;
210   And he that is approved in this offense,
Though he had twinned with me, both at a birth,
Shall lose me. What? In a town of war
Yet wild, the people's hearts brimful of fear,
To manage° private and domestic quarrel?
215   In night, and on the court and guard of safety?
'Tis monstrous. Iago, who began't?

Montano. If partially affined, or leagued in office,°
Thou dost deliver more or less than truth,
Thou art no soldier.

Iago.   Touch me not so near.
220   I had rather have this tongue cut from my mouth
Than it should do offense to Michael Cassio.

---

192 *censure* judgment   193 *unlace* undo (the term refers specifically to the dressing of a wild boar killed in the hunt)   194 *opinion* reputation 198 *offends* harms, hurts   205 *collied* darkened   214 *manage* conduct 217 *If . . . office* if you are partial because you are related ("affined") or the brother officer (of Cassio)

Yet I persuade myself to speak the truth
Shall nothing wrong him. This it is, general.
Montano and myself being in speech,
There comes a fellow crying out for help, 225
And Cassio following him with determined sword
To execute upon him. Sir, this gentleman
Steps in to Cassio and entreats his pause.
Myself the crying fellow did pursue,
Lest by his clamor—as it so fell out— 230
The town might fall in fright. He, swift of foot,
Outran my purpose; and I returned then rather
For that I heard the clink and fall of swords,
And Cassio high in oath; which till tonight
I ne'er might say before. When I came back— 235
For this was brief—I found them close together
At blow and thrust, even as again they were
When you yourself did part them.
More of this matter cannot I report;
But men are men; the best sometimes forget. 240
Though Cassio did some little wrong to him,
As men in rage strike those that wish them best,
Yet surely Cassio I believe received
From him that fled some strange indignity,
Which patience could not pass.°

Othello. I know, Iago, 245
Thy honesty and love doth mince° this matter,
Making it light to Cassio. Cassio, I love thee;
But never more be officer of mine.

Enter Desdemona, attended.

Look if my gentle love be not raised up.
I'll make thee an example.

Desdemona. What is the matter, dear. 250

Othello. All's well, sweeting; come away to bed.
[*To Montano*] Sir, for your hurts, myself will be
your surgeon.
Lead him off. [*Montano led off.*]

---

²⁴⁵ *pass* allow to pass ²⁴⁶ *mince* cut up (i.e., tell only part of)

Iago, look with care about the town
255   And silence those whom this vile brawl distracted.
Come, Desdemona: 'tis the soldiers' life
To have their balmy slumbers waked with strife.

> *Exit [with all but Iago and Cassio].*

Iago. What, are you hurt, lieutenant?

Cassio. Ay, past all surgery.

260   *Iago.* Marry, God forbid!

Cassio. Reputation, reputation, reputation! O, I have
lost my reputation! I have lost the immortal part of
myself, and what remains is bestial. My reputation,
Iago, my reputation.

265   *Iago.* As I am an honest man, I had thought you had
received some bodily wound. There is more sense°
in that than in reputation. Reputation is an idle and
most false imposition,° oft got without merit and
lost without deserving. You have lost no reputation
270   at all unless you repute yourself such a loser. What,
man, there are more ways to recover the general
again. You are but now cast in his mood°—a
punishment more in policy° than in malice—even
so as one would beat his offenseless dog to affright
275   an imperious lion. Sue to him again, and he's yours.

Cassio. I will rather sue to be despised than to deceive
so good a commander with so slight, so drunken,
and so indiscreet an officer. Drunk! And speak
parrot!° And squabble! Swagger! Swear! and dis-
280   course fustian° with one's own shadow! O thou
invisible spirit of wine, if thou hast no name to be
known by, let us call thee devil!

Iago. What was he that you followed with your sword?
What had he done to you?

285   *Cassio.* I know not.

Iago. Is't possible?

---

266 *sense* physical feeling   268 *imposition* external thing   272 *cast in his
mood* dismissed because of his anger   273 *in policy* politically necessary
278–79 *speak parrot* gabble without sense   279–80 *discourse fustian* speak
nonsense ("fustian" was a coarse cotton cloth used for stuffing)

Cassio. I remember a mass of things, but nothing distinctly: a quarrel, but nothing wherefore. O God, that men should put an enemy in their mouths to steal away their brains! that we should with joy, 290 pleasance, revel, and applause transform ourselves into beasts!

Iago. Why, but you are now well enough. How came you thus recovered?

Cassio. It hath pleased the devil drunkenness to give 295 place to the devil wrath. One unperfectness shows me another, to make me frankly despise myself.

Iago. Come, you are too severe a moraler. As the time, the place, and the condition of this country stands, I could heartily wish this had not befall'n; but since 300 it is as it is, mend it for your own good.

Cassio. I will ask him for my place again: he shall tell me I am a drunkard. Had I as many mouths as Hydra, such an answer would stop them all. To be now a sensible man, by and by a fool, and presently 305 a beast! O strange! Every inordinate cup is unblest, and the ingredient is a devil.

Iago. Come, come, good wine is a good familiar creature if it be well used. Exclaim no more against it. And, good lieutenant, I think you think I love 310 you.

Cassio. I have well approved it, sir. I drunk?

Iago. You or any man living may be drunk at a time, man. I tell you what you shall do. Our general's wife is now the general. I may say so in this respect, 315 for that he hath devoted and given up himself to the contemplation, mark, and devotement of her parts° and graces. Confess yourself freely to her; importune her help to put you in your place again. She is of so free, so kind, so apt, so blessed a disposition she 320 holds it a vice in her goodness not to do more than

---

³¹⁷ *devotement of her parts* devotion to her qualities

she is requested. This broken joint between you
and her husband entreat her to splinter;° and my
fortunes against any lay° worth naming, this crack
325 of your love shall grow stronger than it was before.

Cassio. You advise me well.

Iago. I protest, in the sincerity of love and honest
kindness.

Cassio. I think it freely; and betimes in the morning I
330 will beseech the virtuous Desdemona to undertake
for me. I am desperate of my fortunes if they check°
me.

Iago. You are in the right. Good night, lieutenant; I
must to the watch.

335 *Cassio.* Good night, honest Iago.   *Exit Cassio.*

Iago. And what's he then that says I play the villain,
When this advice is free° I give, and honest,
Probal to° thinking, and indeed the course
To win the Moor again? For 'tis most easy
340 Th' inclining° Desdemona to subdue
In any honest suit; she's framed as fruitful°
As the free elements.° And then for her
To win the Moor—were't to renounce his baptism,
All seals and symbols of redeemèd sin—
345 His soul is so enfettered to her love
That she may make, unmake, do what she list,
Even as her appetite° shall play the god
With his weak function.° How am I then a villain
To counsel Cassio to this parallel course,
350 Directly to his good? Divinity of hell!
When devils will the blackest sins put on,°
They do suggest at first with heavenly shows,°
As I do now. For whiles this honest fool
Plies Desdemona to repair his fortune,
355 And she for him pleads strongly to the Moor,

---

323 *splinter* splint   324 *lay* wager   331 *check* repulse   337 *free* generous
and open   338 *Probal to* provable by   340 *inclining* inclined (to be helpful)   341 *framed as fruitful* made as generous   342 *elements* i.e., basic
nature   347 *appetite* liking   348 *function* thought   351 *put on* advance,
further   352 *shows* appearances

unimportant soliloquy

I'll pour this pestilence into his ear:
That she repeals him° for her body's lust;
And by how much she strives to do him good,
She shall undo her credit with the Moor.
So will I turn her virtue into pitch,   360
And out of her own goodness make the net
That shall enmesh them all. How now, Roderigo?

Enter Roderigo.

Roderigo. I do follow here in the chase, not like a
hound that hunts, but one that fills up the cry.° My
money is almost spent; I have been tonight exceed-   365
ingly well cudgeled; and I think the issue will be,
I shall have so much experience for my pains; and
so, with no money at all, and a little more wit,
return again to Venice.

Iago. How poor are they that have not patience!   370
What wound did ever heal but by degrees?
Thou know'st we work by wit, and not by witch-
    craft;
And wit depends on dilatory time.
Does't not go well? Cassio hath beaten thee,
And thou by that small hurt hath cashiered Cassio.   375
Though other things grow fair against the sun,
Yet fruits that blossom first will first be ripe.
Content thyself awhile. By the mass, 'tis morning!
Pleasure and action make the hours seem short.
Retire thee; go where thou art billeted.   380
Away, I say! Thou shalt know more hereafter.
Nay, get thee gone!   *Exit Roderigo.*
                    Two things are to be done:
My wife must move° for Cassio to her mistress;
I'll set her on;
Myself awhile° to draw the Moor apart   385
And bring him jump° when he may Cassio find
Soliciting his wife. Ay, that's the way!
Dull not device by coldness and delay.   *Exit.*

---

357 *repeals him* asks for (Cassio's reinstatement)   364 *fills up the cry*
makes up one of the hunting pack, adding to the noise but not actually tracking   383 *move* petition   385 *awhile* at the same time
386 *jump* at the precise moment and place

ACT III

Scene I. [*A street.*]

Enter Cassio [and] Musicians.

Cassio. Masters, play here. I will content your pains.°
Something that's brief; and bid "Good morrow,
general."   [*They play.*]

[*Enter Clown.°*]

Clown. Why, masters, have your instruments been in
Naples° that they speak i' th' nose thus?

5 *Musician.* How, sir, how?

Clown. Are these, I pray you, wind instruments?

Musician. Ay, marry, are they, sir.

Clown. O, thereby hangs a tale.

Musician. Whereby hangs a tale, sir?

10 *Clown.* Marry, sir, by many a wind instrument that I
know. But, masters, here's money for you; and the
general so likes your music that he desires you,
for love's sake, to make no more noise with it.

Musician. Well, sir, we will not.

15 *Clown.* If you have any music that may not be heard,
to't again. But, as they say, to hear music the
general does not greatly care.

III.i.[1] *content your pains* reward your efforts [2] s.d. *Clown* fool
[4] *Naples* (this may refer either to the Neapolitan nasal tone, or to syph-
ilis—rife in Naples—which breaks down the nose)

Musician. We have none such, sir.

Clown. Then put up your pipes in your bag, for I'll
    away. Go, vanish into air, away!   20

                  Exit Musicians.

Cassio. Dost thou hear me, mine honest friend?

Clown. No. I hear not your honest friend. I hear you.

Cassio. Prithee keep up thy quillets.° There's a poor
    piece of gold for thee. If the gentlewoman that
    attends the general's wife be stirring, tell her there's   25
    one Cassio entreats her a little favor of speech.
    Wilt thou do this?

Clown. She is stirring, sir. If she will stir hither, I shall
    seem to notify unto her.°   *Exit Clown.*

              Enter Iago.

Cassio. In happy time, Iago.

Iago.   You have not been abed then?   30

Cassio. Why no, the day had broke before we parted.
    I have made bold, Iago, to send in to your wife;
    My suit to her is that she will to virtuous Desdemona
    Procure me some access.

Iago.   I'll send her to you presently,
    And I'll devise a mean to draw the Moor   35
    Out of the way, that your converse and business
    May be more free.

Cassio. I humbly thank you for 't.   *Exit [Iago].*
                  I never knew
    A Florentine° more kind and honest.

              Enter Emilia.

Emilia. Good morrow, good lieutenant. I am sorry   40
    For your displeasure;° but all will sure be well.
    The general and his wife are talking of it,

²³ *quillets* puns ²⁹ *seem . . . her* (the Clown is mocking Cassio's
overly elegant manner of speaking) ³⁹ *Florentine* i.e., Iago is as kind
as if he were from Cassio's home town, Florence ⁴¹ *displeasure* dis-
comforting

And she speaks for you stoutly. The Moor replies
That he you hurt is of great fame in Cyprus
45 And great affinity,° and that in wholesome wisdom
He might not but refuse you. But he protests he loves
    you,
And needs no other suitor but his likings
To bring you in again.

Cassio.   Yet I beseech you,
If you think fit, or that it may be done,
50 Give me advantage of some brief discourse
With Desdemona alone.

Emilia.   Pray you come in.
I will bestow you where you shall have time
To speak your bosom° freely.

Cassio.   I am much bound to you.
                                   [*Exeunt.*]

Scene II. [*The citadel.*]

Enter Othello, Iago, and Gentlemen.

Othello. These letters give, Iago, to the pilot
And by him do my duties to the Senate.
    That done, I will be walking on the works;
    Repair° there to me.

Iago.   Well, my good lord, I'll do't.

5 *Othello.* This fortification, gentlemen, shall we see't?

Gentlemen. We'll wait upon your lordship.   *Exeunt.*

---

45 *affinity* family   53 *bosom* inmost thoughts   III.ii.4 *Repair* go

Scene III. [*The citadel.*]

Enter Desdemona, Cassio, and Emilia.

Desdemona. Be thou assured, good Cassio, I will do
  All my abilities in thy behalf.

Emilia. Good madam, do. I warrant it grieves my hus-
    band
  As if the cause were his.

Desdemona. O, that's an honest fellow. Do not doubt,
    Cassio,   5
  But I will have my lord and you again
  As friendly as you were.

Cassio.   Bounteous madam,
  Whatever shall become of Michael Cassio,
  He's never anything but your true servant.

Desdemona. I know't; I thank you. You do love my   10
    lord.
  You have known him long, and be you well assured
  He shall in strangeness stand no farther off
  Than in a politic distance.°

Cassio.   Ay, but, lady,
  That policy may either last so long,
  Or feed upon such nice° and waterish diet,   15
  Or breed itself so out of circumstances,°
  That, I being absent, and my place supplied,°
  My general will forget my love and service.

Desdemona. Do not doubt° that; before Emilia here
  I give thee warrant of thy place. Assure thee,   20
  If I do vow a friendship, I'll perform it

III.iii.¹²⁻¹³ *He . . . distance* i.e., he shall act no more distant to you
than is necessary for political reasons ¹⁵ *nice* trivial ¹⁶ *Or . . . circumstances* i.e., or grow so on the basis of accidental happenings and
political needs ¹⁷ *supplied* filled ¹⁹ *doubt* imagine

To the last article. My lord shall never rest;
I'll watch him tame° and talk him out of patience;
His bed shall seem a school, his board a shrift;°
25   I'll intermingle everything he does
With Cassio's suit. Therefore be merry, Cassio,
For thy solicitor shall rather die
Than give thy cause away.

>   *Enter Othello and Iago [at a distance].*

Emilia. Madam, here comes my lord.

30   *Cassio.* Madam, I'll take my leave.

Desdemona. Why, stay, and hear me speak.

Cassio. Madam, not now. I am very ill at ease,
Unfit for mine own purposes.

Desdemona. Well, do your discretion.   *Exit Cassio.*

Iago. Ha! I like not that.

35   *Othello.*   What dost thou say?

Iago. Nothing, my lord; or if—I know not what.

Othello. Was not that Cassio parted from my wife?

Iago. Cassio, my lord? No, sure, I cannot think it
That he would steal away so guilty-like,
Seeing your coming.

40   *Othello.*   I do believe 'twas he.

Desdemona. [*Coming to them*] How now, my lord?
I have been talking with a suitor here,
A man that languishes in your displeasure.

Othello. Who is't you mean?

Desdemona. Why, your lieutenant, Cassio. Good my
45   lord,
If I have any grace or power to move you,
His present° reconciliation take.
For if he be not one that truly loves you,

---

²³ *watch him tame* (animals were tamed by being kept awake)
²⁴ *board a shrift* table (seem) a confessional   ⁴⁷ *present* immediate

That errs in ignorance, and not in cunning,
I have no judgment in an honest face.   50
I prithee call him back.

Othello.   Went he hence now?

Desdemona. I' sooth so humbled
That he hath left part of his grief with me
To suffer with him. Good love, call him back.

Othello. Not now, sweet Desdemon; some other time.   55

Desdemona. But shall't be shortly?

Othello.   The sooner, sweet, for you.

Desdemona. Shall't be tonight at supper?

Othello.   No, not tonight.

Desdemona. Tomorrow dinner then?

Othello.   I shall not dine at home;
I meet the captains at the citadel.

Desdemona. Why then, tomorrow night, on Tuesday
    morn,   60
On Tuesday noon, or night, on Wednesday morn.
I prithee name the time, but let it not
Exceed three days. In faith, he's penitent;
And yet his trespass, in our common reason
(Save that, they say, the wars must make example   65
Out of her best), is not almost a fault
T' incur a private check.° When shall he come?
Tell me, Othello. I wonder in my soul
What you would ask me that I should deny
Or stand so mamm'ring° on. What? Michael Cassio,   70
That came awooing with you, and so many a time,
When I have spoke of you dispraisingly,
Hath ta'en your part—to have so much to do
To bring him in? By'r Lady, I could do much—

Othello. Prithee no more. Let him come when he will!   75
I will deny thee nothing.

66–67 *is . . . check* is almost not serious enough for a private rebuke
(let alone a public disgrace)   70 *mamm'ring* hesitating

Desdemona.   Why, this is not a boon;
'Tis as I should entreat you wear your gloves,
Or feed on nourishing dishes, or keep you warm,
Or sue to you to do a peculiar profit°
80 To your own person. Nay, when I have a suit
Wherein I mean to touch your love indeed,
It shall be full of poise° and difficult weight,
And fearful to be granted.

Othello.   I will deny thee nothing!
Whereon I do beseech thee grant me this,
85 To leave me but a little to myself.

Desdemona. Shall I deny you? No. Farewell, my lord.

Othello. Farewell, my Desdemona: I'll come to thee
    straight.°

Desdemona. Emilia, come. Be as your fancies teach
    you;
    Whate'er you be, I am obedient. *Exit* [*with Emilia*].

90 *Othello.* Excellent wretch! Perdition catch my soul
But I do love thee! And when I love thee not,
Chaos is come again.

Iago. My noble lord——

Othello.   What dost thou say, Iago?

Iago. Did Michael Cassio, when you wooed my lady,
95 Know of your love?

Othello. He did, from first to last. Why dost thou ask?

Iago. But for a satisfaction of my thought,
No further harm.

Othello.   Why of thy thought, Iago?

Iago. I did not think he had been acquainted with her.

100 *Othello.* O, yes, and went between us° very oft.

Iago. Indeed?

Othello. Indeed? Ay, indeed! Discern'st thou aught in
    that?

---

79 *peculiar profit*   particularly personal good   82 *poise*   weight
87 *straight* at once   100 *between us* i.e., as messenger

Is he not honest?

Iago.　　　　　　　　Honest, my lord?

Othello.　　　　　　　　　Honest? Ay, honest.

Iago. My lord, for aught I know.

Othello. What dost thou think?

Iago.　　　　　　　　Think, my lord?

Othello.　　　　　　　　Think, my lord? *105*
By heaven, thou echoest me,
As if there were some monster in thy thought
Too hideous to be shown. Thou dost mean some-
　thing.
I heard thee say even now, thou lik'st not that,
When Cassio left my wife. What didst not like? *110*
And when I told thee he was of my counsel°
Of my whole course of wooing, thou cried'st "In-
　deed?"
And didst contract and purse thy brow together,
As if thou then hadst shut up in thy brain
Some horrible conceit.° If thou dost love me, *115*
Show me thy thought.

Iago. My lord, you know I love you.

Othello.　　　　　　　　I think thou dost;
And, for I know thou'rt full of love and honesty
And weigh'st thy words before thou giv'st them
　breath,
Therefore these stops° of thine fright me the more; *120*
For such things in a false disloyal knave
Are tricks of custom;° but in a man that's just
They're close dilations,° working from the heart
That passion cannot rule.

Iago.　　　　　　　　For Michael Cassio,
I dare be sworn, I think that he is honest. *125*

Othello. I think so too.

---

111 *of my counsel* in my confidence　115 *conceit* thought　120 *stops*
interruptions　122 *of custom* customary　123 *close dilations* expressions
of hidden thoughts

Iago.   Men should be what they seem;
 Or those that be not, would they might seem none!

Othello. Certain, men should be what they seem.

Iago. Why then, I think Cassio's an honest man.

130 *Othello.* Nay, yet there's more in this?
 I prithee speak to me as to thy thinkings,
 As thou dost ruminate, and give thy worst of
  thoughts
 The worst of words.

Iago.   Good my lord, pardon me:
 Though I am bound to every act of duty,
135 I am not bound to that all slaves are free to.
 Utter my thoughts? Why, say they are vile and false,
 As where's that palace whereinto foul things
 Sometimes intrude not? Who has that breast so pure
 But some uncleanly apprehensions
140 Keep leets and law days,° and in sessions sit
 With meditations lawful?

Othello. Thou dost conspire against thy friend, Iago,
 If thou but think'st him wronged, and mak'st his ear
 A stranger to thy thoughts.

Iago.   I do beseech you—
145 Though I perchance am vicious in my guess
 (As I confess it is my nature's plague
 To spy into abuses, and of my jealousy
 Shape faults that are not), that your wisdom
 From one that so imperfectly conceits
150 Would take no notice, nor build yourself a trouble
 Out of his scattering and unsure observance.
 It were not for your quiet nor your good,
 Nor for my manhood, honesty, and wisdom,
 To let you know my thoughts.

Othello.   What dost thou mean?

155 *Iago.* Good name in man and woman, dear my lord,
 Is the immediate jewel of their souls.

---

140 *leets and law days* meetings of local courts

Who steals my purse steals trash; 'tis something,
   nothing;
'Twas mine, 'tis his, and has been slave to thousands;
But he that filches from me my good name
Robs me of that which not enriches him   160
And makes me poor indeed.

Othello. By heaven, I'll know thy thoughts!

Iago. You cannot, if my heart were in your hand;
   Nor shall not whilst 'tis in my custody.

Othello. Ha!

Iago.   O, beware, my lord, of jealousy!   165
   It is the green-eyed monster, which doth mock
   The meat it feeds on. That cuckold lives in bliss
   Who, certain of his fate, loves not his wronger;
   But O, what damnèd minutes tells° he o'er
   Who dotes, yet doubts—suspects, yet fondly° loves! 170

Othello. O misery.

Iago. Poor and content is rich, and rich enough;
   But riches fineless° is as poor as winter
   To him that ever fears he shall be poor.
   Good God the souls of all my tribe defend   175
   From jealousy!

Othello.   Why? Why is this?
   Think'st thou I'd make a life of jealousy,
   To follow still° the changes of the moon
   With fresh suspicions? No! To be once in doubt
   Is to be resolved. Exchange me for a goat   180
   When I shall turn the business of my soul
   To such exsufflicate and blown° surmises,
   Matching thy inference. 'Tis not to make me jealous
   To say my wife is fair, feeds well, loves company,
   Is free of speech, sings, plays, and dances;   185
   Where virtue is, these are more virtuous.
   Nor from mine own weak merits will I draw
   The smallest fear or doubt of her revolt,

---

¹⁶⁹ *tells* counts   ¹⁷⁰ *fondly* foolishly   ¹⁷³ *fineless* infinite   ¹⁷⁸ *To follow still* to change always (as the phases of the moon)   ¹⁸² *exsufflicate and blown* inflated and flyblown

For she had eyes, and chose me. No, Iago;
190 I'll see before I doubt; when I doubt, prove;
And on the proof there is no more but this:
Away at once with love or jealousy!

Iago. I am glad of this; for now I shall have reason
To show the love and duty that I bear you
195 With franker spirit. Therefore, as I am bound,
Receive it from me. I speak not yet of proof.
Look to your wife; observe her well with Cassio;
Wear your eyes thus: not jealous nor secure.
I would not have your free and noble nature
200 Out of self-bounty° be abused. Look to't.
I know our country disposition well:
In Venice they do let heaven see the pranks
They dare not show their husbands; their best con-
science
Is not to leave't undone, but kept unknown.°

205 *Othello.* Dost thou say so?

Iago. She did deceive her father, marrying you;
And when she seemed to shake and fear your looks,
She loved them most.

Othello. And so she did.

Iago. Why, go to then!
She that so young could give out such a seeming
210 To seel° her father's eyes up close as oak°—
He thought 'twas witchcraft. But I am much to
blame.
I humbly do beseech you of your pardon
For too much loving you.

Othello. I am bound to thee forever.

Iago. I see this hath a little dashed your spirits.

Othello. Not a jot, not a jot.

215 *Iago.* Trust me, I fear it has.

---

²⁰⁰ *self-bounty* innate kindness (which attributes his own motives to
others) ²⁰³⁻⁴ *their . . . unknown* i.e., their morality does not forbid
adultery, but it does forbid being found out ²¹⁰ *seel* hoodwink ²¹⁰ *oak*
(a close-grained wood)

I hope you will consider what is spoke
Comes from my love. But I do see y' are moved.
I am to pray you not to strain° my speech
To grosser issues, nor to larger reach°
Than to suspicion.   220

Othello. I will not.

Iago.   Should you do so, my lord,
My speech should fall into such vile success
Which my thoughts aimed not. Cassio's my worthy
    friend—
My lord, I see y' are moved.

Othello.   No, not much moved.
I do not think but Desdemona's honest.   225

Iago. Long live she so. And long live you to think so.

Othello. And yet, how nature erring from itself——

Iago. Ay, there's the point, as (to be bold with you)
Not to affect many proposèd matches
Of her own clime, complexion, and degree,°   230
Whereto we see in all things nature tends° —
Foh! one may smell in such a will most rank,
Foul disproportions, thoughts unnatural.
But, pardon me, I do not in position°
Distinctly° speak of her; though I may fear   235
Her will, recoiling to her better judgment,
May fall to match° you with her country forms,°
And happily° repent.

Othello.   Farewell, farewell!
If more thou dost perceive, let me know more.
Set on thy wife to observe. Leave me, Iago.   240

Iago. My lord, I take my leave.   [*Going.*]

²¹⁸ *strain* enlarge the meaning of ²¹⁹ *reach* meaning ²³⁰ *degree* social
station ²³¹ *in . . . tends* i.e., all things in nature seek out their own
kind ²³⁴ *position* general argument ²³⁵ *Distinctly* specifically ²³⁷ *fall
to match* happen to compare ²³⁷ *country forms* i.e., the familiar
appearances of her countrymen ²³⁸ *happily* by chance

Othello. Why did I marry? This honest creature doubt-
    less
    Sees and knows more, much more, than he unfolds.

Iago. [*Returns.*] My lord, I would I might entreat your
    honor
245   To scan this thing no farther. Leave it to time.
    Although 'tis fit that Cassio have his place,
    For sure he fills it up with great ability,
    Yet, if you please to hold him off awhile,
    You shall by that perceive him and his means.
250   Note if your lady strain his entertainment°
    With any strong or vehement importunity;
    Much will be seen in that. In the meantime
    Let me be thought too busy in my fears
    (As worthy cause I have to fear I am)
255   And hold her free, I do beseech your honor.

Othello. Fear not my government.°

Iago.   I once more take my leave.
                                    Exit.

Othello. This fellow's of exceeding honesty,
    And knows all qualities,° with a learnèd spirit
    Of human dealings. If I do prove her haggard,°
260   Though that her jesses° were my dear heartstrings,
    I'd whistle her off and let her down the wind°
    To prey at fortune. Haply for° I am black
    And have not those soft parts° of conversation
    That chamberers° have, or for I am declined
265   Into the vale of years—yet that's not much—
    She's gone. I am abused, and my relief
    Must be to loathe her. O curse of marriage,
    That we can call these delicate creatures ours,
    And not their appetites! I had rather be a toad

---

250 *strain his entertainment* urge strongly that he be reinstated
256 *government* self-control 258 *qualities* natures, types of people
259 *haggard* a partly trained hawk which has gone wild again 260 *jesses*
straps which held the hawk's legs to the trainer's wrist 261 *I'd . . .
wind* I would release her (like an untamable hawk) and let her fly free
262 *Haply for* it may be because 263 *soft parts* gentle qualities and
manners 264 *chamberers* courtiers—or perhaps, accomplished seducers

And live upon the vapor of a dungeon   270
Than keep a corner in the thing I love
For others' uses. Yet 'tis the plague to great ones;
Prerogatived are they less than the base.
'Tis destiny unshunnable, like death.
Even then this forkèd° plague is fated to us   275
When we do quicken.° Look where she comes.

              Enter Desdemona and Emilia.

If she be false, heaven mocked itself!
I'll not believe't.

Desdemona.   How now, my dear Othello?
Your dinner, and the generous islanders
By you invited, do attend° your presence.   280

Othello. I am to blame.

Desdemona.   Why do you speak so faintly?
Are you not well?

Othello. I have a pain upon my forehead, here.°

Desdemona. Why, that's with watching; 'twill away
     again.
Let me but bind it hard, within this hour   285
It will be well.

Othello.   Your napkin° is too little;
     [*He pushes the handkerchief away, and it falls.*]
Let it° alone. Come, I'll go in with you.

Desdemona. I am very sorry that you are not well.
                              Exit [*with Othello*].

Emilia. I am glad I have found this napkin;
This was her first remembrance from the Moor.   290
My wayward husband hath a hundred times
Wooed me to steal it; but she so loves the token

---

²⁷⁵ *forkèd* horned (the sign of the cuckold was horns)   ²⁷⁶ *do quicken*
are born   ²⁸⁰ *attend* wait   ²⁸³ *here* (he points to his imaginary horns)
²⁸⁶ *napkin* elaborately worked handkerchief   ²⁸⁷ *it* (it makes a considerable difference in the interpretation of later events whether this
"it" refers to Othello's forehead or to the handkerchief; nothing in the
text makes the reference clear)

(For he conjured her she should ever keep it)
That she reserves it evermore about her
295   To kiss and talk to. I'll have the work ta'en out°
And give't Iago. What he will do with it,
Heaven knows, not I; I nothing° but to please his
     fantasy.°

Enter Iago.

Iago. How now? What do you here alone?

Emilia. Do not you chide; I have a thing for you.

Iago. You have a thing for me? It is a common
300   thing——

Emilia. Ha?

Iago. To have a foolish wife.

Emilia. O, is that all? What will you give me now
     For that same handkerchief?

Iago.   What handkerchief?

305 *Emilia.* What handkerchief!
Why, that the Moor first gave to Desdemona,
That which so often you did bid me steal.

Iago. Hast stol'n it from her?

Emilia. No, but she let it drop by negligence,
310   And to th' advantage,° I, being here, took't up.
Look, here 't is.

Iago.   A good wench. Give it me.

Emilia. What will you do with't, that you have been
     so earnest
To have me filch it?

Iago.   Why, what is that to you?

                             [*Takes it.*]

Emilia. If it be not for some purpose of import,°
315   Give't me again. Poor lady, she'll run mad
When she shall lack° it.

---

295 *work ta'en out* needlework copied   297 *I nothing* I wish nothing
297 *fantasy* fancy, whim   310 *to th' advantage* being lucky   314 *import*
importance   316 *lack* miss

Iago.   Be not acknown on't.° *Soliloquy*
  I have use for it. Go, leave me.   *Exit Emilia.*
  I will in Cassio's lodging lose this napkin   *Iago setting up*
  And let him find it. Trifles light as air   *Cassio*
  Are to the jealous confirmations strong   *320*
  As proofs of Holy Writ. This may do something.
  The Moor already changes with my poison:
  Dangerous conceits are in their natures poisons,
  Which at the first are scarce found to distaste,°
  But, with a little,° act upon the blood,   *325*
  Burn like the mines of sulfur. I did say so.

Enter Othello.

  Look where he comes! Not poppy nor mandragora,°
  Nor all the drowsy syrups of the world,
  Shall ever medicine thee to that sweet sleep
  Which thou owedst° yesterday.

Othello.   Ha! ha! False to me?   *330*

Iago. Why, how now, general? No more of that.

Othello. Avaunt! be gone! Thou hast set me on the
    rack.
  I swear 'tis better to be much abused
  Than but to know't a little.

Iago.   How now, my lord?

Othello. What sense had I of her stol'n hours of lust?   *335*
  I saw't not, thought it not, it harmed not me;
  I slept the next night well, fed well, was free and
    merry;
  I found not Cassio's kisses on her lips.
  He that is robbed, not wanting° what is stol'n,
  Let him not know't, and he's not robbed at all.   *340*

Iago. I am sorry to hear this.

---

³¹⁶ *Be not acknown on't* forget you ever saw it   ³²⁴ *are scarce found
to distaste* scarcely can be tasted   ³²⁵ *with a little* in a short time
³²⁷ *poppy nor mandragora* (soporifics)   ³³⁰ *owedst* possessed   ³³⁹ *want-
ing* missing

Othello. I had been happy if the general camp,
  Pioners° and all, had tasted her sweet body,
  So I had nothing known. O now, forever
345 Farewell the tranquil mind! Farewell content!
  Farewell the plumèd troops, and the big wars
  That makes ambition virtue! O, farewell!
  Farewell the neighing steed and the shrill trump,
  The spirit-stirring drum, th' ear-piercing fife,
350 The royal banner, and all quality,
  Pride, pomp, and circumstance° of glorious war!
  And O you mortal engines° whose rude throats
  Th' immortal Jove's dread clamors° counterfeit,
  Farewell! Othello's occupation's gone!

355 *Iago.* Is't possible, my lord?

Othello. Villain, be sure thou prove my love a whore!
  Be sure of it; give me the ocular proof;
  Or, by the worth of mine eternal soul,
  Thou hadst been better have been born a dog
  Than answer my waked wrath!

360 *Iago.*   Is't come to this?

Othello. Make me to see't; or at the least so prove it
  That the probation° bear no hinge nor loop
  To hang a doubt on—or woe upon thy life!

Iago. My noble lord——

365 *Othello.* If thou dost slander her and torture me,
  Never pray more; abandon all remorse;
  On horror's head horrors accumulate;
  Do deeds to make heaven weep, all earth amazed;
  For nothing canst thou to damnation add
  Greater than that.

370 *Iago.*   O grace! O heaven forgive me!
  Are you a man? Have you a soul or sense?
  God b' wi' you! Take mine office. O wretched fool,
  That lov'st to make thine honesty a vice!
  O monstrous world! Take note, take note, O world,

³⁴³ *Pioners* (the basest manual laborers in the army, who dug trenches and mines) ³⁵¹ *circumstance* pageantry ³⁵² *mortal engines* lethal weapons, i.e., cannon ³⁵³ *clamors* i.e., thunder ³⁶² *probation* proof

To be direct and honest is not safe.   375
I thank you for this profit, and from hence
I'll love no friend, sith° love breeds such offense.

Othello. Nay, stay. Thou shouldst be honest.

Iago. I should be wise; for honesty's a fool
   And loses that it works for.

Othello.   By the world,   *He is completely confused* 380
I think my wife be honest, and think she is not;
I think that thou art just, and think thou art not.
I'll have some proof. My name, that was as fresh
As Dian's° visage, is now begrimed and black
As mine own face. If there be cords, or knives,   385
Poison, or fire, or suffocating streams,
I'll not endure it. Would I were satisfied!
Iago. I see you are eaten up with passion.
I do repent me that I put it to you.
You would be satisfied?

Othello.   Would? Nay, and I will.   390

Iago. And may; but how? How satisfied, my lord?
Would you, the supervisor,° grossly gape on?
Behold her topped?

Othello.   Death and damnation! O!

Iago. It were a tedious° difficulty, I think,
To bring them to that prospect.° Damn them then,   395
If ever mortal eyes do see them bolster°
More than their own! What then? How then?
What shall I say? Where's satisfaction?
It is impossible you should see this,
Were they as prime° as goats, as hot as monkeys,   400
As salt° as wolves in pride,° and fools as gross
As ignorance made drunk. But yet, I say,

---

377 *sith* since   384 *Dian's* Diana's (goddess of the moon and of chastity)   392 *supervisor* onlooker   394 *tedious* hard to arrange   395 *prospect* sight (where they can be seen)   396 *bolster* go to bed   400–01 *prime, salt* lustful   401 *pride* heat

If imputation and strong circumstances
Which lead directly to the door of truth
405   Will give you satisfaction, you might have't.

Othello. Give me a living reason she's disloyal.

Iago. I do not like the office.°
    But sith I am entered in this cause so far,
    Pricked° to't by foolish honesty and love,
410   I will go on. I lay with Cassio lately,
    And being troubled with a raging tooth,
    I could not sleep.
    There are a kind of men so loose of soul
    That in their sleeps will mutter their affairs.
415   One of this kind is Cassio.
    In sleep I heard him say, "Sweet Desdemona,
    Let us be wary, let us hide our loves!"
    And then, sir, would he gripe° and wring my hand,
    Cry "O sweet creature!" Then kiss me hard,
420   As if he plucked up kisses by the roots
    That grew upon my lips; laid his leg o'er my thigh,
    And sigh, and kiss, and then cry, "Cursèd fate
    That gave thee to the Moor!"

Othello. O monstrous! monstrous!

Iago.   Nay, this was but his dream.

425 *Othello.* But this denoted a foregone conclusion,°
    'Tis a shrewd doubt,° though it be but a dream.

Iago. And this may help to thicken other proofs
    That do demonstrate° thinly.

Othello.   I'll tear her all to pieces!

Iago. Nay, yet be wise. Yet we see nothing done;
430   She may be honest yet. Tell me but this:
    Have you not sometimes seen a handkerchief
    Spotted with strawberries in your wife's hand?

Othello. I gave her such a one; 'twas my first gift.

---

⁴⁰⁷ *office* duty   ⁴⁰⁹ *Pricked* spurred   ⁴¹⁸ *gripe* seize   ⁴²⁵ *foregone con-clusion* consummated fact   ⁴²⁶ *shrewd doubt* penetrating guess   ⁴²⁸ *demonstrate* show, appear

Iago. I know not that; but such a handkerchief—
  I am sure it was your wife's—did I today   *435*
  See Cassio wipe his beard with.

Othello.   If it be that——

Iago. If it be that, or any that was hers,
  It speaks against her with the other proofs.

Othello. O, that the slave had forty thousand lives!
  One is too poor, too weak for my revenge.   *440*
  Now do I see 'tis true. Look here, Iago:
  All my fond love thus do I blow to heaven.
  'Tis gone.
  Arise, black vengeance, from the hollow hell!
  Yield up, O Love, thy crown and hearted° throne   *445*
  To tyrannous hate! Swell, bosom, with thy fraught,°
  For 'tis of aspics'° tongues.

Iago.   Yet be content.°

Othello. O, blood, blood, blood!

Iago. Patience, I say. Your mind may change.

Othello. Never, Iago. Like to the Pontic Sea,°   *450*
  Whose icy current and compulsive course
  Nev'r keeps retiring ebb, but keeps due on
  To the Propontic and the Hellespont,
  Even so my bloody thoughts, with violent pace,
  Shall nev'r look back, nev'r ebb to humble love,   *455*
  Till that a capable and wide° revenge
  Swallow them up. [*He kneels.*] Now, by yond marble heaven,
  In the due reverence of a sacred vow
  I here engage my words.

Iago.   Do not rise yet.

                    [*Iago kneels.*]
  Witness, you ever-burning lights above,   *460*

---

445 *hearted* seated in the heart   **446** *fraught* burden   **447** *aspics'* asps'
447 *content* patient, quiet   **450** *Pontic Sea* the Black Sea (famous for
the strong and constant current with which it flows through the Bosporus
into the Mediterranean, where the water level is lower)   **456** *capable
and wide* sufficient and far-reaching

　　You elements that clip° us round about,
　　Witness that here Iago doth give up
　　The execution° of his wit, hands, heart
　　To wronged Othello's service! Let him command,
465　And to obey shall be in me remorse,°
　　What bloody business ever.°　　　　　[*They rise.*]

Othello.　　　　　　　　　　　I greet thy love,
　　Not with vain thanks but with acceptance boun-
　　　teous,°
　　And will upon the instant put thee to't.°
　　Within these three days let me hear thee say
470　That Cassio's not alive.

Iago. My friend is dead. 'Tis done at your request.
　　But let her live.

Othello.　　　　　　Damn her, lewd minx! O, damn her!
　　Damn her!
　　Come, go with me apart. I will withdraw
　　To furnish me with some swift means of death
475　For the fair devil. Now art thou my lieutenant.

Iago. I am your own forever.　　　　　　　*Exeunt.*

Scene IV. [*A street.*]

Enter Desdemona, Emilia, and Clown.

Desdemona. Do you know, sirrah, where Lieutenant
　　Cassio lies?°

Clown. I dare not say he lies anywhere.

Desdemona. Why, man?

5　*Clown.* He's a soldier, and for me to say a soldier lies,
　　'tis stabbing.

⁴⁶¹ *clip* enfold ⁴⁶³ *execution* workings, action ⁴⁶⁵ *remorse* pity
⁴⁶⁶ *ever* soever ⁴⁶⁷ *bounteous* absolute ⁴⁶⁸ *to't* i.e., to the work you
have said you are prepared to do III.iv.² *lies* lodges

Desdemona. Go to. Where lodges he?

Clown. To tell you where he lodges is to tell you where
I lie.

Desdemona. Can anything be made of this?   10

Clown. I know not where he lodges, and for me to
devise a lodging, and say he lies here or he lies there,
were to lie in mine own throat.°

Desdemona. Can you enquire him out, and be edified°
by report?   15

Clown. I will catechize the world for him; that is, make
questions, and by them answer.

Desdemona. Seek him, bid him come hither. Tell him
I have moved° my lord on his behalf and hope all
will be well.   20

Clown. To do this is within the compass° of man's wit,
and therefore I will attempt the doing it. *Exit Clown.*

Desdemona. Where should° I lose the handkerchief,
Emilia?

Emilia. I know not, madam.

Desdemona. Believe me, I had rather have lost my
purse   25
Full of crusadoes.° And but my noble Moor
Is true of mind, and made of no such baseness
As jealous creatures are, it were enough
To put him to ill thinking.

Emilia.   Is he not jealous?

Desdemona. Who? He? I think the sun where he was
born   30
Drew all such humors° from him.

Emilia.   Look where he comes.

---

[18] *lie in mine own throat* (to lie in the throat is to lie absolutely and
completely) [14] *edified* enlightened (Desdemona mocks the Clown's
overly elaborate diction) [19] *moved* pleaded with [21] *compass* reach
[23] *should* might [26] *crusadoes* Portuguese gold coins [31] *humors* characteristics

Enter Othello.

Desdemona. I will not leave him now till Cassio
Be called to him. How is't with you, my lord?

Othello. Well, my good lady. [*Aside*] O, hardness to
dissemble!° —
How do you, Desdemona?

35 **Desdemona.**   Well, my good lord.

Othello. Give me your hand. This hand is moist,°
my lady.

Desdemona. It hath felt no age nor known no sorrow.

Othello. This argues° fruitfulness and liberal° heart.
Hot, hot, and moist. This hand of yours requires
40 A sequester° from liberty; fasting and prayer;
Much castigation; exercise devout;
For here's a young and sweating devil here
That commonly rebels. 'Tis a good hand,
A frank one.

Desdemona.   You may, indeed, say so;
45 For 'twas that hand that gave away my heart.

Othello. A liberal hand! The hearts of old gave hands,
But our new heraldry° is hands, not hearts.

Desdemona. I cannot speak of this. Come now, your
promise!

Othello. What promise, chuck?

Desdemona. I have sent to bid Cassio come speak with
50 you.

Othello. I have a salt and sorry rheum° offends me.
Lend me thy handkerchief.

---

34 *hardness to dissemble* (Othello may refer here either to the difficulty he has in maintaining his appearance of composure, or to
what he believes to be Desdemona's hardened hypocrisy) **36** *moist*
(a moist, hot hand was taken as a sign of a lustful nature) **38** *argues*
suggests **38** *liberal* free, open (but also with a suggestion of "licentious";
from here on in this scene Othello's words bear a double meaning,
seeming to be normal but accusing Desdemona of being unfaithful)
40 *sequester* separation **47** *heraldry* heraldic symbolism **51** *a salt and
sorry rheum* a heavy, running head cold

Desdemona.   Here, my lord.

Othello. That which I gave you.

Desdemona.   I have it not about me.

Othello. Not?

Desdemona. No, indeed, my lord.

Othello.   That's a fault.
That handkerchief   55
Did an Egyptian to my mother give.
She was a charmer,° and could almost read
The thoughts of people. She told her, while she
 kept it
'Twould make her amiable° and subdue my father
Entirely to her love; but if she lost it   60
Or made a gift of it, my father's eye
Should hold her loathèd, and his spirits should hunt
After new fancies. She, dying, gave it me,
And bid me, when my fate would have me wived,
To give it her. I did so; and take heed on't; 65
Make it a darling like your precious eye.
To lose't or give't away were such perdition
As nothing else could match.

Desdemona.   Is't possible?

Othello. 'Tis true. There's magic in the web° of it.
A sibyl that had numbered in the world   70
The sun to course two hundred compasses,
In her prophetic fury° sewed the work;
The worms were hallowed that did breed the silk,
And it was dyed in mummy° which the skillful
Conserved of maidens' hearts.

Desdemona.   Indeed? Is't true? 75

Othello. Most veritable. Therefore look to't well.

Desdemona. Then would to God that I had never
 seen't!

---

⁵⁷ *charmer* magician ⁵⁹ *amiable* desirable ⁶⁹ *web* weaving ⁷² *prophetic fury* seized by the spirit and able to prophesy ⁷⁴ *mummy* liquid drained from embalmed bodies

Othello. Ha! Wherefore?

Desdemona. Why do you speak so startingly and rash?

80 *Othello.* Is't lost? Is't gone? Speak, is it out o' th' way?

Desdemona. Heaven bless us!

Othello. Say you?

Desdemona. It is not lost. But what an if it were?

Othello. How?

85 *Desdemona.* I say it is not lost.

Othello. Fetch't, let me see't!

Desdemona. Why, so I can; but I will not now.
  This is a trick to put me from my suit:
  Pray you let Cassio be received again.

90 *Othello.* Fetch me the handkerchief! My mind misgives.

Desdemona. Come, come!
  You'll never meet a more sufficient° man——

Othello. The handkerchief!

Desdemona.   A man that all his time
  Hath founded his good fortunes on your love,
95 Shared dangers with you——

Othello. The handkerchief!

Desdemona. I'faith, you are to blame.

Othello. Away!   *Exit Othello.*

Emilia. Is not this man jealous?

100 *Desdemona.* I nev'r saw this before.
  Sure there's some wonder in this handkerchief;
  I am most unhappy in the loss of it.

Emilia. 'Tis not a year or two shows us a man.
  They are all but stomachs, and we all but food;
105 They eat us hungerly, and when they are full,
  They belch us.

---

⁹² *sufficient* complete, with all proper qualities

Enter Iago and Cassio.

             Look you, Cassio and my husband.

Iago. There is no other way; 'tis she must do't.
And lo the happiness! Go and importune her.

Desdemona. How now, good Cassio? What's the news
  with you?

Cassio. Madam, my former suit. I do beseech you   *110*
That by your virtuous means I may again
Exist, and be a member of his love
Whom I with all the office° of my heart
Entirely honor. I would not be delayed.
If my offense be of such mortal kind   *115*
That nor my service past, nor present sorrows,
Nor purposed merit in futurity,
Can ransom me into his love again,
But to know so must be my benefit.°
So shall I clothe me in a forced content,   *120*
And shut myself up in some other course
To fortune's alms.

Desdemona.   Alas, thrice-gentle Cassio,
My advocation° is not now in tune.
My lord is not my lord; nor should I know him
Were he in favor° as in humor altered.   *125*
So help me every spirit sanctified
As I have spoken for you all my best
And stood within the blank° of his displeasure
For my free speech. You must awhile be patient.
What I can do I will; and more I will   *130*
Than for myself I dare. Let that suffice you.

Iago. Is my lord angry?

Emilia.   He went hence but now,
And certainly in strange unquietness.

Iago. Can he be angry? I have seen the cannon
When it hath blown his ranks into the air   *135*
And, like the devil, from his very arm

---

¹¹³ *office* duty   ¹¹⁹ *benefit* good   ¹²³ *advocation* advocacy   ¹²⁵ *favor*
countenance   ¹²⁸ *blank* bull's-eye of a target

Puffed his own brother. And is he angry?
Something of moment° then. I will go meet him.
There's matter in't indeed if he be angry.

Desdemona. I prithee do so.   *Exit* [*Iago*].
140   Something sure of state,°
Either from Venice or some unhatched practice°
Made demonstrable here in Cyprus to him,
Hath puddled° his clear spirit; and in such cases
Men's natures wrangle with inferior things,
145   Though great ones are their object. 'Tis even so.
For let our finger ache, and it endues°
Our other, healthful members even to a sense
Of pain. Nay, we must think men are not gods,
Nor of them look for such observancy
150   As fits the bridal. Beshrew me much, Emilia,
I was, unhandsome warrior as I am,
Arraigning his unkindness with my soul;
But now I find I had suborned the witness,
And he's indicted falsely.

Emilia.   Pray heaven it be
155   State matters, as you think, and no conception
Nor no jealous toy° concerning you.

Desdemona. Alas the day! I never gave him cause.

Emilia. But jealous souls will not be answered so;
They are not ever jealous for the cause,
160   But jealous for they're jealous. It is a monster
Begot upon itself, born on itself.

Desdemona. Heaven keep the monster from Othello's
    mind!

Emilia. Lady, amen.

Desdemona. I will go seek him. Cassio, walk here
    about.
165   If I do find him fit,° I'll move your suit
And seek to effect it to my uttermost.

---

138 *moment* importance   140 *of state* state affairs   141 *unhatched prac-*
tice undisclosed plot   143 *puddled* muddied   146 *endues* leads   156 *toy*
trifle   165 *fit* receptive

Cassio. I humbly thank your ladyship.
       Exit [Desdemona with Emilia].

     Enter Bianca.

Bianca. Save you, friend Cassio!

Cassio.   What make you from
 home?
 How is't with you, my most fair Bianca?
 I' faith, sweet love, I was coming to your house. 170

Bianca. And I was going to your lodging, Cassio.
 What, keep a week away? Seven days and nights?
 Eightscore eight hours? And lovers' absent hours
 More tedious than the dial eightscore times?
 O weary reck'ning.°

Cassio.   Pardon me, Bianca. 175
 I have this while with leaden thoughts been pressed,
 But I shall in a more continuate° time
 Strike off this score° of absence. Sweet Bianca,
    [Gives her Desdemona's handkerchief.]
 Take me this work out.

Bianca.   O Cassio, whence came this?
 This is some token from a newer friend. 180
 To the felt absence now I feel a cause.
 Is't come to this? Well, well.

Cassio.   Go to, woman!
 Throw your vile guesses in the devil's teeth,
 From whence you have them. You are jealous now
 That this is from some mistress, some remembrance. 185
 No, by my faith, Bianca.

Bianca.   Why, whose is it?

Cassio. I know not neither; I found it in my chamber.
 I like the work well; ere it be demanded,°
 As like enough it will, I would have it copied.
 Take it and do't, and leave me for this time. 190

---

¹⁷⁵ *reck'ning* addition ¹⁷⁷ *continuate* uninterrupted ¹⁷⁸ *Strike off this score* i.e., pay this bill (the *score* being the account of drinks kept in a tavern) ¹⁸⁸ *demanded* asked for (by the person who lost it)

Bianca. Leave you? Wherefore?

Cassio. I do attend here on the general
  And think it no addition, nor my wish,
  To have him see me womaned.

Bianca.   Why, I pray you?

Cassio. Not that I love you not.

195 *Bianca.*   But that you do not love me!
  I pray you bring° me on the way a little,
  And say if I shall see you soon at night.

Cassio. 'Tis but a little way that I can bring you,
  For I attend here; but I'll see you soon.

200 *Bianca.* 'Tis very good. I must be circumstanced.°

                                             Exeunt omnes.

---

196 *bring* accompany   200 *circumstanced* accept things as they are

ACT IV

Scene I. [*A street.*]

Enter Othello and Iago.

Iago. Will you think so?

Othello.   Think so, Iago?

Iago.   What,
  To kiss in private?

Othello.   An unauthorized° kiss?

Iago. Or to be naked with her friend in bed
  An hour or more, not meaning any harm?

Othello. Naked in bed, Iago, and not mean harm?   *5*
  It is hypocrisy against the devil.
  They that mean virtuously, and yet do so,
  The devil their virtue tempts, and they tempt heaven.

Iago. If they do nothing, 'tis a venial slip.
  But if I give my wife a handkerchief——   *10*

Othello. What then?

Iago. Why, then 'tis hers, my lord; and being hers,
  She may, I think, bestow't on any man.

Othello. She is protectress of her honor too.
  May she give that?   *15*

Iago. Her honor is an essence that's not seen;
  They have it very oft that have it not.
  But for the handkerchief——

IV.i.² *unauthorized* illicit

Othello. By heaven, I would most gladly have forgot it!
20 Thou said'st—O, it comes o'er my memory
As doth the raven° o'er the infected house,
Boding to all—he had my handkerchief.

Iago. Ay, what of that?

Othello.   That's not so good now.

Iago. What if I had said I had seen him do you wrong?
25 Or heard him say—as knaves be such abroad°
Who having, by their own importunate suit,
Or voluntary dotage° of some mistress,
Convincèd or supplied° them, cannot choose
But they must blab——

Othello.   Hath he said anything?

30 *Iago.* He hath, my lord; but be you well assured,
No more than he'll unswear.

Othello.   What hath he said?

Iago. Why, that he did—I know not what he did.

Othello. What? what?

Iago. Lie——

Othello. With her?

35 *Iago.*   With her, on her; what you will.

Othello. Lie with her? Lie on her?—We say lie on her
when they belie her.—Lie with her! Zounds, that's
fulsome.° —Handkerchief—confessions—handkerchief!—To confess, and be hanged for his labor—
40 first to be hanged, and then to confess! I tremble at
it. Nature would not invest herself in such shadowing passion without some instruction.° It is not
words that shakes me thus.—Pish! Noses, ears, and

[21] *raven* (a harbinger of death) [25] *abroad* i.e., in the world [27] *voluntary dotage* weakness of the will [28]*Convincèd or supplied* persuaded or gratified (the mistress) [38] *fulsome* foul, repulsive [41-42] *Nature . . . instruction* i.e., my mind would not become so darkened (with anger) unless there were something in this (accusation); (it should be remembered that Othello believes in the workings of magic and supernatural forces)

lips? Is't possible?—Confess?—Handkerchief?—O
devil!   *Falls in a trance.*   45

Iago. Work on.
  My med'cine works! Thus credulous fools are
    caught,
  And many worthy and chaste dames even thus,
  All guiltless, meet reproach.° What, ho! My lord!
  My lord, I say! Othello!

             Enter Cassio.

               How now, Cassio?   50
Cassio. What's the matter?

Iago. My lord is fall'n into an epilepsy.
  This is his second fit; he had one yesterday.

Cassio. Rub him about the temples.

Iago. The lethargy° must have his quiet course.   55
  If not, he foams at mouth, and by and by
  Breaks out to savage madness. Look, he stirs.
  Do you withdraw yourself a little while.
  He will recover straight. When he is gone,
  I would on great occasion° speak with you.   60
                  [Exit Cassio.]
  How is it, general? Have you not hurt your head?

Othello. Dost thou mock° me?

Iago.   I mock you not, by heaven.
  Would you would bear your fortune like a man.

Othello. A hornèd man's a monster and a beast.

Iago. There's many a beast then in a populous city,   65
  And many a civil° monster.

Othello. Did he confess it?

Iago.   Good, sir, be a man.
  Think every bearded fellow that's but yoked
  May draw° with you. There's millions now alive

---

⁴⁹ *reproach* shame ⁵⁵ *lethargy* coma ⁶⁰ *great occasion* very important matter ⁶² *mock* (Othello takes Iago's comment as a reference to
his horns—which it is) ⁶⁶ *civil* city-dwelling ⁶⁹ *draw* i.e., like the
horned ox

70 That nightly lie in those unproper° beds
Which they dare swear peculiar.° Your case is
        better.
O, 'tis the spite of hell, the fiend's arch-mock,
To lip a wanton in a secure couch,
And to suppose her chaste. No, let me know;
75 And knowing what I am, I know what she shall be.

Othello. O, thou art wise! 'Tis certain.

Iago.   Stand you awhile apart;
Confine yourself but in a patient list.°
Whilst you were here, o'erwhelmèd with your
        grief—
A passion most unsuiting such a man—
80 Cassio came hither. I shifted him away°
And laid good 'scuses upon your ecstasy;°
Bade him anon return, and here speak with me;
The which he promised. Do but encave° yourself
And mark the fleers,° the gibes, and notable°
        scorns
85 That dwell in every region of his face.
For I will make him tell the tale anew:
Where, how, how oft, how long ago, and when
He hath, and is again to cope your wife.
I say, but mark his gesture. Marry patience,
90 Or I shall say you're all in all in spleen,°
And nothing of a man.

Othello.   Dost thou hear, Iago?
I will be found most cunning in my patience;
But—dost thou hear?—most bloody.

Iago.   That's not amiss;
But yet keep time in all. Will you withdraw?

*[Othello moves to one side, where his remarks are not
                        audible to Cassio and Iago.]*

---

⁷⁰ *unproper* i.e., not exclusively the husband's ⁷¹ *peculiar* their own alone
⁷⁷ *a patient list* the bounds of patience ⁸⁰ *shifted him away* got rid of
him by a stratagem ⁸¹ *ecstasy* trance (the literal meaning, "outside oneself," bears on the meaning of the change Othello is undergoing)
⁸³ *encave* hide ⁸⁴ *fleers* mocking looks or speeches ⁸⁴ *notable* obvious
⁹⁰ *spleen* passion, particularly anger

Now will I question Cassio of Bianca,   *95*
A huswife° that by selling her desires
Buys herself bread and cloth. It is a creature
That dotes on Cassio, as 'tis the strumpet's plague
To beguile many and be beguiled by one.
He, when he hears of her, cannot restrain   *100*
From the excess of laughter. Here he comes.

Enter Cassio.

As he shall smile, Othello shall go mad;
And his unbookish° jealousy must conster°
Poor Cassio's smiles, gestures, and light behaviors
Quite in the wrong. How do you, lieutenant?   *105*

Cassio. The worser that you give me the addition°
Whose want even kills me.

Iago. Ply Desdemona well, and you are sure on't.
Now, if this suit lay in Bianca's power,
How quickly should you speed!

Cassio.   Alas, poor caitiff!°   *110*

Othello. Look how he laughs already!

Iago. I never knew woman love man so.

Cassio. Alas, poor rogue! I think, i' faith, she loves me.

Othello. Now he denies it faintly, and laughs it out.

Iago. Do you hear, Cassio?

Othello.   Now he importunes him   *115*
To tell it o'er. Go to! Well said, well said!

Iago. She gives it out that you shall marry her.
Do you intend it?

Cassio. Ha, ha, ha!

Othello. Do ye triumph, Roman? Do you triumph?   *120*

Cassio. I marry? What, a customer?° Prithee bear

---

⁹⁶ *huswife* housewife (but with the special meaning here of "prostitute")
¹⁰³ *unbookish* ignorant ¹⁰³ *conster* construe ¹⁰⁶ *addition* title
¹¹⁰ *caitiff* wretch ¹²¹ *customer* one who sells, a merchant (here, a prostitute)

some charity to my wit; do not think it so unwholesome. Ha, ha, ha!

Othello. So, so, so, so. They laugh that win.

125 *Iago.* Why, the cry goes that you marry her.

Cassio. Prithee, say true.

Iago. I am a very villain else.

Othello. Have you scored° me? Well.

Cassio. This is the monkey's own giving out. She is
130 persuaded I will marry her out of her own love and
flattery, not out of my promise.

Othello. Iago beckons me; now he begins the story.
[*Othello moves close enough to hear.*]

Cassio. She was here even now; she haunts me in every
place. I was the other day talking on the sea bank
135 with certain Venetians, and thither comes the
bauble,° and falls me thus about my neck——

Othello. Crying "O dear Cassio!" as it were. His gesture imports it.

Cassio. So hangs, and lolls, and weeps upon me; so
140 shakes and pulls me! Ha, ha, ha!

Othello. Now he tells how she plucked him to my
chamber. O, I see that nose of yours, but not that
dog I shall throw it to.

Cassio. Well, I must leave her company.

145 *Iago.* Before me!° Look where she comes.

Enter Bianca.

Cassio. 'Tis such another fitchew!° Marry a perfumed
one? What do you mean by this haunting of me?

Bianca. Let the devil and his dam haunt you! What did
you mean by that same handkerchief you gave me
150 even now? I was a fine fool to take it. I must take

---

¹²⁸ *scored* marked, defaced   ¹³⁶ *bauble* plaything   ¹⁴⁵ *Before me!* (an
exclamation of surprise)   ¹⁴⁶ *fitchew* polecat, i.e., strong-smelling
creature

out the work? A likely piece of work that you should
find it in your chamber and know not who left it
there! This is some minx's token, and I must take
out the work? There! [*She throws down the handkerchief.*] Give it your hobbyhorse.° Wheresoever   155
you had it, I'll take out no work on't.

Cassio. How now, my sweet Bianca? How now? how
now?

Othello. By heaven, that should be my handkerchief!

Bianca. If you'll come to supper tonight, you may; if   160
you will not, come when you are next prepared
for.°   *Exit.*

Iago. After her, after her!

Cassio. Faith, I must; she'll rail in the streets else.

Iago. Will you sup there?   165

Cassio. Yes, I intend so.

Iago. Well, I may chance to see you, for I would very
fain speak with you.

Cassio. Prithee come. Will you?

Iago. Go to, say no more.   [*Exit Cassio.*]   170

Othello. [*Comes forward.*] How shall I murder him,
Iago?

Iago. Did you perceive how he laughed at his vice?

Othello. O Iago!

Iago. And did you see the handkerchief?   175

Othello. Was that mine?

Iago. Yours, by this hand! And to see how he prizes
the foolish woman your wife! She gave it him, and
he hath giv'n it his whore.

Othello. I would have him nine years a-killing!—A   180
fine woman, a fair woman, a sweet woman?

---

155 *hobbyhorse* prostitute   161-62 *next prepared for* next expected—i.e.,
never

Iago: Nay, you must forget that.

Othello. Ay, let her rot, and perish, and be damned
    tonight; for she shall not live. No, my heart is turned
185 to stone; I strike it, and it hurts my hand. O, the
    world hath not a sweeter creature! She might lie by
    an emperor's side and command him tasks.

Iago. Nay, that's not your way.°

Othello. Hang her! I do but say what she is. So deli-
190 cate with her needle. An admirable musician. O, she
    will sing the savageness out of a bear! Of so high
    and plenteous wit and invention° ——

Iago. She's the worse for all this.

Othello. O, a thousand, a thousand times. And then,
195 of so gentle a condition?°

Iago. Ay, too gentle.

Othello. Nay, that's certain. But yet the pity of it,
    Iago. O Iago, the pity of it, Iago.

Iago. If you are so fond over her iniquity, give her
200 patent to offend; for if it touch° not you, it comes
    near nobody.

Othello. I will chop her into messes!° Cuckold me!

Iago. O, 'tis foul in her.

Othello. With mine officer!

205 *Iago.* That's fouler.

Othello. Get me some poison, Iago, this night. I'll not
    expostulate with her, lest her body and beauty un-
    provide my mind° again. This night, Iago!

Iago. Do it not with poison. Strangle her in her bed,
210 even the bed she hath contaminated.

Othello. Good, good! The justice of it pleases. Very
    good!

---

188 *way* proper course   192 *invention* imagination   195 *gentle a condition*
(1) well born (2) of a gentle nature   200 *touch* affects   202 *messes* bits
207–08 *unprovide my mind* undo my resolution

Iago. And for Cassio, let me be his undertaker.° You
  shall hear more by midnight.

Othello. Excellent good!   *[A trumpet.]*
                  What trumpet is that same?   213

Iago. I warrant something from Venice.

    Enter Lodovico, Desdemona, and Attendants.

                      'Tis Lodovico.
  This comes from the Duke. See, your wife's with
  him.

Lodovico. God save you, worthy general.

Othello.   With° all my heart, sir.

Lodovico. The Duke and the senators of Venice greet
  you.   *[Gives him a letter.]*

Othello. I kiss the instrument of their pleasures.   220
            [Opens the letter and reads.]

Desdemona. And what's the news, good cousin Lodovico?

Iago. I am very glad to see you, signior.
  Welcome to Cyprus.

Lodovico. I thank you. How does Lieutenant Cassio?

Iago.   Lives, sir.

Desdemona. Cousin, there's fall'n between him and
  my lord
  An unkind° breach; but you shall make all well.   225

Othello. Are you sure of that?

Desdemona. My lord?

Othello. *[Reads]* "This fail you not to do, as you
  will——"

Lodovico. He did not call; he's busy in the paper.   230
  Is there division 'twixt my lord and Cassio?

---

²¹³ *undertaker* (not "burier" but "one who undertakes to do something") ²¹⁸ *With* i.e., I greet you with ²²⁶ *unkind* unnatural

Desdemona. A most unhappy one. I would do much
  T' atone° them, for the love I bear to Cassio.

Othello. Fire and brimstone!

Desdemona.   My lord?

Othello.   Are you wise?

Desdemona. What, is he angry?

235 *Lodovico.*   May be th' letter moved him;
  For, as I think, they do command him home,
  Deputing Cassio in his government.°

Desdemona. Trust me, I am glad on't.

Othello.   Indeed?

Desdemona.   My lord?

Othello. I am glad to see you mad.

Desdemona.   Why, sweet Othello——

240 *Othello.* Devil!   [*Strikes her.*]

Desdemona. I have not deserved this.

Lodovico. My lord, this would not be believed in
      Venice,
  Though I should swear I saw't. 'Tis very much.
  Make her amends; she weeps.

Othello.   O devil, devil!
245 If that the earth could teem° with woman's tears,
  Each drop she falls° would prove a crocodile.°
  Out of my sight!

Desdemona.   I will not stay to offend you. [*Going.*]

Lodovico. Truly, an obedient lady.
  I do beseech your lordship call her back.

Othello. Mistress!

Desdemona.   My lord?

250 *Othello.*   What would you with her, sir?

---

²³³ *atone* reconcile ²³⁷ *government* office ²⁴⁵ *teem* conceive ²⁴⁶ *falls*
drops ²⁴⁶ *crocodile* (the crocodile was supposed to shed false tears to
lure its victims)

Lodovico. Who? I, my lord?

Othello. Ay! You did wish that I would make her turn.
  Sir, she can turn, and turn, and yet go on
  And turn again; and she can weep, sir, weep;
  And she's obedient; as you say, obedient.
  Very obedient. Proceed you in your tears.   255
  Concerning this, sir—O well-painted passion!
  I am commanded home.—Get you away;
  I'll send for you anon.—Sir, I obey the mandate
  And will return to Venice.—Hence, avaunt!   260
                       [Exit Desdemona.]
  Cassio shall have my place. And, sir, tonight
  I do entreat that we may sup together.
  You are welcome, sir, to Cyprus.—Goats and mon-
    keys!   *Exit.*

Lodovico. Is this the noble Moor whom our full Senate
  Call all in all sufficient? Is this the nature   265
  Whom passion could not shake? whose solid virtue
  The shot of accident nor dart of chance
  Could neither graze nor pierce?

Iago.   He is much changed.

Lodovico. Are his wits safe? Is he not light of brain?

Iago. He's that he is; I may not breathe my censure.   270
  What he might be (if, what he might, he is not)
  I would to heaven he were!

Lodovico.   What, strike his wife?

Iago. Faith, that was not so well; yet would I knew
  That stroke would prove the worst.

Lodovico.   Is it his use?°
  Or did the letters work upon his blood°   275
  And new-create his fault?

Iago.   Alas, alas!
  It is not honesty in me to speak
  What I have seen and known. You shall observe
    him,

274 *use* habit   275 *blood* passion

And his own courses° will denote him so
280　That I may save my speech. Do but go after
And mark how he continues.

Lodovico. I am sorry that I am deceived in him.

Exeunt.

Scene II. [*The citadel.*]

Enter Othello and Emilia.

Othello. You have seen nothing then?

Emilia. Nor ever heard, nor ever did suspect.

Othello. Yes, you have seen Cassio and she together.

Emilia. But then I saw no harm, and then I heard
5　　Each syllable that breath made up° between them.

Othello. What, did they never whisper?

Emilia.   Never, my lord.

Othello. Nor send you out o' th' way?

Emilia. Never.

Othello. To fetch her fan, her gloves, her mask, nor
nothing?

10　*Emilia.* Never, my lord.

Othello. That's strange.

Emilia. I durst, my lord, to wager she is honest,
Lay down my soul at stake.° If you think other,
Remove your thought. It doth abuse your bosom.
15　If any wretch have put this in your head,
Let heaven requite it with the serpent's curse,°
For if she be not honest,° chaste, and true,

---

²⁷⁹ *courses* actions IV.ii.⁵ *that breath made up* spoken ¹³ *at stake* as the wager ¹⁶ *serpent's curse* (God's curse on the serpent after the fall in Eden) ¹⁷ *honest* chaste

There's no man happy. The purest of their wives
Is foul as slander.

Othello.   Bid her come hither. Go.

Exit Emilia.

She says enough; yet she's a simple bawd°   20
That cannot say as much. This is a subtle whore,
A closet lock and key of villainous secrets,
And yet she'll kneel and pray; I have seen her do't.

Enter Desdemona and Emilia.

Desdemona. My lord, what is your will?

Othello.   Pray you, chuck, come hither.

Desdemona. What is your pleasure?

Othello.   Let me see your eyes.   25
Look in my face.

Desdemona.   What horrible fancy's this?

Othello. [*To Emilia*] Some of your function,° mis-
tress:
Leave procreants alone and shut the door;
Cough or cry hem if anybody come.
Your mystery,° your mystery! Nay, dispatch!   30

Exit Emilia.

Desdemona. Upon my knee, what doth your speech
import?
I understand a fury in your words.°

Othello. Why, what art thou?

Desdemona.   Your wife, my lord; your true
And loyal wife.

Othello.   Come, swear it, damn thyself;
Lest, being like one of heaven, the devils themselves   85
Should fear to seize thee. Therefore be double-
damned:
Swear thou art honest.

Desdemona.   Heaven doth truly know it.

²⁰ *bawd* procuress ²⁷ *Some of your function* do your proper work (as
the operator of a brothel) ³⁰ *mystery* trade ³² *words* (Q1 adds to
this line, "But not the words")

Othello. Heaven truly knows that thou art false as hell.

Desdemona. To whom, my lord? With whom? How am
    I false?

40   *Othello.* Ah, Desdemon! Away! Away! Away!

Desdemona. Alas the heavy day! Why do you weep?
    Am I the motive° of these tears, my lord?
    If haply° you my father do suspect
    An instrument of this your calling back,
45   Lay not your blame on me. If you have lost him,
    I have lost him too.

Othello.   Had it pleased heaven
    To try me with affliction, had they rained
    All kinds of sores and shames on my bare head,
    Steeped° me in poverty to the very lips,
50   Given to captivity me and my utmost hopes,
    I should have found in some place of my soul
    A drop of patience. But, alas, to make me
    The fixèd figure for the time of scorn°
    To point his slow and moving finger at.
55   Yet could I bear that too, well, very well.
    But there where I have garnered up my heart,
    Where either I must live or bear no life,
    The fountain from the which my current runs
    Or else dries up—to be discarded thence,
60   Or keep it as a cistern for foul toads
    To knot and gender° in—turn thy complexion there,
    Patience, thou young and rose-lipped cherubin!
    I here look grim as hell!°

Desdemona. I hope my noble lord esteems me honest.

65   *Othello.* O, ay, as summer flies are in the shambles,°
    That quicken even with blowing.° O thou weed,

---

⁴²*motive* cause   ⁴³*haply* by chance   ⁴⁹*Steeped* submerged   ⁵³*The
. . . scorn* the very image of scorn in our time   ⁶¹*knot and gender*
twist in bunches and procreate   ⁶¹⁻⁶³*turn . . . hell* (the rough sense
would seem to be, "even Patience would grow pale, turn complexion, at
Desdemona's perfidy, but that Othello looks grimly on")   ⁶⁵*shambles*
abattoirs   ⁶⁶*quicken even with blowing* become impregnated as soon
as they lay their eggs

Who art so lovely fair, and smell'st so sweet,
That the sense aches at thee, would thou hadst never
  been born!

Desdemona. Alas, what ignorant° sin have I committed?

Othello. Was this fair paper, this most goodly book,   *70*
Made to write "whore" upon? What committed?
Committed? O thou public commoner,°
I should make very forges of my cheeks
That would to cinders burn up modesty,
Did I but speak thy deeds. What committed?   *75*
Heaven stops the nose at it, and the moon winks;°
The bawdy wind that kisses all it meets
Is hushed within the hollow mine of earth
And will not hear 't. What committed?

Desdemona. By heaven, you do me wrong!   *80*

Othello. Are not you a strumpet?

Desdemona.   No, as I am a Christian!
If to preserve this vessel for my lord
From any other foul unlawful touch
Be not to be a strumpet, I am none.

Othello. What, not a whore?

Desdemona.   No, as I shall be saved!   *85*

Othello. Is't possible?

Desdemona. O, heaven forgive us!

Othello.   I cry you mercy° then.
I took you for that cunning whore of Venice
That married with Othello. [*Calling*] You, mistress,

                    Enter Emilia.

That have the office opposite to Saint Peter   *90*
And keep the gate of hell! You, you, ay, you!
We have done our course; there's money for your
  pains.   [*Throws her some coins.*]

⁶⁹ *ignorant* unknowing ⁷² *commoner* prostitute ⁷⁶ *winks* closes its
eyes (the moon was the symbol of chastity) ⁸⁷ *cry you mercy* ask
your pardon

I pray you turn the key and keep our counsel.

Exit.

Emilia. Alas, what does this gentleman conceive?

95 How do you, madam? How do you, my good lady?

Desdemona. Faith, half asleep.

Emilia. Good madam, what's the matter with my lord?

Desdemona. With who?

Emilia. Why, with my lord, madam.

Desdemona. Who is thy lord?

100 *Emilia.* He that is yours, sweet lady.

Desdemona. I have none. Do not talk to me, Emilia.
I cannot weep, nor answers have I none
But what should go by water.° Prithee tonight
Lay on my bed my wedding sheets, remember;
And call thy husband hither.

105 *Emilia.* Here's a change indeed!

Exit.

Desdemona. 'Tis meet I should be used so, very meet.
How have I been behaved, that he might stick
The small'st opinion on my least misuse?°

Enter Iago and Emilia.

Iago. What is your pleasure, madam? How is't with
you?

Desdemona. I cannot tell. Those that do teach young

110 babes
Do it with gentle means and easy tasks.
He might have chid me so; for, in good faith,
I am a child to chiding.

Iago. What is the matter, lady?

Emilia. Alas, Iago, my lord hath so bewhored her,

---

103 *water* tears   107–08 *stick . . . misuse* base any doubt on my smallest
fault

Thrown such despite° and heavy terms upon her   *115*
That true hearts cannot bear it.

Desdemona. Am I that name, Iago?

Iago.   What name, fair lady?

Desdemona. Such as she said my lord did say I was.

Emilia. He called her whore. A beggar in his drink
Could not have laid such terms upon his callet.°   *120*

Iago. Why did he so?

Desdemona. I do not know; I am sure I am none such.

Iago. Do not weep, do not weep. Alas the day.

Emilia. Hath she forsook so many noble matches,
Her father and her country, and her friends,   *125*
To be called whore? Would it not make one weep?

Desdemona. It is my wretched fortune.

Iago.   Beshrew° him for 't!
How comes this trick upon him?

Desdemona.   Nay, heaven doth know.

Emilia. I will be hanged if some eternal villain,
Some busy and insinuating rogue,
Some cogging,° cozening slave, to get some office,   *130*
Have not devised this slander. I will be hanged else.

Iago. Fie, there is no such man! It is impossible.

Desdemona. If any such there be, heaven pardon him.

Emilia. A halter pardon him! And hell gnaw his bones!   *135*
Why should he call her whore? Who keeps her com-
    pany?
What place? What time? What form? What likeli-
    hood?
The Moor's abused by some most villainous knave,
Some base notorious knave, some scurvy fellow.
O heavens, that such companions° thou'dst unfold,°   *140*
And put in every honest hand a whip
To lash the rascals naked through the world
Even from the east to th' west!

---

¹¹⁵ *despite* abuse   ¹²⁰ *callet* slut   ¹²⁷ *Beshrew* curse   ¹³¹ *cogging* cheat-
ing   ¹⁴⁰ *companions* fellows, rogues   ¹⁴⁰ *unfold* disclose

Iago.   Speak within door.°

Emilia. O, fie upon them! Some such squire° he was
145   That turned your wit the seamy side without
        And made you to suspect me with the Moor.

Iago. You are a fool. Go to.

Desdemona.   Alas, Iago,
        What shall I do to win my lord again?
        Good friend, go to him, for, by this light of heaven,
150   I know not how I lost him. Here I kneel:
        If e'er my will did trespass 'gainst his love
        Either in discourse of thought° or actual deed,
        Or that mine eyes, mine ears, or any sense
        Delighted them in any other form;
155   Or that I do not yet, and ever did,
        And ever will (though he do shake me off
        To beggarly divorcement) love him dearly,
        Comfort forswear me. Unkindness may do much,
        And his unkindness may defeat° my life,
160   But never taint my love. I cannot say "whore."
        It does abhor me now I speak the word;
        To do the act that might the addition earn
        Not the world's mass of vanity could make me.

Iago. I pray you be content. 'Tis but his humor.°
165 .   The business of the state does him offense.

Desdemona. If 'twere no other.

Iago.   It is but so, I warrant.
                                    [*Trumpets within.*]
        Hark how these instruments summon to supper.
        The messengers of Venice stay the meat.°
        Go in, and weep not. All things shall be well.
                          [*Exeunt Desdemona and Emilia.*]

                    Enter Roderigo.

170   How now, Roderigo?

---

¹⁴³ *within door* more quietly and moderately   ¹⁴⁴ *squire* (a term of
contempt)   ¹⁵² *discourse of thought* thinking   ¹⁵⁹ *defeat* destroy
¹⁶⁴ *humor* mood   ¹⁶⁸ *stay the meat* await the meal

Roderigo. I do not find that thou deal'st justly with me.

Iago. What in the contrary?

Roderigo. Every day thou daff'st° me with some device,° Iago, and rather, as it seems to me now,
keep'st from me all conveniency° than suppliest me   *175*
with the least advantage of hope. I will indeed no
longer endure it; nor am I yet persuaded to put up°
in peace what already I have foolishly suffered.

Iago. Will you hear me, Roderigo?

Roderigo. I have heard too much, and your words   *180*
and performances are no kin together.

Iago. You charge me most unjustly.

Roderigo. With naught but truth. I have wasted myself out of my means. The jewels you have had from
me to deliver Desdemona would half have corrupted   *185*
a votarist.° You have told me she hath received
them, and returned me expectations and comforts
of sudden respect° and acquaintance; but I find
none.

Iago. Well, go to; very well.   *190*

Roderigo. Very well? Go to? I cannot go to, man; nor
'tis not very well. Nay, I think it is scurvy, and begin
to find myself fopped° in it.

Iago. Very well.

Roderigo. I tell you 'tis not very well. I will make my-   *195*
self known to Desdemona. If she will return me
my jewels, I will give over my suit and repent my
unlawful solicitation. If not, assure yourself I will
seek satisfaction of you.

Iago. You have said now?   *200*

Roderigo. Ay, and said nothing but what I protest°
intendment of doing.

---

¹⁷³ *daff'st* put off   ¹⁷³⁻⁷⁴ *device* scheme   ¹⁷⁵ *conveniency* what is needful   ¹⁷⁷ *put up* accept   ¹⁸⁶ *votarist* nun   ¹⁸⁸ *sudden respect* immediate
consideration   ¹⁹³ *fopped* duped   ²⁰¹ *protest* aver

Iago. Why, now I see there's mettle° in thee, and even
from this instant do build on thee a better opinion
205   than ever before. Give me thy hand, Roderigo. Thou
hast taken against me a most just exception;° but
yet I protest I have dealt most directly° in thy
affair.

Roderigo. It hath not appeared.

210   *Iago.* I grant indeed it hath not appeared, and your
suspicion is not without wit and judgment. But,
Roderigo, if thou hast that in thee indeed which I
have greater reason to believe now than ever—I
mean purpose, courage, and valor—this night show
215   it. If thou the next night following enjoy not Desdemona, take me from this world with treachery and
devise engines for° my life.

Roderigo. Well, what is it? Is it within reason and
compass?°

220   *Iago.* Sir, there is especial commission come from
Venice to depute Cassio in Othello's place.

Roderigo. Is that true? Why, then Othello and Desdemona return again to Venice.

Iago. O, no; he goes into Mauritania and taketh away
225   with him the fair Desdemona, unless his abode be
lingered here by some accident; wherein none can
be so determinate° as the removing of Cassio.

Roderigo. How do you mean, removing him?

Iago. Why, by making him uncapable of Othello's
230   place—knocking out his brains.

Roderigo. And that you would have me to do?

Iago. Ay, if you dare do yourself a profit and a right.
He sups tonight with a harlotry,° and thither will I
go to him. He knows not yet of his honorable for-
235   tune. If you will watch his going thence, which I

---

²⁰³ *mettle* spirit   ²⁰⁶ *exception* objection   ²⁰⁷ *directly* straightforwardly
²¹⁷ *engines for* schemes against   ²¹⁹ *compass* possibility   ²²⁷ *determi-
nate* effective   ²³³ *harlotry* female

will fashion to fall out° between twelve and one,
you may take him at your pleasure. I will be near
to second° your attempt, and he shall fall between
us. Come, stand not amazed at it, but go along with
me. I will show you such a necessity in his death 240
that you shall think yourself bound to put it on him.
It is now high supper time, and the night grows
to waste. About it.

Roderigo. I will hear further reason for this.

Iago. And you shall be satisfied.   *Exeunt.* 245

Scene III. [*The citadel.*]

*Enter Othello, Lodovico, Desdemona, Emilia, and
Attendants.*

Lodovico. I do beseech you, sir, trouble yourself no
further.

Othello. O, pardon me; 'twill do me good to walk.

Lodovico. Madam, good night. I humbly thank your
ladyship.

Desdemona. Your honor is most welcome.

Othello. Will you walk, sir? O, Desdemona.   5

Desdemona. My lord?

Othello. Get you to bed on th' instant; I will be returned forthwith. Dismiss your attendant there.
Look 't be done.

Desdemona. I will, my lord.   10
          Exit [Othello, with Lodovico and Attendants].

Emilia. How goes it now? He looks gentler than he did.

²³⁶ *fall out* occur   ²³⁸ *second* support

Desdemona. He says he will return incontinent,°
And hath commanded me to go to bed,
And bade me to dismiss you.

Emilia.   Dismiss me?

15 *Desdemona.* It was his bidding; therefore, good Emilia,
Give me my nightly wearing, and adieu.
We must not now displease him.

Emilia. I would you had never seen him!

Desdemona. So would not I. My love doth so approve
    him
That even his stubbornness, his checks,° his
20 frowns—
Prithee unpin me—have grace and favor.

Emilia. I have laid these sheets you bade me on the
    bed.

Desdemona. All's one.° Good Father, how foolish
    are our minds!
If I do die before, prithee shroud me
In one of these same sheets.

25 *Emilia.*   Come, come! You talk.

Desdemona. My mother had a maid called Barbary.
She was in love; and he she loved proved mad
And did forsake her. She had a song of "Willow";
An old thing 'twas, but it expressed her fortune,
30 And she died singing it. That song tonight
Will not go from my mind; I have much to do
But to go hang my head all at one side
And sing it like poor Barbary. Prithee dispatch.

Emilia. Shall I go fetch your nightgown?

35 *Desdemona.* No, unpin me here.
This Lodovico is a proper man.

Emilia. A very handsome man.

Desdemona. He speaks well.

IV.iii.¹² *incontinent* at once   ²⁰ *checks* rebukes   ²³ *All's one* no matter

Emilia. I know a lady in Venice would have walked
  barefoot to Palestine for a touch of his nether lip.   40

Desdemona. [*Sings*]
    "The poor soul sat singing by a sycamore tree,
      Sing all a green willow;
    Her hand on her bosom, her head on her knee,
      Sing willow, willow, willow.
    The fresh streams ran by her and murmured
        her moans;   45
      Sing willow, willow, willow;
    Her salt tears fell from her, and soft'ned the
        stones—
      Sing willow, willow, willow—"
  Lay by these.   [*Gives Emilia her clothes.*]
    "Willow, Willow"——   50
  Prithee hie° thee; he'll come anon.°
    "Sing all a green willow must be my garland.
    Let nobody blame him; his scorn I approve"——
  Nay, that's not next. Hark! Who is't that knocks?

Emilia. It is the wind.   55

Desdemona. [*Sings*]
    "I called my love false love; but what said he
        then?
      Sing willow, willow, willow:
    If I court moe° women, you'll couch with moe
        men."
  So, get thee gone; good night. Mine eyes do itch.
  Doth that bode weeping?

Emilia.   'Tis neither here nor there.   60

Desdemona. I have heard it said so. O, these men,
  these men.
  Dost thou in conscience think, tell me, Emilia,
  That there be women do abuse their husbands
  In such gross kind?

Emilia.   There be some such, no question.

51 *hie* hurry   51 *anon* at once   58 *moe* more

Desdemona. Wouldst thou do such a deed for all the
65   world?

Emilia. Why, would not you?

Desdemona.   No, by this heavenly light!

Emilia. Nor I neither by this heavenly light.
I might do't as well i' th' dark.

Desdemona. Wouldst thou do such a deed for all the
world?

70   *Emilia.* The world's a huge thing; it is a great price for
a small vice.

Desdemona. In troth, I think thou wouldst not.

Emilia. In troth, I think I should; and undo't when I
had done. Marry, I would not do such a thing for
75   a joint-ring,° nor for measures of lawn,° nor for
gowns, petticoats, nor caps, nor any petty exhibition,° but for all the whole world? Why, who
would not make her husband a cuckold to make him
a monarch? I should venture purgatory for't.

80   *Desdemona.* Beshrew me if I would do such a wrong
for the whole world.

Emilia. Why, the wrong is but a wrong i' th' world;
and having the world for your labor, 'tis a wrong
in your own world, and you might quickly make
85   it right.

Desdemona. I do not think there is any such woman.

Emilia. Yes, a dozen; and as many to th' vantage as
would store° the world they played for.
But I do think it is their husbands' faults
90   If wives do fall. Say that they slack their duties
And pour our treasures into foreign° laps;
Or else break out in peevish jealousies,
Throwing restraint upon us; or say they strike us,

---

⁷⁵ *joint-ring* (a ring with two interlocking halves)   ⁷⁵ *lawn* fine linen
⁷⁶⁻⁷⁷ *exhibition* payment   ⁸⁷⁻⁸⁸ *to . . . store* in addition as would fill
⁹¹ *foreign* alien, i.e., other than the wife

Or scant our former having in despite°—
Why, we have galls; and though we have some
    grace,   95
Yet have we some revenge. Let husbands know
Their wives have sense like them. They see, and
    smell,
And have their palates both for sweet and sour,
As husbands have. What is it that they do
When they change° us for others? Is it sport?   *100*
I think it is. And doth affection° breed it?
I think it doth. Is't frailty that thus errs?
It is so too. And have not we affections?
Desires for sport? and frailty? as men have?
Then let them use us well; else let them know,   *105*
The ills we do, their ills instruct us so.°

Desdemona. Good night, good night. Heaven me such
    uses° send,
Not to pick bad from bad, but by bad mend. *Exeunt.*

---

⁹⁴ *scant . . . despite* reduce, in spite, our household allowance (?)
¹⁰⁰ *change* exchange   ¹⁰¹ *affection* strong feeling, desire   ¹⁰⁶ *instruct
us so* teach us to do likewise   ¹⁰⁷ *uses* practices

ACT V

Scene I. [*A street.*]

Enter Iago and Roderigo.

Iago. Here, stand behind this bulk;° straight will he
    come.
    Wear thy good rapier bare, and put it home.
    Quick, quick! Fear nothing; I'll be at thy elbow.
    It makes us, or it mars us, think on that,
5   And fix most firm thy resolution.

Roderigo. Be near at hand; I may miscarry in't.

Iago. Here, at thy hand. Be bold, and take thy stand.
                        [*Moves to one side.*]

Roderigo. I have no great devotion to the deed,
    And yet he hath given me satisfying reasons.
10   'Tis but a man gone. Forth my sword! He dies!

Iago. I have rubbed this young quat° almost to the
    sense,°
    And he grows angry. Now, whether he kill Cassio,
    Or Cassio him, or each do kill the other,
    Every way makes my gain. Live Roderigo,
15   He calls me to a restitution large
    Of gold and jewels that I bobbed° from him
    As gifts to Desdemona.
    It must not be. If Cassio do remain,

V.i.[1] *bulk* projecting stall of a shop   [11] *quat* pimple   [11] *to the sense*
raw   [16] *bobbed* swindled

He hath a daily beauty in his life
That makes me ugly; and besides, the Moor   20
May unfold me to him; there stand I in much peril.
No, he must die. But so, I hear him coming.

Enter Cassio.

Roderigo. I know his gait. 'Tis he. Villain, thou diest!
                              [*Thrusts at Cassio.*]

Cassio. That thrust had been mine enemy indeed
But that my coat° is better than thou know'st.   25
I will make proof of thine.   [*Fights with Roderigo.*]

Roderigo.   O, I am slain!°

Cassio. I am maimed forever. Help, ho! Murder!
    Murder!

Enter Othello [to one side].

Othello. The voice of Cassio. Iago keeps his word.

Roderigo. O, villain that I am!

Othello.   It is even so.

Cassio. O help, ho! Light! A surgeon!   30

Othello. 'Tis he. O brave Iago, honest and just,
    That hast such noble sense of thy friend's wrong!
    Thou teachest me. Minion,° your dear lies dead,
    And your unblest° fate hies.° Strumpet, I come.
    Forth of my heart those charms, thine eyes, are
        blotted.   35
    Thy bed, lust-stained, shall with lust's blood be
        spotted.
                              Exit Othello.

²⁵ *coat* i.e., a mail shirt or bulletproof vest ²⁶ *slain* (most editors add
here a stage direction which has Iago wounding Cassio in the leg from
behind, but remaining unseen. However, nothing in the text requires
this, and Cassio's wound can be given him in the fight with Roderigo,
for presumably when Cassio attacks Roderigo the latter would not
simply accept the thrust but would parry. Since Iago enters again at
line 46, he must exit at some point after line 22) ³³ *Minion* hussy, i.e.,
Desdemona ³⁴ *unblest* unsanctified ³⁴ *hies* approaches swiftly

Enter Lodovico and Gratiano.

Cassio. What, ho? No watch? No passage?° Murder!
Murder!

Gratiano. 'Tis some mischance. The voice is very
direful.

Cassio. O, help!

40   *Lodovico.* Hark!

Roderigo. O wretched villain!

Lodovico. Two or three groan. 'Tis heavy night.
These may be counterfeits. Let's think't unsafe
To come into the cry without more help.

45   *Roderigo.* Nobody come? Then shall I bleed to death.

Lodovico. Hark!

Enter Iago [with a light].

Gratiano. Here's one comes in his shirt, with light and
weapons.

Iago. Who's there? Whose noise is this that cries on
murder?

Lodovico. We do not know.

Iago.   Do not you hear a cry?

Cassio. Here, here! For heaven's sake, help me!

50   *Iago.*   What's the matter?

Gratiano. This is Othello's ancient, as I take it.

Lodovico. The same indeed, a very valiant fellow.

Iago. What are you here that cry so grievously?

Cassio. Iago? O, I am spoiled, undone by villains.
55   Give me some help.

Iago. O me, lieutenant! What villains have done this?

Cassio. I think that one of them is hereabout
And cannot make away.

---

87 *passage* passers-by

Iago.   O treacherous villains!
  [*To Lodovico and Gratiano*] What are you there?
    Come in, and give some help.

Roderigo. O, help me there!   60

Cassio. That's one of them.

Iago.   O murd'rous slave! O vil-
    lain!   [*Stabs Roderigo.*]

Roderigo. O damned Iago! O inhuman dog!

Iago. Kill men i' th' dark?——Where be these bloody
    thieves?——
  How silent is this town!——Ho! Murder! Murder!——
  What may you be? Are you of good or evil?   65

Lodovico. As you shall prove us, praise us.

Iago. Signior Lodovico?

Lodovico. He, sir.

Iago. I cry you mercy. Here's Cassio hurt by villains.

Gratiano. Cassio?   70

Iago. How is't, brother?

Cassio. My leg is cut in two.

Iago.   Marry, heaven forbid!
  Light, gentlemen. I'll bind it with my shirt.

                    Enter Bianca.

Bianca. What is the matter, ho? Who is't that cried?

Iago. Who is't that cried?   75

Bianca. O my dear Cassio! My sweet Cassio!
    O Cassio, Cassio, Cassio!

Iago. O notable strumpet!——Cassio, may you suspect
  Who they should be that have thus mangled you?

Cassio. No.   80

Gratiano. I am sorry to find you thus. I have been to
    seek you.

Iago. Lend me a garter. So. O for a chair
  To bear him easily hence.

Bianca. Alas, he faints! O Cassio, Cassio, Cassio!

85 *Iago.* Gentlemen all, I do suspect this trash
  To be a party in this injury.—
  Patience awhile, good Cassio.—Come, come.
  Lend me a light. Know we this face or no?
  Alas, my friend and my dear countryman
90 Roderigo? No.—Yes, sure.—Yes, 'tis Roderigo!

Gratiano. What, of Venice?

Iago. Even he, sir. Did you know him?

Gratiano.   Know him? Ay.

Iago. Signior Gratiano? I cry your gentle pardon.
  These bloody accidents must excuse my manners
  That so neglected you.

95 *Gratiano.*   I am glad to see you.

Iago. How do you, Cassio?—O, a chair, a chair!

Gratiano. Roderigo?

Iago. He, he, 'tis he! [*A chair brought in.*] O, that's
  well said;° the chair.
  Some good man bear him carefully from hence.
  I'll fetch the general's surgeon. [*To Bianca*] For you,
100 mistress,
  Save you your labor. [*To Cassio*] He that lies slain
  here, Cassio,
  Was my dear friend. What malice was between you?

Cassio. None in the world; nor do I know the man.

Iago. What, look you pale?—O, bear him out o' th'
  air.   [*Cassio is carried off.*]
  Stay you, good gentlemen.—Look you pale, mis-
105 tress?
  Do you perceive the gastness° of her eye?
  Nay, if you stare, we shall hear more anon.
  Behold her well; I pray you look upon her.

⁹⁸ *well said* well done   ¹⁰⁶ *gastness* terror

Do you see, gentlemen? Nay, guiltiness will speak,
Though tongues were out of use.°   110

[Enter Emilia.]

Emilia. Alas, what is the matter? What is the matter,
   husband?

Iago. Cassio hath here been set on in the dark
   By Roderigo and fellows that are scaped.
   He's almost slain, and Roderigo quite dead.

Emilia. Alas, good gentleman! Alas, good Cassio!   115

Iago. This is the fruits of whoring. Prithee, Emilia,
   Go know of Cassio where he supped tonight.
   [To Bianca] What, do you shake at that?

Bianca. He supped at my house; but I therefore shake
   not.

Iago. O, did he so? I charge° you go with me.   120

Emilia. Oh fie upon thee, strumpet!

Bianca. I am no strumpet, but of life as honest
   As you that thus abuse me.

Emilia.   As I? Fie upon thee!

Iago. Kind gentlemen, let's go see poor Cassio
   dressed.°
   [To Bianca] Come, mistress, you must tell's another
   tale.   125
   Emilia, run you to the citadel
   And tell my lord and lady what hath happed.
                                      [Exit Emilia.]
   Will you go on afore?   *Exeunt [all but Iago].*
                    This is the night
   That either makes me or fordoes me quite.° *[Exit.]*

---

¹¹⁰ *tongues were out of use* men no longer spoke ¹²⁰ *charge* command
¹²⁴ *dressed* bandaged ¹²⁹ *fordoes me quite* completely ruins me

Scene II. [*Desdemona's chamber.*]

*Enter Othello [with a light]; and Desdemona
in her bed.*

Othello. It is the cause, it is the cause, my soul.
Let me not name it to you, you chaste stars.
It is the cause. Yet I'll not shed her blood,
Nor scar that whiter skin of hers than snow,
5   And smooth as monumental alabaster.
Yet she must die, else she'll betray more men.
Put out the light, and then put out the light.
If I quench thee, thou flaming minister,°
I can again thy former light restore,
10 Should I repent me; but once put out thy light,
Thou cunning'st° pattern of excelling nature,
I know not where is that Promethean heat°
That can thy light relume.° When I have plucked
   the rose,
I cannot give it vital° growth again;
15 It needs must wither. I'll smell thee on the tree.
                          [*He kisses her.*]
O balmy breath, that dost almost persuade
Justice to break her sword. One more, one more!
Be thus when thou art dead, and I will kill thee,
And love thee after. One more, and that's the last!
20 So sweet was ne'er so fatal. I must weep,
But they are cruel tears. This sorrow's heavenly;
It strikes where it doth love. She wakes.

Desdemona. Who's there? Othello?

Othello.   Ay, Desdemona.

V.ii.[8] *minister* worker, servant [11] *cunning'st* most intricate and skill-fully wrought (by nature excelling itself) [12] *Promethean heat* divine fire (Prometheus is the Titan who stole fire from heaven and gave it to man) [13] *relume* relight [14] *vital* living

Desdemona. Will you come to bed, my lord?

Othello. Have you prayed tonight, Desdemon?

Desdemona.   Ay, my lord.   25

Othello. If you bethink yourself of any crime
    Unreconciled as yet to heaven and grace,
    Solicit for it straight.

Desdemona. Alack, my lord, what may you mean by
    that?

Othello. Well, do it, and be brief; I will walk by.°   30
    I would not kill thy unpreparèd spirit.
    No, heavens forfend! I would not kill thy soul.

Desdemona. Talk you of killing?

Othello.   Ay, I do.

Desdemona.   Then heaven
    Have mercy on me!

Othello.   Amen, with all my heart.

Desdemona. If you say so, I hope you will not kill me.   35

Othello. Humh.

Desdemona. And yet I fear you; for you're fatal then
    When your eyes roll so. Why I should fear I know
        not,
    Since guiltiness I know not; but yet I feel I fear.

Othello. Think on thy sins.

Desdemona.   They are loves I bear to you.   40

Othello. Ay, and for that thou diest.

Desdemona. That death's unnatural that kills for
    loving.
    Alas, why gnaw you so your nether lip?
    Some bloody passion shakes your very frame.
    These are portents; but yet I hope, I hope,   45
    They do not point on me.

Othello.   Peace and be still.

³⁰ *by* nearby

Desdemona. I will so. What's the matter?

Othello. That handkerchief which I so loved and gave
    thee,
Thou gav'st to Cassio.

Desdemona.   No, by my life and soul!
Send for the man and ask him.

50 *Othello.*   Sweet soul, take heed,
Take heed of perjury; thou art on thy deathbed.

Desdemona. Ay, but not yet to die.

Othello.   Presently.°
Therefore confess thee freely of thy sin,
For to deny each article° with oath
55   Cannot remove nor choke the strong conception
That I do groan withal. Thou art to die.

Desdemona. Then Lord have mercy on me.

Othello.   I say, amen.

Desdemona. And have you mercy too. I never did
Offend you in my life; never loved Cassio
60   But with such general warranty° of heaven
As I might love. I never gave him token.

Othello. By heaven, I saw my handkerchief in's hand!
O perjured woman! thou dost stone° my heart,
And mak'st me call what I intend to do
65   A murder, which I thought a sacrifice.
I saw the handkerchief.

Desdemona.   He found it then.
I never gave it him. Send for him hither.
Let him confess a truth.

Othello.   He hath confessed.

Desdemona. What, my lord?

Othello. That he hath used thee.

Desdemona.   How? Unlawfully?

---

[52] *Presently* immediately   [54] *article* item (of the charge of adultery. Othello makes heavy use of legal terms in this scene)   [60] *warranty* allowance   [63] *stone* turn to stone

Othello.　　　　　　　　　　　　　　　　　Ay.　　*70*

Desdemona. He will not say so.

Othello.　　　　　　　　No, his mouth is stopped.
　Honest Iago hath ta'en order for't.°

Desdemona. O, my fear interprets. What, is he dead?

Othello. Had all his hairs been lives, my great revenge
　Had stomach° for them all.　　　　　　　　　　*75*

Desdemona. Alas, he is betrayed, and I undone!

Othello. Out, strumpet! Weep'st thou for him to my
　face?

Desdemona. O, banish me, my lord, but kill me not!

Othello. Down, strumpet!

Desdemona. Kill me tomorrow; let me live tonight!　*80*

Othello. Nay, if you strive——

Desdemona. But half an hour!

Othello.　　　　　　Being done, there is no pause.

Desdemona. But while I say one prayer!

Othello.　　　　　　　　　　　It is too late.
　　　　　　　　　　　　　　　　Smothers her.

　　　　　　Emilia at the door.

Emilia. [*Calls within.*] My lord, my lord! What, ho, my
　lord, my lord!

Othello. What noise is this? Not dead? Not yet quite
　dead?　　　　　　　　　　　　　　　　　　*85*
　I that am cruel am yet merciful;
　I would not have thee linger in thy pain.
　So, so.

Emilia. [*Within*] What, ho! My lord, my lord!

Othello.　　　　　　　　　　　Who's there?

Emilia. [*Within*] O, good my lord, I would speak a
　word with you.

---

⁷² *ta'en order for't* made sure of it　⁷⁵ *stomach* appetite

90 *Othello.* Yes, 'tis Emilia.—By and by.—She's dead.—
'Tis like she comes to speak of Cassio's death.
The noise was high.° Ha! No more moving?
Still as the grave.—Shall she come in? Were't
good?—
I think she stirs again. No.— What's best to do?
95 If she come in, she'll sure speak to my wife.
My wife! My wife! What wife? I have no wife.
O, insupportable! O heavy hour!
Methinks it should be now a huge eclipse
Of sun and moon, and that th' affrighted globe
Should yawn° at alteration.

100 *Emilia.*   [*Within*] I do beseech you
That I may speak with you, O good my lord!

Othello. I had forgot thee. O, come in, Emilia.
Soft, by and by.—Let me the curtains draw.—
[*Draws the bed hangings and then opens the door.*]
Where art thou?

             Enter Emilia.

             What's the matter with thee now?

105 *Emilia.* O my good lord, yonder's foul murders done!

Othello. What? Now?

Emilia. But now, my lord.

Othello. It is the very error° of the moon.
She comes more nearer earth than she was wont
110 And makes men mad.

Emilia. Cassio, my lord, hath killed a young Venetian
Called Roderigo.

Othello.   Roderigo killed?
And Cassio killed?

---

⁹² *high* loud (Q1 reads "here")   ⁹⁸⁻¹⁰⁰ *Methinks . . . alteration* (the
Elizabethans believed that great changes in human affairs were reflected
by disorders in nature)   ¹⁰⁰ *yawn* gape open (as in an earthquake)
¹⁰⁸ *error* wandering out of regular course (disorders in the heavens
were believed by some to cause disorders on earth, as well as vice
versa)

Emilia. No, Cassio is not killed.

Othello. Not Cassio killed? Then murder's out of tune,
  And sweet revenge grows harsh.   115

Desdemona. O, falsely, falsely murdered!

Emilia. O Lord! What cry is that?

Othello. That? What?

Emilia. Out and alas! that was my lady's voice.
  Help! Help, ho! Help! O lady, speak again!
  Sweet Desdemona! O sweet mistress, speak!   120

Desdemona. A guiltless death I die.

Emilia. O, who hath done this deed?

Desdemona. Nobody—I myself. Farewell.
  Commend me to my kind lord. O, farewell!
                                          [*She dies.*]

Othello. Why, how should she be murd'red?

Emilia. Alas, who knows?   125

Othello. You heard her say herself, it was not I.

Emilia. She said so. I must needs report the truth.

Othello. She's like a liar gone to burning hell!
  'Twas I that killed her.

Emilia. O, the more angel she,
  And you the blacker devil!   130

Othello. She turned to folly, and she was a whore.

Emilia. Thou dost belie her, and thou art a devil.

Othello. She was false as water.

Emilia. Thou art rash as fire to say
  That she was false. O, she was heavenly true!

Othello. Cassio did top her. Ask thy husband else.   135
  O, I were damned beneath all depth in hell
  But that I did proceed upon just grounds
  To this extremity. Thy husband knew it all.

Emilia. My husband?

Othello. Thy husband.

Emilia.   That she was false to wedlock?

140 *Othello.* Ay, with Cassio. Had she been true,
      If heaven would make me such another world
      Of one entire and perfect chrysolite,°
      I'd not have sold her for it.

Emilia.   My husband?

Othello. Ay, 'twas he that told me on her first.
145   An honest man he is, and hates the slime
      That sticks on filthy deeds.

Emilia.   My husband?

Othello. What needs this iterance? Woman, I say thy
      husband.

Emilia. O mistress, villainy hath made mocks with
      love!
      My husband say she was false?

Othello.   He, woman.
150   I say, thy husband. Dost understand the word?
      My friend, thy husband; honest, honest Iago.

Emilia. If he say so, may his pernicious soul
      Rot half a grain a day! He lies to th' heart.
      She was too fond of her most filthy bargain.

155 *Othello.* Hah?

Emilia. Do thy worst.
      This deed of thine is no more worthy heaven
      Than thou wast worthy her.

Othello.   Peace, you were best.°

Emilia. Thou hast not half that pow'r to do me harm
160   As I have to be hurt. O gull! O dolt!
      As ignorant as dirt! Thou hast done a deed—
                  [*Othello moves to draw his sword.*]
      I care not for thy sword; I'll make thee known,
      Though I lost twenty lives. Help! Help! Ho! Help!
      The Moor hath killed my mistress! Murder! murder!

---

142 *chrysolite* topaz   158 *Peace, you were best* i.e., you had better be silent

Enter Montano, Gratiano, and Iago [and Others].

Montano. What is the matter? How now, general?   165

Emilia. O, are you come, Iago? You have done well,
    That men must lay their murders on your neck.

Gratiano. What is the matter?

Emilia. Disprove this villain, if thou be'st a man.
    He says thou told'st him that his wife was false.   170
    I know thou didst not; thou'rt not such a villain.
    Speak, for my heart is full.

Iago. I told him what I thought, and told no more
    Than what he found himself was apt and true.

Emilia. But did you ever tell him she was false?   175

Iago. I did.

Emilia. You told a lie, an odious damnèd lie!
    Upon my soul, a lie! A wicked lie!
    She false with Cassio? Did you say with Cassio?

Iago. With Cassio, mistress. Go to, charm° your
    tongue.   180

Emilia. I will not charm my tongue; I am bound to
    speak:
    My mistress here lies murdered in her bed.

All. O heavens forfend!

Emilia. And your reports have set the murder on.

Othello. Nay, stare not, masters. It is true indeed.   185

Gratiano. 'Tis a strange truth.

Montano. O monstrous act!

Emilia.   Villainy, villainy, villainy!
    I think upon't—I think I smell't!—O villainy!
    I thought so then.—I'll kill myself for grief.—
    O villainy, villainy!   190

Iago. What, are you mad? I charge you get you home.

Emilia. Good gentlemen, let me have leave to speak.

180 *charm* control

'Tis proper I obey him, but not now.
Perchance, Iago, I will ne'er go home.

Othello. O! O! O!   [*Falls on the bed.*]

195 *Emilia.*   Nay, lay thee down and roar,
For thou hast killed the sweetest innocent
That e'er did lift up eye.

Othello.   O, she was foul!   [*Rises.*]
I scarce did know you, uncle. There lies your niece,
Whose breath, indeed, these hands have newly
          stopped.
200 I know this act shows horrible and grim.

Gratiano. Poor Desdemon! I am glad thy father's dead.
Thy match was mortal to him, and pure grief
Shore his old thread in twain. Did he live now,
This sight would make him do a desperate turn;
205 Yea, curse his better angel from his side,
And fall to reprobation.°

Othello. 'Tis pitiful; but yet Iago knows
That she with Cassio hath the act of shame
A thousand times committed. Cassio confessed it;
210 And she did gratify his amorous works
With that recognizance and pledge of love,
Which I first gave her. I saw it in his hand.
It was a handkerchief, an antique token
My father gave my mother.

215 *Emilia.* O God! O heavenly God!

Iago. Zounds, hold your peace!

Emilia.   'Twill out, 'twill out! I peace?
No, I will speak as liberal as the north.°
Let heaven and men and devils, let them all,
All, all, cry shame against me, yet I'll speak.

Iago. Be wise, and get you home.

220 *Emilia.*   I will not.
          [*Iago draws and threatens Emilia.*]

²⁰⁶ *reprobation* damnation   ²¹⁷ *liberal as the north* freely (and bitingly)
as the north wind blows

Gratiano. Fie! Your sword upon a woman?

Emilia. O thou dull Moor, that handkerchief thou
    speak'st of
  I found by fortune, and did give my husband;
  For often with a solemn earnestness—
  More than indeed belonged to such a trifle—   225
  He begged of me to steal't.

Iago.   Villainous whore!

Emilia. She give it Cassio? No, alas, I found it,
  And I did give't my husband.

Iago.   Filth, thou liest!

Emilia. By heaven, I do not, I do not, gentlemen.
  O murd'rous coxcomb! What should such a fool   230
  Do with so good a wife?

Othello.   Are there no stones° in heaven
  But what serves for the thunder? Precious villain!
  [*The Moor runs at Iago, but is disarmed by Montano.*
                    Iago kills his wife.]

Gratiano. The woman falls. Sure he hath killed his
  wife.

Emilia. Ay, ay. O, lay me by my mistress' side.
                        [*Exit Iago.*]

Gratiano. He's gone, but his wife's killed.   235

Montano. 'Tis a notorious° villain. Take you this
    weapon,
  Which I have recovered from the Moor.
  Come, guard the door without. Let him not pass,
  But kill him rather. I'll after that same villain,
  For 'tis a damnèd slave.
          Exit [with all but Othello and Emilia].

Othello.   I am not valiant neither;   240
  But every puny whipster° gets my sword.
  But why should honor outlive honesty?
  Let it go all.

231 *stones* thunderbolts   236 *notorious* out-and-out   241 *puny whipster*
small top-whipping boy (?)

Emilia.   What did thy song bode, lady?
          Hark, canst thou hear me? I will play the swan,
245   And die in music. [*Sings*] "Willow, willow, willow."
          Moor, she was chaste. She loved thee, cruel Moor,
          So come my soul to bliss as I speak true.
          So speaking as I think, alas, I die.   [*She dies.*]

Othello. I have another weapon in this chamber;
250   It was a sword of Spain, the ice-brook's temper.
          O, here it is.—Uncle, I must come forth.

Gratiano. [*Within*] If thou attempt it, it will cost thee
          dear.
          Thou hast no weapon, and perforce must suffer.

Othello. Look in upon me then and speak with me,
255   Or, naked as I am, I will assault thee.

                    [*Enter Gratiano.*]

Gratiano. What is the matter?

Othello.   Behold, I have a weapon;
          A better never did itself sustain
          Upon a soldier's thigh. I have seen the day
          That with this little arm and this good sword
260   I have made my way through more impediments
          Than twenty times your stop. But O vain boast!
          Who can control his fate? 'Tis not so now.
          Be not afraid, though you do see me weaponed.
          Here is my journey's end, here is my butt,°
265   And very seamark of my utmost sail.°
          Do you go back dismayed? 'Tis a lost fear.
          Man but a rush° against Othello's breast,
          And he retires. Where should Othello go?
          Now, how dost thou look now? O ill-starred wench!
270   Pale as thy smock! When we shall meet at compt,°
          This look of thine will hurl my soul from heaven,
          And fiends will snatch at it. Cold, cold, my girl?
          Even like thy chastity.
          O cursèd, cursèd slave! Whip me, ye devils,

²⁶⁴ *butt* target, stopping place   ²⁶⁵ *seamark of my utmost sail* marker
of my farthest journey   ²⁶⁷ *Man but a rush* attack with only a reed
²⁷⁰ *compt* Judgment Day

From the possession of° this heavenly sight!　　*275*
Blow me about in winds! roast me in sulfur!
Wash me in steep-down gulfs of liquid fire!
O Desdemon! Dead Desdemon; dead. O! O!

　　Enter Lodovico, Cassio, Montano, and Iago
　　　　[as prisoner,] with Officers.

Lodovico. Where is this rash and most unfortunate
　　man?

Othello. That's he that was Othello; Here I am.　　*280*

Lodovico. Where is that viper? Bring the villain forth.

Othello. I look down towards his feet°——but that's a
　　fable.
If that thou be'st a devil, I cannot kill thee.
　　　　　　　　　　　　　　　[Wounds Iago.]

Lodovico. Wrench his sword from him.
　　　　　　　　　　　　[Othello is disarmed.]

Iago.　　　　　　　　I bleed, sir, but not killed.

Othello. I am not sorry neither. I'd have thee live;　　*285*
For in my sense, 'tis happiness to die.

Lodovico. O thou Othello that was once so good,
Fall'n in the practice° of a cursèd slave,
What shall be said to thee?

Othello.　　　　　　　　Why, anything:
An honorable murderer, if you will;　　*290*
For naught I did in hate, but all in honor.

Lodovico. This wretch hath part confessed his villainy.
Did you and he consent in Cassio's death?

Othello. Ay.

Cassio. Dear general, I never gave you cause.　　*295*

Othello. I do believe it, and I ask your pardon.
Will you, I pray, demand that demi-devil
Why he hath thus ensnared my soul and body?

---

275 *the possession of* being possessed by　282 *towards his feet* i.e., for
his cloven hoofs　288 *practice* plotting

Iago. Demand me nothing. What you know, you know.
300   From this time forth I never will speak word.

Lodovico. What, not to pray?

Gratiano.   Torments will ope your lips.

Othello. Well, thou dost best.

Lodovico. Sir, you shall understand what hath befall'n,
    Which, as I think, you know not. Here is a letter
305   Found in the pocket of the slain Roderigo;
    And here another. The one of them imports
    The death of Cassio to be undertook
    By Roderigo.

Othello. O villain!

Cassio.   Most heathenish and most gross!

310 *Lodovico.* Now here's another discontented paper
    Found in his pocket too; and this, it seems,
    Roderigo meant t' have sent this damnèd villain;
    But that, belike, Iago in the interim
    Came in and satisfied him.

Othello.   O thou pernicious caitiff!
315   How came you, Cassio, by that handkerchief
    That was my wife's?

Cassio.   I found it in my chamber;
    And he himself confessed it but even now
    That there he dropped it for a special purpose
    Which wrought to his desire.

Othello.   O fool! Fool! Fool!

320 *Cassio.* There is besides in Roderigo's letter,
    How he upbraids Iago that he made him
    Brave me upon the watch; whereon it came
    That I was cast; and even but now he spake,
    After long seeming dead—Iago hurt him,
325   Iago set him on.

Lodovico. You must forsake this room and go with
       us.
    Your power and your command is taken off,
    And Cassio rules in Cyprus. For this slave,

If there be any cunning cruelty
That can torment him much and hold him long,   *830*
It shall be his. You shall close prisoner rest
Till that the nature of your fault be known
To the Venetian state. Come, bring away.

Othello. Soft you, a word or two before you go.
I have done the state some service, and they know't.   *835*
No more of that. I pray you, in your letters,
When you shall these unlucky deeds relate,
Speak of me as I am. Nothing extenuate,
Nor set down aught in malice. Then must you speak
Of one that loved not wisely, but too well;   *840*
Of one not easily jealous, but, being wrought,
Perplexed in the extreme; of one whose hand,
Like the base Judean,° threw a pearl away
Richer than all his tribe; of one whose subdued
     eyes,
Albeit unusèd to the melting mood,   *845*
Drops tears as fast as the Arabian trees
Their med'cinable gum. Set you down this.
And say besides that in Aleppo once,
Where a malignant and a turbaned Turk
Beat a Venetian and traduced the state,   *850*
I took by th' throat the circumcisèd dog
And smote him—thus.   [*He stabs himself.*]

Lodovico. O bloody period!°

Gratiano.   All that is spoke is marred.

Othello. I kissed thee ere I killed thee. No way but this,
Killing myself, to die upon a kiss.   *355*
                    [*He falls over Desdemona and dies.*]

Cassio. This did I fear, but thought he had no weapon;
For he was great of heart.

Lodovico.   [*To Iago*] O Spartan dog,
More fell° than anguish, hunger, or the sea!

---

843 *Judean* (most editors use the Q1 reading, "Indian," here, but F is
clear; both readings point toward the infidel, the unbeliever) **353** *period*
end **358** *fell* cruel

Look on the tragic loading of this bed.
860 This is thy work. The object poisons sight;
Let it be hid.   [*Bed curtains drawn.*]
        Gratiano, keep° the house,
And seize upon the fortunes of the Moor,
For they succeed on you. To you, lord governor,
Remains the censure of this hellish villain,
365 The time, the place, the torture. O, enforce it!
Myself will straight aboard, and to the state
This heavy act with heavy heart relate.   *Exeunt.*

FINIS

---

361 *keep* remain in

Textual Note

Othello contains some of the most difficult editorial problems of any Shakespearean play. The play was entered in *The Stationer's Register* on 6 October, 1621, and printed in a quarto edition, Q1, by Thomas Walkley in 1622, some eighteen or nineteen years after it was first staged. More curiously, at the time that Walkley printed his quarto edition, the plans for printing the folio edition of Shakespeare's collected works were completed and printing was well along. The Folio, F, appeared in late 1623, and the text of *Othello* included in it differs considerably from Q1. A second quarto, Q2, was printed from F in 1630. The chief differences between the two major texts, Q1 and F, are: (1) There are 160 lines in F that are not in Q1; some of these omissions affect the sense in Q1, but others seem to be either intentional cuts in Q1 or additions in F. (2) There are a number of oaths in Q1 that are not in F; this fact can be interpreted in a number of ways, but all arguments go back to the prohibition in 1606 of swearing on stage—but apparently not in printed editions. (3) The stage directions in Q1 are much fuller than in F. (4) There are a large number of variant readings in the two texts, in single words, in phrases, and in lineation; where Q1, for example, reads "toged" (i.e., wearing a toga), F reads "tongued"; where Q1 reads "Worships," F reads "Moorships."

These may seem petty problems, but they present an editor with a series of most difficult questions about what to print at any given point where the two texts are in disagreement. The usual solution in the past has been for the editor to include all material in F and Q1, and where the two texts are in disagreement to select the reading he prefers. The result is what is known as an eclectic text. But modern bibliographical studies have demonstrated that it is possible to proceed, in some cases at least, in a more precise manner by examining the conflicting texts carefully in order to arrive at something like a reasonable judgment about their relative authority. Shakespearean bibliography has become a most elaborate affair, however, and in most cases it has become necessary to take the word of specialists on these matters. Unfortunately, in the case of *Othello* the experts are not in agreement, and none of their arguments has the ring of certainty. Here is, however, the most general opinion of how the two different texts came into being and how they are related.

After Shakespeare wrote the play, his original draft, usually termed "foul papers," was copied, around 1604, by a scribe and made into what is known as the "promptbook," the official copy of the play used in the theater as the basis for production. This promptbook was the property of the players' company, the King's Men in this case, and remained in their possession to be used, and perhaps revised, whenever they produced *Othello*. Being a repertory company they would present a play for a few performances, then drop it for a time, and then present it again when conditions seemed favorable. At some time around 1620, another copy was made of the original foul papers, or some later copy of them, and this served as the basis for the 1622 Quarto. Later, when the publishers of the Folio got around to printing *Othello*, they took a copy of Q1 and corrected it by the original promptbook, and this corrected copy was then given to the compositors who were setting type for F. There are genuine objections to this theory, the most telling raised by the most recent editor of the play, M. R. Ridley, in *The Arden Shakespeare* edition of *Othello;* but the theory does explain certain difficult facts, and most bibliographers seem to accept some version of it.

The end of this line of argument is to establish fairly

reasonably the authority of the F text as being the closest either to what Shakespeare wrote originally or to the play as he finally left it after playhouse revisions. This agrees with what most scholars find in reading the two texts. Sir Walter Greg puts this common belief in the superiority of F in the strongest terms: "In the great majority of cases there can be no doubt that F has preserved the more Shakespearean reading." (*The Shakespeare First Folio*, Oxford, 1955, p. 365.) For practical purposes what this means is that where an F reading makes sense, then an editor has no choice but to accept it—even though he "likes" the Q reading better and would have used it if he had *written,* instead of only edited, the play. But while an editor may be aided and comforted by the bibliographers' decision that F is more authoritative than Q1, his problems are by no means solved. There are places where F does not make sense but Q1 does, places where F is deficient in some way and Q is clear and complete, and places where both fail to make sense or seem to point to a common failure to transcribe correctly their original. When this occurs an editor must try to understand how the trouble occurred and then fall back on his judgment. This will force him to try to reconstruct the original manuscript from which we are told Q and F both derive, and he must attempt to deduce the original reading which both scribes mangled or which the typesetters in the different printing houses misread or made a mistake in setting.

This editorial process is endlessly complicated, but the general basis of this edition is as follows: F is taken for the copy text and its readings are preserved wherever they make sense. Oaths and stage directions are, however, taken from Q1, since they were presumably part of the original manuscript, but were deleted by the promptbook transcriber to comply with the prohibition against swearing on stage and because the prompt copy did not require such elaborate stage directions as a reading version—somewhat contrary to common sense, this last, but the bibliographers insist upon it. Where mislineation occurs in F, but Q1 has it correctly, the Q1 lineation is used on the theory that it has a better chance of being the original than any hypo-

thetical reconstruction of my own. Finally, where F and
Q1 both produce nonsense, changes, based on the above
theory about the transmission of the text and on the work
of previous editors, have been made.

Where F is deficient, the reading adopted and printed in
this text is given below first in italics; unless otherwise
stated it is taken from Q1. The original F reading that has
been changed follows in roman. Obvious typographical
errors in F, expansions of abbreviations, spelling variants
("murder," "murther"), and changes in punctuation and
lineation are not noted. The act and scene divisions are
translated from Latin, and the division at II.iii is from the
Globe edition rather than from F; otherwise the divisions
of F and the Globe edition are identical. "The Names of
the Actors," here printed at the beginning of the play, in
F follows the play.

I.i.1 *Tush!* Never   Never   4 *'Sblood, but* But   26 *other* others
27 *Christian* Christen'd   30 *God bless* blesse   63 *full* fall   *thick-
lips* Thicks-lips   83 *Zounds, sir* Sir   105 *Zounds, sir* Sir   111 *germans* Germaines   143 *produced* producted   151 *hell pains* (emendation) hell apines [hells paines Q1]

I.ii.33 *Duke* Dukes   37 *Even* enen   49 *carack* (emendation) Car-
ract [Carrick Q1]   50 *he's made* he' made   57 *Come* Cme
67 *darlings* Deareling   74 *weaken* weakens   83 *Whither* Whether
86 *if I do* if do

I.iii.53 *nor* hor   74 *your* yonr   99 *maimed* main'd   106 *Duke* [F
omits]   107 *overt test* oer Test   110 *First Senator* Sen.   122 *till*
tell   138 *travel's* trauellours   140 *rocks, and hills* Rocks, Hills
heads head   142 *other* others   146 *thence* hence   154 *intentively*
instinctively   203 *preserved* preserv'd   227 *couch* (emendation)
Coach [Cooch Q1]   229 *alacrity* Alacartie   259 *me* my [F and Q1]
273 *First Senator* Sen.   286 *First Senator* Sen.   321–22 *balance*
braine   328 *scion* (emendation) Seyen [seyen Q1]   376 *snipe* snpe
379 *H'as* She ha's

II.i.9 *mortise* (emendation) morties [morties Q1]   33 *prays* praye
40 *Third Gentleman* Gent.   53 *First Gentleman* Gent.   56 *Second
Gentleman* Gent.   59 *Second Gentleman* Gent.   65 *ingener* In-
geniuer   66 *Second Gentleman* Gent.   94 *Second Gentleman*
Gent.   168 *gyve* (emendation) giue [catch Q1]   173 *an* and
175 *clyster* cluster   212 *hither* thither   242 *has* he's   261 *mutualities* mutabilities   299 *wife* wist   307 *nightcap* Night-Cape

II.iii.39 *unfortunate* infortunate 57 *to put* put to 61 *God* heauen 72 *God* Heauen 77 *Englishman* Englishmen 93 *thine* thy 95 *'Fore God* Why 99 *God's* heaven's 108 *God forgive* Forgiue 141 *Within . . . help* [F omits; Q1 reads "Helpe, helpe, within"] 142 *Zounds, you* You 156 *God's will* Alas 160 *God's will* Fie, fie 162 *Zounds, I* I 217 *leagued* (emendation) [league F and Q1] 260 *God* Heauen 274 *to* ro 288 *O God* Oh 343 *were 't* were to 362 *enmesh* en-mash 378 *By the mass* In troth

III.i.1s.d. [F includes the Clown] 20 *Exeunt Musicians* Exit Mu. 25 *general's wife* Generall 30 *Cassio* [no speech ascription in F]

III.ii.6 *We'll* Well

III.iii.74 *By'r Lady* Trust me 94 *you* he 106 *By heaven* Alas 135 *free to* free 136 *vile* vild 139 *But some* Wherein 148 *Shape* (emendation) Shapes 162 *By heaven I'll* Ile 170 *fondly* (emendation) soundly [strongly Q1] 175 *God* heauen 182 *exsufflicate* (emendation) exufflicate (F and Q1) *blown* blowd 217 *my* your 222 *vile* vilde 248 *hold him* him 258 *qualities* Quantities 259 *human* humane 281 *to* too 335 *of* in 347 *make* makes 372 *b' wi'* buy 392 *supervisor* supervision 437 *that was* (Malone's emendation) it was [F and Q1]

III.iv.77 *God* Heauen 81 *Heaven* Blesse 97 *I'faith* In sooth 170 *I'faith* Indeed 186 *by my faith* in good troth

IV.i.21 *infected* infectious 37 *Zounds, that's* that's 79 *unsuiting* resulting 103 *conster* conserue 109 *power* dowre 113 *i'faith* indeed 124 *win* winnes 132 *beckons* becomes 164 *Faith, I* I 218 *God save* Save 248 *an obedient* obedient

IV.ii.16 *requite* requit 30 *Nay* May 48 *kinds* kind 154 *in* [Q2] or 168 *stay* stays

IV.iii.14 *bade* bid 51 *hie* high

V.i.1 *bulk* Barke 22 *hear* heard 34 *hies* highes 35 *Forth* For 50 *heaven's* heaven 104 *out o' th'* o' th'

V.ii.13 *the rose* thy Rose 35 *say so* say 57 *Then Lord* O Heauen 100 *Should* Did 116 *O Lord* Alas 126 *heard* heare 206 *reprobation* Reprobance 215 *O God! O heavenly God* O Heauen! Oh heauenly powres 216 *Zounds* Come

The Source of *Othello*

Shakespeare's play is based on a story in Giraldi Cinthio's *Hecatommithi* (III, 7), a collection of a hundred tales printed in Italy in the sixteenth century. So far as is known, there was no English translation of the source story in Shakespeare's time, and while he may have read it in a French translation of Gabriel Chappuys, it seems probable that he read the original Italian. For a discussion of the evidence for this view and a good comparison of the story and the play, see Kenneth Muir, *Shakespeare's Sources* (London, 1957), Vol. I, "Comedies and Tragedies," pp. 122–23. The translation reprinted here is that of J. E. Taylor, done in 1855.

Selection from Giraldi Cinthio
Hecatommithi

There once lived in Venice a Moor, who was very valiant and of a handsome person; and having given proofs in war of great skill and prudence, he was highly esteemed by the Signoria of the Republic, who in rewarding deeds of valor advanced the interests of the state.

It happened that a virtuous lady of marvelous beauty, named Disdemona, fell in love with the Moor, moved thereto by his valor; and he, vanquished by the beauty and the noble character of Disdemona, returned her love; and their affection was so mutual that, although the parents of the lady strove all they could to induce her to take another husband, she consented to marry the Moor; and they lived in such harmony and peace in Venice that no word ever passed between them that was not affectionate and kind.

Now it happened at this time that the Signoria of Venice made a change in the troops whom they used to maintain in Cyprus, and they appointed the Moor commander of the soldiers whom they dispatched thither. Joyful as was the Moor at the honor proffered him, such dignity being only conferred on men of noble rank and well-tried faith, and who had displayed bravery in arms—yet his pleasure was lessened when he reflected on the length and dangers of the voyage, fearing that Disdemona would be pained at his absence. But Disdemona, who had no other happiness in the world than the Moor, and who rejoiced to witness the testimony of his valor her husband had received from so powerful and noble a republic, was all impatient that he should embark with his troops, and longed to accompany him to so honorable a post. And all the more it vexed her to see the Moor so troubled; and not knowing what could be the reason, one day, when they were at dinner, she said to him, "How is it, O Moor, that when so honorable a post has been conferred on you by the Signoria, you are thus melancholy?"

The Moor answered Disdemona, "My pleasure at the honor I have received is disturbed by the love I bear you; for I see that of necessity one of two things must happen— either that I take you with me to encounter the perils of the sea, or, to save you from this danger, I must leave you here in Venice. The first could not be otherwise than serious to me, for all the toil you would have to bear and every danger that might befall you would cause me extreme anxiety and pain, yet, were I to leave you behind me, I should be hateful to myself, since in parting from you I should part from my own life."

Disdemona, on hearing this, replied: "My husband, what thoughts are these that wander through your mind? Why let such things disturb you? I will accompany you whithersoe'er you go, were it to pass through fire, as now to cross the water in a safe and well-provided ship; if indeed there are toils and perils to encounter, I will share them with you. And in truth I should think you loved me little were you to leave me here in Venice, denying me to bear you company, or could believe that I would liefer bide in safety here than share the dangers that await you. Prepare then for the voyage with all the readiness which the dignity of the post you hold deserves."

The Moor, in the fullness of his joy, threw his arms around his wife's neck, and with an affectionate and tender kiss exclaimed, "God keep you long in such love, dear wife!" Then speedily donning his armor, and having prepared everything for his expedition, he embarked on board the galley with his wife and all his troops, and, setting sail, they pursued their voyage, and with a perfectly tranquil sea arrived safely at Cyprus.

Now amongst the soldiery there was an Ensign, a man of handsome figure, but of the most depraved nature in the world. This man was in great favor with the Moor, who had not the slightest idea of his wickedness; for, despite the malice lurking in his heart, he cloaked with proud and valorous speech and with a specious presence the villainy of his soul with such art that he was to all outward show another Hector or Achilles. This man had likewise taken with him his wife to Cyprus, a young, and fair, and virtuous lady; and being of Italian birth she was much loved by Disdemona, who spent the greater part of every day with her.

In the same Company there was a certain Captain of a troop, to whom the Moor was much affectioned. And Disdemona, for this cause, knowing how much her husband valued him, showed him proofs of the greatest kindness, which was all very grateful to the Moor. Now the wicked Ensign, regardless of the faith that he had pledged his wife, no less than of the friendship, fidelity, and obligation which he owed the Moor, fell passionately in love with Disdemona, and bent all his thoughts to achieve his conquest; yet he dared not to declare his passion openly, fearing that, should the Moor perceive it, he would at once kill him. He therefore sought in various ways, and with secret guile, to betray his passion to the lady; but she, whose every wish was centered in the Moor, had no thought for this Ensign more than for any other man; and all the means he tried to gain her love had no more effect than if he had not tried them. But the Ensign imagined that the cause of his ill success was that Disdemona loved the Captain of the troop; and he pondered how to remove him from her sight. The love which he had borne the lady now changed into the bitterest hate, and, having failed in his purposes, he devoted all his thoughts to plot the death of the Captain of the troop and to divert the affection of the Moor from Disdemona. After revolving in his mind various schemes, all alike wicked, he at length resolved to accuse her of unfaithfulness to her husband, and to represent the Captain as her paramour. But knowing the singular love the Moor bore to Disdemona, and the friendship which he had for the Captain, he was well aware that, unless he practiced an artful fraud upon the Moor, it were impossible to make him give ear to either accusation; wherefore he resolved to wait until time and circumstance should open a path for him to engage in his foul project.

Not long afterwards it happened that the Captain, having drawn his sword upon a soldier of the guard, and struck him, the Moor deprived him of his rank; whereat Disdemona was deeply grieved, and endeavored again and again to reconcile her husband to the man. This the Moor told to the wicked Ensign, and how his wife importuned him so much about the Captain that he feared he should be forced at last to receive him back to service. Upon this hint the Ensign resolved to act, and began to work his web of intrigue. "Perchance," said he, "the lady Disdemona may have good reason to look kindly on him."

"And wherefore?" said the Moor.

"Nay, I would not step 'twixt man and wife," replied the Ensign, "but let your eyes be witness to themselves."

In vain the Moor went on to question the officer—he

would proceed no further; nevertheless, his words left a sharp, stinging thorn in the Moor's heart, who could think of nothing else, trying to guess their meaning and lost in melancholy. And one day, when his wife had been endeavoring to pacify his anger toward the Captain, and praying him not to be unmindful of ancient services and friendship for one small fault, especially since peace had been made between the Captain and the soldier he had struck, the Moor was angered, and exclaimed, "Great cause have you, Disdemona, to care so anxiously about this man! Is he a brother, or your kinsman, that he should be so near your heart?"

The lady, with all gentleness and humility, replied, "Be not angered, my dear lord; I have no other cause to bid me speak than sorrow that I see you lose so dear a friend as, by your own words, this Captain has been to you; nor has he done so grave a fault that you should bear him so much enmity. Nay, but you Moors are of so hot a nature that every little trifle moves you to anger and revenge."

Still more enraged at these words, the Moor replied, "I could bring proofs—by heaven it mocks belief! but for the wrongs I have endured revenge must satisfy my wrath."

Disdemona, in astonishment and fright, seeing her husband's anger kindled against her, so contrary to his wont, said humbly and with timidness, "None save a good intent has led me thus to speak with you, my lord; but to give cause no longer for offense, I'll never speak a word more on the subject."

The Moor, observing the earnestness with which his wife again pleaded for the Captain, began to guess the meaning of the Ensign's words; and in deep melancholy he went to seek that villain and induce him to speak more openly of what he knew. Then the Ensign, who was bent upon injuring the unhappy lady, after feigning at first great reluctance to say aught that might displease the Moor, at length pretended to yield to his entreaties, and said, "I can't deny it pains me to the soul to be thus forced to say what needs must be more hard to hear than any other grief; but since you will it so, and that the regard I owe your honor compels me to confess the truth, I will no longer refuse to satisfy your questions and my duty. Know, then, that for no other reason is your lady vexed to see the Captain in disfavor than the pleasure that she has in his company whenever he comes to your house, and all the more since she has taken an aversion to your blackness."

These words went straight to the Moor's heart; but in order to hear more (now that he believed true all that the Ensign had told him) he replied, with a fierce glance, "By heavens, I scarce can hold this hand from plucking out that tongue of thine, so bold, which dares to speak such slander of my wife!"

"Captain," replied the Ensign, "I looked for such reward for these my faithful officers—none else; but since my duty, and the jealous care I bear your honor, have carried me thus far, I do repeat, so stands the truth, as you have heard it from these lips; and if the lady Disdemona hath, with a false show of love for you, blinded your eyes to what you should have seen, this is no argument but that I speak the truth. Nay, this same Captain told it me himself, like one whose happiness is incomplete until he can declare it to another; and, but that I feared your anger, I should have given him, when he told it me, his merited reward, and slain him. But since informing you of what concerns you more than any other man brings me so undeserved a recompense, would I had held my peace, since silence might have spared me your displeasure."

Then the Moor, burning with indignation and anguish, said, "Make thou these eyes self-witnesses of what thou tell'st, or on thy life I'll make thee wish thou hadst been born without a tongue."

"An easy task it would have been," replied the villain, "when he was used to visit at your house; but now that you have banished him, not for just cause, but for mere frivolous pretext, it will be hard to prove the truth. Still, I do not forgo the hope to make you witness of that which you will not credit from my lips."

Thus they parted. The wretched Moor, struck to the heart as by a barbed dart, returned to his home, and awaited the day when the Ensign should disclose to him the truth which was to make him miserable to the end of his

days. But the evil-minded Ensign was, on his part, not less
troubled by the chastity which he knew the lady Disdemona observed inviolate; and it seemed to him impossible
to discover a means of making the Moor believe what he
had falsely told him; and, turning the matter over in his
thoughts in various ways, the villain resolved on a new
deed of guilt.

Disdemona often used to go, as I have already said, to
visit the Ensign's wife, and remained with her a good part
of the day. Now, the Ensign observed that she carried
about with her a handkerchief, which he knew the Moor
had given her, finely embroidered in the Moorish fashion,
and which was precious to Disdemona, nor less so to the
Moor. Then he conceived the plan of taking this kerchief
from her secretly, and thus laying the snare for her final
ruin. The Ensign had a little daughter, a child three years
of age, who was much loved by Disdemona, and one day,
when the unhappy lady had gone to pay a visit at the house
of this vile man, he took the little child up in his arms and
carried her to Disdemona, who took her and pressed her to
her bosom; whilst at the same instant this traitor, who had
extreme dexterity of hand, drew the kerchief from her sash
so cunningly that she did not notice him, and overjoyed he
took his leave of her.

Disdemona, ignorant of what had happened, returned
home, and, busy with other thoughts, forgot the handkerchief. But a few days afterwards, looking for it and not
finding it, she was in alarm, lest the Moor should ask her
for it, as he oft was wont to do. Meanwhile, the wicked
Ensign, seizing a fit opportunity, went to the Captain of
the troop, and with crafty malice left the handkerchief at the
head of his bed without his discovering the trick, until
the following morning, when, on his getting out of bed,
the handkerchief fell upon the floor, and he set his foot
upon it. And not being able to imagine how it had come
to his house, knowing that it belonged to Disdemona, he
resolved to give it to her; and waiting until the Moor had
gone from home, he went to the back door and knocked.
It seemed as if fate conspired with the Ensign to work the
death of the unhappy Disdemona. Just at that time the

Moor returned home, and hearing a knocking at the back door, he went to the window, and in a rage exclaimed, "Who knocks there?" The Captain, hearing the Moor's voice, and fearing lest he should come downstairs and attack him, took to flight without answering a word. The Moor went down, and opening the door hastened into the street and looked about, but in vain. Then, returning into the house in great anger, he demanded of his wife who it was that had knocked at the door. Disdemona replied, as was true, that she did not know; but the Moor said, "It seemed to me the Captain."

"I know not," answered Disdemona, "whether it was he or another person."

The Moor restrained his fury, great as it was, wishing to do nothing before consulting the Ensign, to whom he hastened instantly, and told him all that had passed, praying him to gather from the Captain all he could respecting the affair. The Ensign, overjoyed at the occurrence, promised the Moor to do as he requested, and one day he took occasion to speak with the Captain when the Moor was so placed that he could see and hear them as they conversed. And whilst talking to him of every other subject than of Disdemona, he kept laughing all the time aloud, and feigning astonishment, he made various movements with his head and hands, as if listening to some tale of marvel. As soon as the Moor saw the Captain depart, he went up to the Ensign to hear what he had said to him. And the Ensign, after long entreaty, at length said, "He has hidden from me nothing, and has told me that he has been used to visit your wife whenever you went from home, and that on the last occasion she gave him this handkerchief which you presented to her when you married her."

The Moor thanked the Ensign, and it seemed now clear to him that, should he find Disdemona not to have the handkerchief, it was all true that the Ensign had told to him. One day, therefore, after dinner, in conversation with his wife on various subjects, he asked her for the kerchief. The unhappy lady, who had been in great fear of this, grew red as fire at this demand; and to hide the scarlet of her cheeks, which was closely noted by the Moor, she ran to a chest and pretended to seek the handkerchief, and after hunting for it a long time, she said, "I know not how it is—I cannot find it; can you, perchance, have taken it?"

"If I had taken it," said the Moor, "why should I ask it of you? but you will look better another time."

On leaving the room, the Moor fell to meditating how he should put his wife to death, and likewise the Captain of the troop, so that their deaths should not be laid to his charge. And as he ruminated over this day and night, he could not prevent his wife's observing that he was not the same towards her as he had been wont; and she said to him again and again, "What is the matter? What troubles you? How comes it that you, who were the most light-hearted man in the world, are now so melancholy?"

The Moor feigned various reasons in reply to his wife's questioning, but she was not satisfied, and, although conscious that she had given the Moor no cause, by act or deed, to be so troubled, yet she feared that he might have grown wearied of her; and she would say to the Ensign's wife, "I know not what to say of the Moor; he used to be all love towards me; but within these few days he has become another man; and much I fear that I shall prove a warning to young girls not to marry against the wishes of their parents, and that the Italian ladies may learn from me not to wed a man whom nature and habitude of life estrange from us. But as I know the Moor is on such terms of friendship with your husband, and communicates to him all his affairs, I pray you, if you have heard from him aught that you may tell me of, fail not to befriend me." And as she said this, she wept bitterly.

The Ensign's wife, who knew the whole truth (her husband wishing to make use of her to compass the death of Disdemona), but could never consent to such a project, dared not, from fear of her husband, disclose a single circumstance: all she said was, "Beware lest you give any cause of suspicion to your husband, and show to him by every means your fidelity and love."—"Indeed I do so," replied Disdemona, "but it is all of no avail."

Meanwhile the Moor sought in every way to convince himself of what he fain would have found untrue, and he prayed the Ensign to contrive that he might see the handkerchief in the possession of the Captain. This was a difficult matter to the wicked Ensign; nevertheless, he promised to use every means to satisfy the Moor of the truth of what he said.

Now, the Captain had a wife at home who worked the most marvelous embroidery upon lawn, and seeing the handkerchief, which belonged to the Moor's wife, she resolved, before it was returned to her, to work one like it. As she was engaged in this task, the Ensign observed her standing at a window, where she could be seen by all the passers-by in the street, and he pointed her out to the Moor, who was now perfectly convinced of his wife's guilt. Then he arranged with the Ensign to slay Disdemona and the Captain of the troop, treating them as it seemed they both deserved. And the Moor prayed the Ensign that he would kill the Captain, promising eternal gratitude to him. But the Ensign at first refused to undertake so dangerous a task, the Captain being a man of equal skill and courage; until at length, after much entreating and being richly paid, the Moor prevailed on him to promise to attempt the deed.

Having formed this resolution, the Ensign, going out one dark night, sword in hand, met the Captain on his way to visit a courtesan, and struck him a blow on his right thigh, which cut off his leg and felled him to the earth. Then the Ensign was on the point of putting an end to his life, when the Captain, who was a courageous man and used to the sight of blood and death, drew his sword, and, wounded as he was, kept on his defense, exclaiming with a loud voice, "I'm murdered!" Thereupon the Ensign, hearing the people come running up, with some of the soldiers who were lodged thereabouts, took to his heels to escape being caught; then turning about again, he joined the crowd, pretending to have been attracted by the noise. And when he saw the Captain's leg cut off, he judged that, if not already dead, the blow must, at all events, end his life; and whilst in his heart he was rejoiced at this, he yet feigned to compassionate the Captain as he had been his brother.

The next morning the tidings of this affair spread through

the whole city, and reached the ears of Disdemona; whereat she, who was kindhearted and little dreamed that any ill would betide her, evinced the greatest grief at the calamity. This served but to confirm the Moor's suspicions, and he went to seek for the Ensign, and said to him, "Do you know that my wife is in such grief at the Captain's accident that she is well nigh gone mad."

"And what could you expect, seeing he is her very soul?" replied the Ensign.

"Ay, soul forsooth!" exclaimed the Moor; "I'll draw the soul from out her body; call me no man if that I fail to shut the world upon this wretch."

Then they consulted of one means and another—poison and daggers—to kill poor Disdemona, but could resolve on nothing. At length the Ensign said, "A plan comes to my mind, which will give you satisfaction and raise cause for no suspicion. It is this: the house in which you live is very old, and the ceiling of your chamber has many cracks; I propose we take a stocking, filled with sand, and beat Disdemona with it till she dies; thus will her body bear no signs of violence. When she is dead we can pull down a portion of the ceiling, and thus make it seem as if a rafter falling on her head had killed the lady. Suspicion cannot rest on you, since all men will impute her death to accident."

This cruel counsel pleased the Moor, and he only waited for a fitting time to execute the plot. One night, when he and Disdemona had retired to bed, the Ensign, whom the Moor had concealed in a closet which opened into the chamber, raised a noise in the closet, according to a concerted plan; whereat the Moor said to his wife, "Did you not hear that noise?"

"Indeed I heard it," she replied.

"Rise," said the Moor, "and see what 'tis."

The unhappy Disdemona rose from bed, and the instant she approached the closet, out rushed the Ensign, and being strong and of stout nerve, he beat her cruelly with the bag of sand across her back; upon which Disdemona fell to the ground, scarce able to draw her breath; but with the little voice she had left, she called upon the Moor for aid.

But the Moor, leaping from bed, exclaimed, "Thou wickedest of women, thus has thy falseness found its just reward, the recompense to wives who, counterfeiting love, place horns upon their husbands' brows."

The wretched lady, hearing these words, and feeling that she was near her end (for the Ensign had given her another blow), appealed to the justice of Heaven, since justice here had failed her, in proof of her fidelity and truth; and as she was thus calling Heaven to witness, the wicked Ensign inflicted a third blow, under which she sank lifeless on the floor.

Then the Ensign and the Moor, laying Disdemona on the bed and wounding her head, pulled down part of the ceiling of the chamber, as they had arranged; whereupon the Moor began to call aloud for help, exclaiming that the house was falling. Hearing this uproar, the neighbors all came running up, and there found Disdemona lying dead beneath a rafter —a sight which, from the good life of that poor lady, did fill all hearts with sorrow.

On the following day Disdemona was buried, followed to the grave by the universal grief of the people. But Heaven, the just regarder of all hearts, willed not that so wicked a deed should go unpunished. Ere long the Moor, whom Disdemona had loved more than her own life, began to feel such sorrow at her loss that he went wandering about as one bereft of reason, searching in every part of the house. And reflecting in his thoughts that the Ensign had been the cause that he had lost, with Disdemona, all joy in life, he conceived so deep a hatred to that wicked man he could not bear to set eyes on him, and had it not been for his fear of the inviolable justice of the Signoria of Venice, he would have slain him openly. But being unable to do this with safety, he deprived him of his rank, and would not allow him to remain in his Company; whereat such an enmity arose between the two that no greater or more deadly can be imagined.

The Ensign, that wickedest of all bad men, now turned his thoughts to injuring the Moor; and seeking out the Captain, whose wound was by this time healed, and who went about with a wooden leg in place of the one that had been cut off, he said to him, " 'Tis time you should be avenged for your lost limb; and if you will come with me to Venice, I'll tell you who the malefactor is, whom I dare not mention to you here for many reasons; and I will bring you proofs."

The Captain of the troop, whose anger returned fiercely, but without knowing why, thanked the Ensign, and went with him to Venice. On arriving there the Ensign told him that it was the Moor who had cut off his leg, on account of the suspicion he had formed of Disdemona's conduct with him; and for that reason he had slain her, and then spread the report that the ceiling had fallen and killed her. Upon hearing which, the Captain accused the Moor to the Signoria, both of having cut off his leg and killed his wife, and called the Ensign to witness the truth of what he said. The Ensign declared both charges to be true, for that the Moor had disclosed to him the whole plot, and had tried to persuade him to perpetrate both crimes; and that, having afterwards killed his wife out of jealousy he had conceived, he had narrated to him the manner in which he had perpetrated her death.

The Signoria of Venice, when they heard of the cruelty inflicted by a barbarian upon a lady of their city, commanded that the Moor's arms should be pinioned in Cyprus, and he be brought to Venice, where, with many tortures, they sought to draw from him the truth. But the Moor, bearing with unyielding courage all the torment, denied the whole charge so resolutely that no confession could be drawn from him. But, although by his constancy and firmness he escaped death, he was, after being confined for several days in prison, condemned to perpetual banishment, in which he was eventually slain by the kinsfolk of Disdemona, as he merited. The Ensign returned to his own country, and, following up his wonted villainy, he accused one of his companions of having sought to persuade him to kill an enemy of his, who was a man of noble rank; whereupon this person was arrested and put to the torture; but when he denied the truth of what his accuser had declared, the Ensign himself was likewise tortured to make him prove the truth of his accusations; and he was tortured so that his body ruptured, upon which he was removed from prison and taken home, where he died a miserable death. Thus did Heaven avenge the innocence of Disdemona; and all these events were narrated by the Ensign's wife, who was privy to the whole, after his death, as I have told them here.

Commentaries

The four critical writings reprinted here give some idea of the range of *Othello* criticism and at the same time provide various insights into the play and critical guidelines for approaching it. Thomas Rymer's discussion of *Othello* from his *A Short View of Tragedy* (1693), is a famous attack on the play by a determined neoclassicist and realist. Rymer's smugness and lack of understanding of the nature of dramatic poetry are ridiculous, but his absurd, and at times infuriating, misinterpretations force a reader to formulate and thus become conscious of his own assumptions about the nature of poetry and drama. The Romantic movement in literature had as one of its by-products a great revival of interest in and a new approach to Shakespeare, and Samuel Taylor Coleridge, besides being a great poet, was the first modern Shakespearean critic. Keats, Byron, Lamb, Hazlitt, and Coleridge were all particularly fascinated by the plays, but it was Coleridge who in several series of public lectures brought Romantic theories of art to bear on Shakespeare and began to create that enthusiasm for the plays so characteristic of the nineteenth century. Coleridge never wrote a book on Shakespeare and his lectures were never printed, but notes and newspaper reports of them have survived, and these along with various marginalia from his books and reports of his "table talk" make it possible to put together at least the outline of his views. Modern criticism grows out of Romantic criticism, though it differs in many of its assumptions about the nature of poetry and in its working techniques. The two pieces of modern criticism here reprinted are distinguished interpretations of *Othello* which offer two different, but complementary, critical approaches. Maynard Mack's "The Jacobean Shakespeare" explores the individual tragedies by defining the "vertebrate characteristics" they share with other Shakespearean tragedies. Mack seeks the common constituent elements and the basic patterns of development of Shakespearean tragedy. Heilman, in contrast, narrows his focus to *Othello* alone and searches for the meaning of the play in certain recurring words, images, and ideas.

Samuel Taylor Coleridge

[Comments on *Othello*]

The admirable preparation, so characteristic of Shakespeare, in the introduction of Roderigo as the dupe on
whom Iago first exercises his art, and in so doing displays
his own character. Roderigo is already fitted and pre-
disposed [to be a dupe] by his own passions—without any
fixed principle or strength of character (the want of
character and the power of the passions—like the wind
loudest in empty houses—form his character)—but yet
not without the moral notions and sympathies with honor
which his rank, connections, had hung upon him. The
very three first lines happily state the nature and foundation of the friendship—the purse—as well as the contrast
of Roderigo's intemperance of mind with Iago's coolness,
the coolness of a preconceiving experimenter. The mere
language of protestation in

> If ever I did dream of such a matter,
> Abhor me—

which, fixing the associative link that determines Roderigo's
continuation of complaint—

> Thou told'st me thou didst hold him in thy hate—

elicits a true feeling of Iago's—the dread of contempt
habit[ual] to those who encourage in themselves and have

From *Shakespearean Criticism* by Samuel Taylor Coleridge. 2nd ed.,
ed. Thomas Middleton Raysor. New York: E. P. Dutton and Company,
Inc., 1960; London: J. M. Dent & Sons, Ltd., 1961. 2 vols.

their keenest pleasure in the feeling and expression of contempt for others. His high self-opinion—and how a wicked man employs his real feelings as well as assumes those most alien from his own, as instruments of his purpose.

> *Iago.* Virtue! a fig! 'tis in ourselves that we are thus or thus.

Iago's passionless character, all will in intellect; therefore a bold partisan here of a truth, but yet of a truth converted into falsehood by absence of all the modifications by the frail nature of man. And the last sentiment—

> . . . our raging motions, our carnal stings, our unbitted lusts; whereof I take this, that you call love, to be a sect or scion—

There lies the Iagoism of how many! And the repetition, "Go make money!"—a pride in it, of an anticipated dupe, stronger than the love of lucre.

> *Iago.* Go to, farewell, put money enough in your purse: Thus do I ever make my fool my purse.

The triumph! Again, "put money," after the effect has been fully produced. The last speech [Iago's soliloquy], the motive-hunting of motiveless malignity—how awful! In itself fiendish; while yet he was allowed to bear the divine image, too fiendish for his own steady view. A being next to devil, only not quite devil—and this Shakespeare has attempted—executed—without disgust, without scandal!

[V. ii. 349–51. Othello's death-speech.]

> . . . of one whose hand,
> Like the base Indian, threw a pearl away
> Richer than all his tribe.

Following, in part, a suggestion of the scholar Warburton, Theobald, in his edition of the play, defends the reading of the first Folio, *Iudean,* which he alters to *Judian.*

Thus it is for no-poets to comment on the greatest of poets! To make Othello say that he, who had killed his wife, was like Herod, who had killed his! Oh, how many beauties in this one line were impenetrable by the *thought*-swarming, ever *idea*less Warburton! Othello wishes to excuse himself—to excuse himself by accusing. This struggle of feeling is finely conveyed in the word "base," which is applied to the *rude* Indian not in his own character, but as the momentary representative of Othello. "Indian" means American or Carib, a savage *in genere.* Othello's *belief* is not caused by jealousy; it is forced upon him by Iago, and is such as any man would and must feel who had believed in Iago as Othello did. His great mistake is that *we* know Iago for a villain from the first moment.

Maynard Mack

The Jacobean Shakespeare:

Some Observations on the Construction of the Tragedies

This chapter aims at being a modest supplement (I cannot too much stress the adjective) to A. C. Bradley's pioneering analysis of the construction of Shakespearean tragedy, the second of his famous lectures, published some fifty-five years ago. Bradley's concern was with what would probably today be called the clearer outlines of Shakespearean practice—the management of exposition, conflict, crisis, catastrophe; the contrasts of pace and scene; the over-all patterns of rise-and-fall, variously modulated; the slackened tension after the crisis and Shakespeare's devices for countering this; and the faults.

Bradley is quite detailed about the faults. Sometimes, he says, there are too rapid shiftings of scene and *dramatis personae,* as in the middle section of *Antony and Cleopatra.* Sometimes there is extraneous matter, not required for plot or character development, like the player's speech in *Hamlet* about the murder of Priam, or Hamlet's advice later to the same player on speaking in the theater. Sometimes there are soliloquies too obviously expositional, as when Edgar disguises to become Poor Tom in *King*

From *Stratford-upon-Avon Studies: Jacobean Theatre* (Vol. I), ed. John Russell Brown and Bernard Harris. London: Edward Arnold (Publishers) Ltd., 1960; New York: St. Martin's Press, Inc., 1961. © Edward Arnold (Publishers) Ltd., 1960. Reprinted by permission of the publishers.

Lear. Or there is contradiction and inconsistency, as the double time in *Othello.* Or flatulent writing: "obscure, inflated, tasteless," or "pestered with metaphors." Or "gnomic" insertions, like the Duke's couplet interchange with Brabantio in *Othello,* used "more freely than, I suppose, a good playwright now would care to do." And finally, to make an end, there is too often sacrificing of dramatic appropriateness to get something said that the author wants said. Thus the comments of the Player King and Claudius on the instability of human purpose arise because Shakespeare "wishes in part simply to write poetry, and partly to impress on the audience thoughts which will help them to understand, not the player-king nor yet King Claudius, but Hamlet himself." These failings, Bradley concludes, belong to an art of drama imperfectly developed, which Shakespeare inherited from his predecessors and acquiesced in, on occasion, from "indifference or want of care."

Though Bradley's analysis is still the best account we have of the outward shape of Shakespearean tragedy, a glance at his list of faults and, especially, his examples reminds us that a vast deal of water has got itself under the critical bridges since 1904. It is not simply that most of the faults he enumerates would no longer be regarded as such, but would, instead, be numbered among the characteristic practices of Shakespearean dramaturgy, even at its most triumphant. Still more striking is the extent to which our conception of the "construction" of the tragedies has itself changed. The matters Bradley described have not ceased to be important—far from it: several of our current interpreters, one feels, would benefit if, like Bottom of Master Mustardseed, they were to desire him "of more acquaintance." Still, it is impossible not to feel that Bradley missed something—that there is another kind of construction in Shakespeare's tragedies than the one he designates, more inward, more difficult to define, but not less significant. This other structure is not, like his, generated entirely by the interplay of plot and character. Nor is it, on the other hand, though it is fashionable nowadays to suppose so, ultimately a verbal matter. It is poetic, but it goes well beyond what in certain quarters today is called (with something like a lump in the throat) "the poetry." Some of its elements arise from the play-wright's visualizing imagination, the consciousness of groupings, gestures, entrances, exits. Others may even be prior to language, in the sense that they appear to belong to a paradigm of tragic "form" that was consciously or un-consciously part of Shakespeare's inheritance and intuition as he worked.

At any rate, it is into this comparatively untraveled and uncharted territory of inward structure that I should like to launch a few tentative explorations. I shall occasionally look backward as far as *Julius Caesar* (1599), *Richard II* (1595–1600), and even *Romeo and Juliet* (1595–6); but in the main I shall be concerned with the tragedies of Shakespeare's prime, from *Hamlet* (1600–1) to *Corio-lanus* (1607–8). In these seven or eight years, Shake-speare's golden period, he consolidated a species of tragic structure that for suggestiveness and flexibility has never been matched.[1] I do not anticipate being able to return with a map of this obscure terrain. I hope only to convince better travelers that there is something out there to be known.

First, the hero. The Shakespearean tragic hero, as every-body knows, is an overstater. His individual accent will vary with his personality, but there is always a residue of hyperbole. This, it would seem, is for Shakespeare the authentic tragic music, mark of a world where a man's reach must always exceed his grasp and everything costs not less than everything.

> Wert thou as far
> As that vast shore wash'd with the farthest sea,
> I would adventure for such merchandise.
>
> (*Romeo*, II.ii.82)

[1] The flexibility of the structure is witnessed by the amazing differences between the tragedies, of which it is, however, the lowest common multiple. In my discussion, I shall necessarily take the differences between the tragedies for granted and stress simply the vertebrate characteristics they share.

'Swounds, show me what thou'lt do:
Woo't weep? woo't fight? woo't fast? woo't tear thyself?
Woo't drink up eisel? eat a crocodile
I'll do't.   (*Hamlet*, V.i.297)

                        Nay, had she been true,
If heaven would make me such another world
Of one entire and perfect chrysolite,
I'ld not have sold her for it.   (*Othello*, V.ii.140)

Death, traitor! nothing could have subdued nature
To such a lowness but his unkind daughters,
                                        (*Lear*, III.iv.72)

Will all great Neptune's ocean wash this blood
Clean from my hand?   (*Macbeth*, II.ii.60)

                        I, that with my sword
Quarter'd the world, and o'er green Neptune's back
With ships made cities, . . .   (*Antony*, IV.xiv.57)

                        I go alone,
Like to a lonely dragon, that his fen
Makes fear'd and talk'd of more than seen.
                                (*Coriolanus*, IV.i.29)

This idiom is not, of course, used by the hero only. It
is the language he is dressed in by all who love him, and
often by those who do not:

This was the noblest Roman of them all: . . .
His life was gentle, and the elements
So mix'd in him that Nature might stand up
And say to all the world "This was a man!"
                                (*Caesar*, V.v.68)

The courtier's, soldier's, scholar's, eye, tongue, sword;
The expectancy and rose of the fair state,
The glass of fashion and the mold of form,
The observed of all observers, . . .
                                (*Hamlet*, III.i.159)

Can he be angry? I have seen the cannon,
When it hath blown his ranks into the air,
And, like the devil, from his very arm
Puff'd his own brother:—and can he be angry?
                              (*Othello*, III.iv.134)

On the Alps
It is reported thou didst eat strange flesh,
Which some did die to look on.
                              (*Antony*, I.iv.66)

Let me twine
Mine arms about that body, where against
My grainèd ash an hundred times hath broke,
And scarr'd the moon with splinters.
                              (*Coriolanus*, IV.v.112)

But by whomever used, it is a language that depends
for its vindication—for the redemption of its paper
promises into gold—upon the hero, and any who stand,
heroically, where he does. It is the mark of his, and their,
commitment to something beyond "the vast waters Of
the petrel and the porpoise," as Mr. Eliot has it in *East
Coker,* a commitment to something—not merely death—
which shackles accidents and bolts up change and palates
no dung whatever.

Thus the hyperbole of tragedy stands at the opposite
end of a tonal scale from the hyperbole of comedy, which
springs from and nourishes detachment:

When I was about thy years, Hal, I was not an eagle's
talon in the waist; I could have crept into any alderman's thumb-ring   (*1 Henry IV*, II.iv.362)

O, she misused me past the endurance of a block! an
oak but with one green leaf on it would have answered
her; my very visor began to assume life, and scold with
her.   (*Much Ado*, II.i.246)

He has a son, who shall be flayed alive; then 'nointed
over with honey, set on the head of a wasp's nest; then

stand till he be three quarters and a dram dead; then
recovered again with aqua-vitae or some other hot in-
fusion; then, raw as he is, and in the hottest day prog-
nostication proclaims, shall he be set against a brick-wall,
the sun looking with a southward eye upon him, where
he is to behold him with flies blown to death.

(Winter's Tale, IV.iv.811)

Comic overstatement aims at being preposterous. Until
it becomes so, it remains flat. Tragic overstatement, on
the other hand, aspires to believed, and unless in some
sense it is so, remains bombast.

Besides the hyperbolist, in Shakespeare's scheme of
things, there is always the opposing voice, which belongs
to the hero's foil. As the night the day, the idiom of
absoluteness demands a vocabulary of a different intensity,
a different rhetorical and moral wave length, to set it off.
This other idiom is not necessarily understatement, though
it often takes the form of a deflating accent and very often
involves colloquialism—or perhaps merely a middling sort
of speech—expressive of a suppler outlook than the hero's,
and of other and less upsetting ways of encountering
experience than his hyperbolic, not to say intransigent,
rigorism. " 'Twere to consider too curiously to consider
so," says Horatio of Hamlet's equation between the dust
of Alexander and a bunghole, and this enunciates perfectly
the foil's role. There is no tragedy in him because he does
not consider "curiously"; there are always more things
in earth and heaven than are dreamt of in his philosophy.

Each of the Shakespearean tragedies contains at least
one personage to speak this part, which is regularly assigned to someone in the hero's immediate entourage—
servitor, wife, friend. In *Romeo and Juliet,* it is of course
Mercutio, with his witty resolution of all love into sex.
In *Julius Caesar,* it is Cassius, whose restless urgent
rhythms, full of flashing images, swirl about Brutus's
rounder and abstracter speech, like dogs that bay the
moon:

> *Brutus.* I do believe that these applauses are
>   For some new honors that are heap'd on Caesar.

> *Cassius.* Why, man, he doth bestride the narrow world
> Like a Colossus, and we petty men
> Walk under his huge legs and peep about
> To find ourselves dishonorable graves. (I.ii.133)

In the famous forum speeches, this second voice is taken
over temporarily by Antony, and there emerges a similar
but yet more powerful contrast between them. Brutus's
prose—in which the actuality of the assassination is in-
tellectualized and held at bay by the strict patterns of an
obtrusively formal rhetoric, almost as though corporal
death were transubstantiated to "a ballet of bloodless
categories"—gives way to Antony's sinewy verse about
the "honorable men," which draws the deed, and its consequence the dead Caesar, ever closer till his own vengeful
emotions are kindled in the mob.

In *Hamlet*, the relation of foil to hero undergoes an
unusual adaptation. Here, since the raciest idiom of the
play belongs to the hero himself, the foil, Horatio, is given
a quite conventional speech, and, to make the contrast
sharper (Hamlet being of all the heroes the most voluble),
as little speech as may be. Like his stoicism, like his "blood
and judgment"—

> so well commingled,
> That they are not a pipe for fortune's finger
> To sound what stop she please—   (III.ii.74)

Horatio's "Here, sweet lord," "O, my dear lord," "Well,
my lord" are, presumably (as the gentleman in *Lear* says
of Cordelia's tears), "a better way" than Hamlet's self-
lacerating virtuosities and verbosities. But of course we
do not believe this and are not mean to: who would be
Horatio if he could be Hamlet?

Plainly, this is one of the two questions that all the tragic
foils exist to make us ask (the other we shall come to
presently). Who, for instance, would be Enobarbus, clear-
sighted as he is, in preference to Antony? His brilliant
sardonic speech, so useful while he can hold his own
career and all about him in the comic focus of detachment,

withers in the face of his engagement to ultimate issues, and he dies speaking with imagery, accent, and feeling which are surely meant to identify him at the last with the absoluteness of the heroic world, the more so since his last syllables anticipate Cleopatra's:

> Throw my heart
> Against the flint and hardness of my fault;
> Which, being dried with grief, will break to powder,
> And finish all foul thoughts. O Antony,
> Nobler than my revolt is infamous,
> Forgive me in thine own particular;
> But let the world rank me in register
> A master-leaver and a fugitive:
> O Antony! O Antony! (IV.ix.15)

Such unequivocal judgments are a change indeed on the part of one who could earlier rally cynically with Menas about "two thieves kissing" when their hands meet.

King Lear is given two foils. The primary one is obviously the Fool, whose rhymes and riddles and jets of humor in the first two acts set off both the old king's brooding silences and his massively articulated longer speeches when aroused. But in the storm scenes, and occasionally elsewhere, one is almost as keenly conscious of the relief into which Lear's outrageous imprecations are thrown by the mute devoted patience of his servant Kent. For both foils—and this of course is their most prominent function as representatives of the opposing voice—the storm itself is only a storm, to be stoically endured, in the one case, and, in the other, if his master would but hear reason, eschewed:

> O nuncle, court holy-water in a dry house is better than this rainwater out o' door. Good nuncle, in, ask thy daughters' blessing: . . . (III.ii.10)

Doubtless the Fool does not wish to be taken quite *au pied de la lettre* in this—his talk is always in the vein of the false daughters', his action quite other. But neither for him nor for Kent does facing the thunder have any kind of transcendent meaning. In Lear's case, it has; the thunder he hears is like the thunder heard over Himavant in *The Waste Land*; it has what the anthropologists call "mana"; and his (and our) consuming questions are what it means—and if it means—and whose side it is on.

In my view, the most interesting uses of the opposing voice occur in *Macbeth* and *Othello*. In *Macbeth*, Shakespeare gives it to Lady Macbeth, and there was never, I think, a more thrilling tragic counterpoint set down for the stage than that in the scene following the murder of Duncan, when her purely physical reading of what has happened to them both is met by his metaphysical intuitions. His "noise" to her is just the owl screaming and the crickets' cry. The voice of one crying "sleep no more" is only his "brain-sickly" fear. The blood on his hands is what "a little water clears us of." "Consider it not so deeply," she says at one point, with an echo of Horatio in the graveyard. "These deeds must not be thought After these ways." But in the tragic world, which always opens on transcendence, they must; and this she herself finds before she dies, a prisoner to the deed, endlessly washing the damned spot that will not out. "What's done cannot be undone" is a language that like Enobarbus she has to learn.

Othello's foil of course is Iago, about whose imagery and speech there hangs, as recent commentators have pointed out, a constructed air, an ingenious, hyperconscious generalizing air, essentially suited to one who, as W. H. Clemen has said, "seeks to poison . . . others with his images" (*The Development of Shakespeare's Imagery*, p. 122). Yet Iago's poison does not work more powerfully through his images than through a corrosive habit of abstraction applied in those unique relations of love and faith where abstraction is most irrelevant and most destructive. Iago has learned to "sickly o'er" the central and irreducible individual with the pale cast of class and kind:

Blessed fig's end! The wine she drinks is made of grapes. . . .   (II.i.251)

These Moors are changeable in their wills. . . . If
sanctimony and a frail vow betwixt an erring barbarian
and a supersubtle Venetian be not too hard for my
wits . . .   (I.iii.342–43, 350–53)

Come on, come on; you are pictures out of doors,
Bells in your parlors, wildcats in your kitchens,
Saints in your injuries, devils being offended,
Players in your housewifery, and housewives in your
    beds.   (II.i.108)

> I know our country disposition well;
> In Venice they do let heaven see the pranks
> They dare not show their husbands.   (III.iii.201)

Othello's downfall is signaled quite as clearly when he
drifts into this rationalized dimension—

>   O curse of marriage,
> That we can call these delicate creatures ours,
> And not their appetites—   (III.iii.267)

leaving behind his true vernacular, the idiom of "My life
upon her faith!", as when his mind fills with Iago's copula-
tive imagery. Shakespeare seems to have been well aware
that love (especially such love as can be reflected only in
the union of a black man with a white woman, East with
West) is the mutual knowing of uniqueness:

> Reason, in itself confounded,
> Saw division grow together,
> To themselves yet either neither,
> Simple were so well compounded,
>
> That it cried, How true a twain
> Seemeth this concordant one!
> Love hath reason, reason none,
> If what parts can so remain.
>
> Whereupon it made this threne
> To the phoenix and the dove,

> Co-supremes and stars of love,
> As chorus to their tragic scene.
> > (*The Phoenix and the Turtle*, 41)

And also that there are areas of experience where, as a great saint once said, one must first believe in order that one may know.

To one who should ask why these paired voices seem to be essential ingredients of Shakespearean tragedy, no single answer can, I think, be given. They occur partly, no doubt, because of their structural utility, the value of complementary personalities in a work of fiction being roughly analogous to the value of thesis and antithesis in a discursive work. Partly too, no doubt, because in stage performance, the antiphonal effects of the two main vocabularies, strengthened by diversity in manner, costume, placing on the stage, supply variety of mood and gratify the eye and ear. But these are superficial considerations. Perhaps we come to something more satisfactory when we consider that these two voices apparently answer to reverberations which reach far back in the human past. *Mutatis mutandis,* Coriolanus and Menenius, Antony and Enobarbus, Macbeth and Lady Macbeth, Lear and his Fool, Othello and Iago, Hamlet and Horatio, Brutus and Cassius, Romeo and Mercutio exhibit a kind of duality that is also exhibited in Oedipus and Jocasta (as well as Creon), Antigone and Ismene, Prometheus and Oceanus, Phaedra and her nurse —and also, in many instances in Greek tragedy, by the protagonist and the chorus.

If it is true, as can be argued, that the Greek chorus functions in large measure as spokesman for the values of the community, and the first actor, in large measure, for the passionate life of the individual, we can perhaps see a philosophical basis for the long succession of opposing voices. What matters to the community is obviously accommodation—all those adjustments and resiliences that enable it to survive; whereas what matters to the individual, at least in his heroic mood, is just as obviously integrity—all that enables him to remain an *individual,* one thing not many.

The confrontation of these two outlooks is therefore a confrontation of two of our most cherished instincts, the instinct to be resolute, autonomous, free, and the instinct to be "realistic," adaptable, secure. If it is also true, as I think most of us believe, that tragic drama is in one way or other a record of man's affair with transcendence (whether this be defined as gods, God, or, as by Malraux, the human "fate," which men must "question" even if they cannot control), we can see further why the hero must have an idiom—such as hyperbole—that establishes him as moving to measures played above, or outside, our normal space and time. For the *reductio ad absurdum* of the tragic confrontation is the comic one, exemplified in Don Quixote and his Sancho, where the comedy arises precisely from the fact that the hero only *imagines* he moves to measures above and outside our normal world; and where, to the extent that we come to identify with his faith, the comedy slides towards pathos and even the tragic absolute.

These considerations, however, remain speculative. What is not in doubt is that dramaturgically the antiphony of two voices and two vocabularies serves Shakespeare well, and in one of its extensions gives rise to a phenomenon as peculiar and personal to him as his signature. Towards the close of a tragic play, or if not towards the close, at the climax, will normally appear a short scene or episode (sometimes more than one) of spiritual cross purposes: a scene in which the line of tragic speech and feeling generated by commitment is crossed by an alien speech and feeling very much detached. Bradley, noting such of these episodes as are "humorous or semi-humorous," places them among Shakespeare's devices for sustaining interest after the crisis, since their introduction "affords variety and relief, and also heightens by contrast the tragic feelings." Another perceptive critic has noted that though such scenes afford "relief," it is not by laughter. "We return for a moment to simple people, a gravedigger, a porter, a countryman, and to the goings on of every day, the feeling for bread and cheese, and when we go back to the high tragic mood we do so with a heightened sense that we are moving in a world fully realized" (F. P. Wilson, *Eliza-*

bethan and Jacobean, p. 122). To such comments, we must add another. For the whole effect of these episodes does not come simply from variety, or from the juxtaposition of bread and cheese with the high tragic mood, though these elements are certainly present in it.

It arises, in the main, I think, from the fact that Shakespeare here lays open to us, in an especially poignant form, what I take to be the central dialogue of tragic experience. It is a dialogue of which the Greek dialogue of individual with community, the seventeenth-century dialogue of soul with body, the twentieth-century dialogue of self with soul are perhaps all versions in their different ways: a dialogue in which each party makes its case in its own tongue, incapable of wholly comprehending what the other means. And Shakespeare objectifies it for us on his stage by the encounter of those by whom, "changed, changed utterly," a terrible beauty has been born, with those who are still players in life's casual comedy. Hamlet and the gravediggers, Desdemona and Emilia, Cleopatra and the clown afford particularly fine examples of Shakespeare's technique in this respect.

In the first instance, the mixture of profoundly imaginative feelings contained in Hamlet's epitaph for Yorick—

> I knew him, Horatio: a fellow of infinite jest, of most excellent fancy; he hath borne me on his back a thousand times; and now, how abhorred in my imagination it is! my gorge rises at it. Here hung those lips that I have kissed I know not how oft. Where be your gibes now? your gambols? your songs? your flashes of merriment, that were wont to set the table on a roar? Not one now, to mock your own grinning? quite chap-fallen? Now get you to my lady's chamber, and tell her, let her paint an inch thick, to this favor she must come; make her laugh at that—   (V.i.203)

is weighed over against the buffoon literalism of the clown—

> *Hamlet.* What man dost thou dig it for?
>
> *First Clown.* For no man, sir.

Hamlet. What woman, then?

First Clown. For none, neither.

Hamlet. Who is to be buried in 't?

First Clown. One that was a woman, sir; but, rest her
soul, she's dead—   (V.i.141)

and against his uncompromising factualism too, his hard
dry vocabulary of detachment, without overtones, by which
he cuts his métier down to a size that can be lived with:

I'faith, if he be not rotten before he die, . . . he will
last you some eight year or nine year: a tanner will last
you nine year.   (V.i.180)

But in this scene Hamlet's macabre thoughts are not
allowed to outweigh the clown. A case is made for factualism and literalism. Horatio is seen to have a point in saying
it is to consider too curiously to consider as Hamlet does.
A man must come to terms with the graveyard; but how
long may he linger in it with impunity, or allow it to linger
in him? Such reckonings the opposing voice, whether
spoken by the primary foil or by another, is calculated to
awake in us: this is the second kind of question that it
exists to make us ask.

In a sense, then, the implicit subject of all these episodes
is the predicament of being human. They bring before us
the grandeur of man's nature, which contains, potentially,
both voices, both ends of the moral and psychic spectrum.
They bring before us the necessity of his choice, because
it is rarely given to him to go through any door without
closing the rest. And they bring before us the sadness, the
infinite sadness of his lot, because, short of the "certain
certainties" that tragedy does not deal with, he has no
sublunar way of knowing whether defiant "heroism" is
really more to be desired than suppler "wisdom." The alabaster innocence of Desdemona's world shines out beside
the crumpled bedsitters of Emilia's—

Desdemona. Wouldst thou do such a deed for all the world?

Emilia. Why, would not you?

Desdemona.   No, by this heavenly light!

Emilia. Nor I neither by this heavenly light;
  I might do't as well i' the dark.

Desdemona. Wouldst thou do such a deed for all the world?

Emilia. The world's a huge thing: it is a great price
  For a small vice.

Desdemona. In troth, I think thou wouldst not.

Emilia. In troth, I think I should . . . who would not
  make her husband a cuckold to make him a monarch? I should venture purgatory for 't.

Desdemona. Beshrew me, if I would do such a wrong
  For the whole world.

Emilia. Why, the wrong is but a wrong i' the world;
  and having the world for your labor, 'tis a wrong in
  your own world, and you might quickly make it
  right.

Desdemona. I do not think there is any such woman—
                              (IV.iii.65)

but the two languages never, essentially, commune—and, for this reason, the dialogue they hold can never be finally adjudicated.

The same effect may be noted in Cleopatra's scene with the countryman who brings her the asps. Her exultation casts a glow over the whole scene of her death. But her language when the countryman has gone would not have the tragic resonance it has, if we could not hear echoing between the lines the gritty accents of the opposing voice:

Give me my robe, put on my crown; I have
Immortal longings in me.

> Truly, I have him: but I would not be the party that should desire you to touch him, for his biting is immortal; those that do die of it do seldom or never recover.

> The stroke of death is as a lover's pinch,
> Which hurts, and is desired.

> I heard of one of them no longer than yesterday: a very honest woman, but something given to lie; as a woman should not do, but in the way of honesty: how she died of the biting of it, what pain she felt.

>   Peace, peace!
> Dost thou not see my baby at my breast,
> That sucks the nurse asleep?
>   (V.ii.283–313)

> Give it nothing, I pray you, for it is not worth the feeding.
>   (V.ii.245–71)

The "worm"—or "my baby"; the Antony Demetrius and Philo see—or the Antony whose face is as the heavens; the "small vice" of Emilia—or the deed one would not do for the whole world; the skull knocked about the mazzard by a sexton's spade—or the skull which "had a tongue in it and could sing once": these are incommensurables, which human nature nevertheless must somehow measure, reconcile, and enclose.

We move now from "character" to "action," and to the question: what happens in a Shakespearean tragedy? Bradley's traditional categories—exposition, conflict, crisis, catastrophe, etc.—give us one side of this, but, as we noticed earlier, largely the external side, and are in any case rather too clumsy for the job we try to do with them. They apply as well to potboilers of the commercial theater as to serious works of art, to prose as well as poetic drama. What is worse, they are unable to register the unique capacity of Shakespearean dramaturgy to hint, evoke, imply, and, in short, by indirections find directions out. The nature of some of Shakespeare's "indirections" is a topic we must explore before we can hope to confront the question posed above with other terms than Bradley's.

To clarify what I mean by indirection, let me cite an instance from *King Lear*. Everybody has noticed, no doubt, that Lear's Fool (apart from being the King's primary foil) gives voice during the first two acts to notations of topsiturviness that are not, one feels, simply his own responses to the inversions of order that have occurred in family and state, but a reflection of the King's; or, to put the matter another way, the situation is so arranged by Shakespeare that we are invited to apply the Fool's comments to Lear's inner experience, and I suspect that most of us do so. The Fool thus serves, to some extent, as a screen on which Shakespeare flashes, as it were, readings from the psychic life of the protagonist, possibly even his subconscious life, which could not otherwise be conveyed in drama at all. Likewise, the Fool's *idée fixe* in this matter, his apparent obsession with one idea (often a clinical symptom of incipient insanity) is perhaps dramatic shorthand, and even sleight-of-hand, for goings-on in the King's brain that only occasionally bubble to the surface in the form of conscious apprehensions: "O let me not be mad, not mad sweet heaven." "O fool, I shall go mad." Conceivably, there may even be significance in the circumstance that the Fool does not enter the play as a speaking character till after King Lear has behaved like a fool, and leaves it before he is cured.

Whatever the truth of this last point, the example of the Fool in Lear introduces us to devices of play construction and ways of recording the progress of inward "action," which, though the traditional categories say nothing about them, are a basic resource of Shakespeare's playwriting, and nowhere more so than in the tragedies. We may now consider a few of them in turn.

First, there are the figures, like the Fool, some part of whose consciousness, as conveyed to us at particular moments, seems to be doing double duty, filling our minds with impressions analogous to those which we may presume to be occupying the conscious or unconscious mind of the hero, whether he is before us on the stage or not. A possible example may be Lady Macbeth's sleepwalking scene. Macbeth is absent at this juncture, has gone "into the field"—has not in fact been visible during two long scenes and will not be visible again till the next scene after this. In the interval, the slaying at Macduff's castle and the conversations between Malcolm and Macduff keep him before us in his capacity as tyrant, murderer, "Hell-kite," seen from the outside. But Lady Macbeth's sleepwalking is, I think, Shakespeare's device for keeping him before us in his capacity as tragic hero and sufferer. The "great perturbation in nature" of which the doctor whispers ("to receive at once the benefit of sleep, and do the effects of watching"), the "slumbery agitation," the "thick-coming fancies That keep her from her rest": these, by a kind of poetical displacement, we may apply to him as well as to her; and we are invited to do so by the fact that from the moment of the first murder all the play's references to sleep, and its destruction, have had reference to Macbeth himself. We are, of course, conscious as we watch the scene, that this is Lady Macbeth suffering the metaphysical aspects of murder that she did not believe in; we may also be conscious that the remorse pictured here tends to distinguish her from her husband, who for some time has been giving his "initiate fear" the "hard use" he said it lacked, with dehumanizing consequences. Yet in some way the pity of this situation suffuses him as well as her, the more so because in every word she utters his presence beside her is supposed; and if we allow this to be true, not only will Menteith's comment in the following scene—

> Who then shall blame
> His pester'd senses to recoil and start,
> When all that is within him does condemn
> Itself for being there—   (V.ii.22)

evoke an image of suffering as well as retribution, but we shall better understand Macbeth's striking expression, at

his next appearance, in words that we are almost bound to
feel have some reference to himself, of corrosive griefs
haunting below the conscious levels of the mind:

> Canst thou not minister to a mind diseased,
> Pluck from the memory a rooted sorrow,
> Raze out the written troubles of the brain
> And with some sweet oblivious antidote
> Cleanse the stuff'd bosom of that perilous stuff
> Which weighs upon the heart?   (V.iii.40)

Such speeches as this, and as Lady Macbeth's while
sleepwalking—which we might call umbrella speeches,
since more than one consciousness may shelter under
them—are not uncommon in Shakespeare's dramaturgy,
as many critics have pointed out. *Lear* affords the classic
examples: in the Fool, as we have seen, and also in Edgar.
Edgar's speech during the storm scenes projects in part his
role of Poor Tom, the eternal outcast; in part, Edmund
(and also Oswald), the vicious servant, self-seeking, with
heart set on lust and proud array; possibly in part, Gloucester, whose arrival with a torch the Fool appropriately
announces (without knowing it) in terms related to Edgar's
themes: "Now a little fire in a wide field were like an old
lecher's heart"; and surely, in some part too, the King, for
the chips and tag-ends of Edgar's speech reflect, as if from
Lear's own mind, not simply mental disintegration, but a
strong sense of a fragmented moral order: "Obey thy
parents; keep thy word justly; swear not; commit not with
man's sworn spouse. . . ."

But in my view, the most interesting of all the umbrella
speeches in the tragedies is Enobarbus's famous description
of Cleopatra in her barge. The triumvirs have gone offstage,
Antony to have his first view of Octavia. When we see him
again, his union with Octavia will have been agreed on all
parts (though not yet celebrated), and he will be saying to
her, with what can hardly be supposed to be insincerity:

> My Octavia,
> Read not my blemishes in the world's report:

I have not kept my square; but that to come
Shall all be done by the rule. Good night, dear lady.
(II.iii.4)

Then the soothsayer appears, reminds Antony that his
guardian angel will always be overpowered when Caesar's
is by, urges him to return to Egypt; and Antony, left alone
after the soothsayer has gone, meditates a moment on the
truth of the pronouncement and then says abruptly:

I will to Egypt:
And though I make this marriage for my peace,
I' the east my pleasure lies.   (II.iii.38)

There is plainly a piece of prestidigitation here. It is
performed in part by means of the soothsayer's entry, which
is evidently a kind of visual surrogate for Antony's own
personal intuition. ("I see it in my motion, have it not in
my tongue," the soothsayer says, when asked for the
reasons he wishes Antony to return; and that is presumably
the way Antony sees it too: in his "motion," i.e., involun-
tarily, intuitively.) But a larger part is played by Enobarbus's account of Cleopatra. Between the exit of the
triumvirs and the reappearance of Antony making unsolic-
ited promises to Octavia, this is the one thing that inter-
venes. And it is the only thing that needs to. Shakespeare
has made it so powerful, so colored our imaginations with
it, that we understand the promises of Antony, not in the
light in which he understands them as he makes them, but
in the riotous brilliance of Enobarbus's evocation of Cleopatra. The psychic gap, in Antony, between "My Octavia"
and "Good night, dear lady," on the one hand, and "I will
to Egypt," on the other, is filled by a vision, given to us, of
irresistible and indeed quasi-unearthly power, of which
the soothsayer's intuition is simply a more abstract formulation. Here again, by indirection, Shakespeare finds direction out.

Not all mirror situations in the tragedies involve reflection of another consciousness. Some, as is well known, em-
phasize the outlines of an action by recapitulating it, as
when Edgar's descent to Poor Tom and subsequent gradual

re-ascent to support the gored state echoes the downward
and upward movement in the lives of both King Lear and
Gloucester; or as when Enobarbus's defection to, and again
from, the bidding of his practical reason repeats that which
Antony has already experienced, and Cleopatra will experience (at least in one way of understanding Act V) between
Antony's death and her own. *Hamlet,* complex in all respects, offers an unusually complex form of this. The three
sons, who are, in various senses, all avengers of dead
fathers, are all deflected, temporarily, from their designs
by the maneuvers of an elder (Claudius for Laertes and
Hamlet; the King of Norway, inspired by Claudius, for
Fortinbras), who in two cases is the young man's uncle.
There are of course important differences between these
three young men which we are not to forget; but with respect to structure, the images in the mirror are chiefly
likenesses. Hamlet, outmaneuvered by Claudius, off to England to be executed, crosses the path of Fortinbras, who
has also been outmaneuvered by Claudius (working through
his uncle), and is off to Poland to make mouths at the
invisible event, while at the same moment Laertes, clam-
oring for immediate satisfaction in the King's palace, is
outmaneuvered in his turn. Likewise, at the play's end, all
three young men are "victorious," in ways they could hardly
have foreseen. The return of Fortinbras, having achieved
his objective in Poland, to find his "rights" in Denmark
achieved without a blow, is timed to coincide with Hamlet's
achieving his objective in exposing and killing the King,
and Laertes' achieving his objective of avenging his father's
death on Hamlet. When this episode is played before us in
the theater, there is little question, to my way of thinking,
but that something of the glow and martial upsurge dramatized in Fortinbras's entrance associates itself to Hamlet,
even as Fortinbras's words associate Hamlet to a soldier's
death. Meantime, Laertes, who has been trapped by the
King and has paid with his life for it, gives us an alterna-
tive reflection of the Prince, which is equally a part of the
truth.

Fortinbras's arrival at the close of *Hamlet* is an instance of an especially interesting type of mirroring to be found everywhere in Shakespeare's work—the emblematic entrance, and exit. Sometimes such exits occur by death, as the death of Gaunt, who takes a sacramental view of kingship and nation, in *Richard II*, at the instant when Richard has destroyed, by his personal conduct and by "farming" his realm, the sacramental relationships which make such a view possible to maintain. Gaunt has to die, we might say, before a usurpation like his son's can even be imagined; and it is, I take it, not without significance that the first word of Bolingbroke's return comes a few seconds after we have heard (from the same speaker, Northumberland) that Gaunt's tongue "is now a stringless instrument." Something similar, it seems clear, occurs with the death of Mamillius in *The Winter's Tale*. Sickening with his father's sickening mind, Mamillius dies in the instant that his father repudiates the message of the oracle; and though, in the end, all else is restored to Leontes, Mamillius is not.

In the tragedies, emblematic entrances and exits assume a variety of forms, ranging from those whose significance is obvious to those where it is uncertain, controversial, and perhaps simply a mirage. One entrance whose significance is unmistakable occurs in the first act of *Macbeth*, when Duncan, speaking of the traitor Cawdor, whom he has slain, laments that there is no art to find the mind's construction in the face, just as the new Cawdor, traitor-to-be, appears before him. Equally unmistakable is the significance of the King's exit, in the first scene of *Lear*, with the man who like himself has put externals first. "Come, noble Burgundy," he says, and in a pairing that can be made profoundly moving on the stage, the two men go out together.

But what are we to say to Antony's freedman Eros, who enters for the first time (at least by name) just before his master's suicide and kills himself rather than kill Antony. This is all from his source, Plutarch's life of Antony; but why did Shakespeare include it? Did Eros's name mean something to him? Are we to see here a shadowing of the other deaths for love, or not? And the carrying off of Lepidus, drunk, from the feast aboard Pompey's galley.

Does this anticipate his subsequent fate? and if it does, what does the intoxication signify which in this scene all the great men are subject to in their degree. Is it ordinary drunkenness; or is it, like the drunkenness that afflicts Caliban, Trinculo, and Stephano in *The Tempest,* a species of self-intoxication, Shakespeare's subdued comment on the thrust to worldly power? Or again, what of the arrival of the players in *Hamlet?* Granted their role in the plot, does Shakespeare make no other profit from them? Are such matters as the speech on Priam's murder and the advice on acting interesting excrescences, as Bradley thought, or does each mirror something that we are to appropriate to our understanding of the play: in the first instance, the strange confederacy of passion and paralysis in the hero's mind,[2] in the second, the question that tolls on all sides through the castle at Elsinore: when is an act not an "act"?[3]

These are questions to which it is not always easy to give a sound answer. The ground becomes somewhat firmer underfoot, I think, if we turn for a concluding instance to Bianca's pat appearances in *Othello.* R. B. Heilman suggests that in rushing to the scene of the night assault on Cassio, when she might have stayed safely within doors, and so exposing herself to vilification as a "notable strumpet," Bianca acts in a manner "thematically relevant, because Othello has just been attacking Desdemona as a strumpet"—both "strumpets," in other words, are faithful (*Magic in the Web,* p. 180). Whether this is true or not, Bianca makes two very striking entrances earlier, when in each case she may be thought to supply in living form on the stage the prostitute figure that Desdemona has become in Othello's mind. Her second entrance is notably expressive. Othello here is partially overhearing while Iago rallies Cassio about Bianca, Othello being under the delusion that the talk is of Desdemona. At the point when, in Othello's mental imagery, Desdemona becomes the soliciting whore

---

[2] See an important comment on this by H. Levin, in *Kenyon Review* (1950), pp. 273–96.

[3] I have touched on this point in *Tragic Themes in Western Literature,* ed. C. Brooks (1953).

—"she tells him how she plucked him to my chamber"—
Bianca enters in the flesh, and not only enters, but flour-
ishes the magic handkerchief, now degenerated, like the
love it was to ensure, to some "minx's," some "hobbyhorse's" token, the subject of jealous bickering. In the
theater, the emblematic effect of this can hardly be ignored.[4]

Further types of mirroring will spring to every reader's
mind. The recapitulation of a motif, for instance, as in the
poisoning episodes in *Hamlet*. *Hamlet* criticism has too
much ignored, I think, the fact that a story of poisoning
forms the climax of the first act, a mime and "play" of
poisoning the climax of the third, and actual poisoning, on
a wide scale, the climax of the fifth. Surely this repetition
was calculated to keep steady for Shakespeare's Elizabethan audiences the political and moral bearings of the play?
We may say what we like about Hamlet's frailties, which
are real, but we can hardly ignore the fact that in each of
the poisoning episodes the poisoner is the King. The King,
who ought to be like the sun, giving warmth, radiance, and
fertility to his kingdom, is actually its destroyer. The "leper-
ous distilment" he pours into Hamlet's father's ear, which
courses through his body with such despatch, has coursed
just as swiftly through the body politic, and what we see in
Denmark as a result is a poisoned kingdom, containing one
corruption upon another of Renaissance ideals: the "wise
councilor," who is instead a tedious windbag; the young
"man of honor," who has no trust in another's honor, as
his advice to his sister shows, and none of his own, as his
own treachery to Hamlet shows; the "friends," who are not
friends but spies; the loved one, the "mistress," who proves
disloyal (a decoy, however reluctant, for villainy), and
goes mad—through poison also, "the poison of deep grief";
the mother and Queen, who instead of being the guardian
of the kingdom's matronly virtues has set a harlot's blister
on love's forehead and made marriage vows "as false as
dicers' oaths"; and the Prince, the "ideal courtier," the

---

[4] Another emblematic entrance is the first entrance of the soothsayer
in *Julius Caesar;* see "The Teaching of Drama," *Essays on the Teaching
of English*, ed. E. J. Gordon and E. S. Noyes (1960).

Renaissance man—once active, energetic, now reduced to anguished introspection; a glass of fashion, now a sloven in antic disarray; a noble mind, now partly unhinged, in fact as well as seeming; the observed of all observers, now observed in a more sinister sense; the mold of form, now capable of obscenities, cruelty, even treachery, mining below the mines of his school friends to hoist them with their own petard. All this, in one way or another, is the poison of the King, and in the last scene, lest we miss the point, we are made to see the spiritual poison become literal and seize on all those whom it has not already destroyed.

> a Prince's Court
> Is like a common Fountaine, whence should flow
> Pure silver-droppes in generall: But if't chance
> Some curs'd example poyson't neere the head,
> Death, and diseases through the whole land spread.

The lines are Webster's, but they state with precision one of the themes of Shakespeare's play.

Finally, in the tragedies as elsewhere in Shakespeare, we have the kinds of replication that have been specifically called "mirror scenes," [5] or (more in Ercles' vein) scenes of "analogical probability." [6] The most impressive examples here are frequently the opening scenes and episodes. The witches of *Macbeth,* whose "foul is fair" and battle that is "won *and* lost" anticipate so much to come. The "great debate" in *Antony and Cleopatra,* initiated in the comments of Philo and the posturings of the lovers, and reverberating thereafter within, as well as around, the lovers till they die. The watchmen on the platform in *Hamlet,* feeling out a mystery—an image that will re-form in our minds again and again as we watch almost every member of the *dramatis personae* engage in similar activity later on. The technique of manipulation established at the outset of *Othello,* the persuading of someone to believe something

---

[5] By H. T. Price, in *Joseph Quincy Adams Memorial Studies,* ed. J. McManaway (1948), pp. 101 ff.

[6] See P. J. Aldus, *Shakespeare Quarterly* (1955), pp. 397 ff. Aldus deals suggestively with the opening scene of *Julius Caesar.*

he is reluctant to believe and which is not true in the sense presented—exemplified in Iago's management of both Roderigo and Brabantio, and prefiguring later developments even to the detail that the manipulator operates by preference through an instrument.

Lear offers perhaps the best of all these instances. Here the "Nature" of which the play is to make so much, ambiguous, double-barreled, is represented in its normative aspect in the hierarchies on the stage before us—a whole political society from its *primum mobile*, the great King, down to lowliest attendant, a whole family society from father down through married daughters and sons-in-law to a third daughter with her wooers—and, in its appetitive aspect, which Edmund will formulate in a few moments, in the overt self-will of the old King and the hidden self-will, the "plighted cunning," of the false daughters. As the scene progresses, in fact, we can see these hierarchies of the normative nature, which at first looked so formidable and solid, crumble away in the repudiation of Cordelia, the banishment of Kent, the exit of Lear and Burgundy, till nothing is left standing on the stage but Nature red in tooth and claw as the false daughters lay their heads together.

I have dwelt a little on these effects of "indirection" in the tragedies because I believe that most of us as playgoers are keenly conscious of their presence. I have perhaps described them badly, in some instances possibly misconceived them; but they are not my invention; this kind of thing has been pointed to more and more widely during the past fifty years by reputable observers. In short, these effects, in some important sense, are "there." And if they are, the question we must ask is, Why? What are they for? How are they used?

I return then to the query with which this section began: what *does* happen in a Shakespearean tragedy? Is it possible to formulate an answer that will, while not repudiating the traditional categories so far as they are useful, take into account the matters we have been examining? In the present state of our knowledge I am not convinced that this is possible: we have been too much concerned in this century with the verbal, which is only part of the picture.

Nevertheless, I should like to make a few exploratory gestures.

Obviously the most important thing that happens in a Shakespearean tragedy is that the hero follows a cycle of change, which is, in part, psychic change. And this seems generally to be constituted in three phases. During the first phase, corresponding roughly to Bradley's exposition, the hero is delineated. Among other things, he is placed in positions that enable him to sound the particular timbre of his tragic music:

> Not so, my lord; I am too much i' the sun.
>
> > (*Hamlet*, I.ii.67)

> Seems, madam! nay, it is; I know not "seems."
>
> > (I.ii.76)

> My father's brother, but no more like my father
> Than I to Hercules.   (I.ii.152)

> > My fate cries out,
> And makes each petty artery in this body
> As hardy as the Nemean lion's nerve.   (I.iv.81)

Chiming against this we are also permitted to hear the particular timbre of the opposing voice, spoken by the foil as well as others:

> > If it be,
> Why seems it so particular with thee?
>
> > > (I.ii.74)

> For what we know must be and is as common
> As any the most vulgar thing to sense,
> Why should we in our peevish opposition
> Take it to heart?   (I.ii.98)

> What if it tempt you toward the flood, my lord,
> Or to the dreadful summit of the cliff
> That beetles o'er his base into the sea,
> And there assume some other horrible form,
> Which might deprive your sovereignty of reason
> And draw you into madness?   (I.iv.69)

From now on, as we saw, these are the differing attitudes towards experience that will supply the essential dialogue of the play.

The second phase is much more comprehensive. It contains the conflict, crisis, and falling action—in short, the heart of the matter. Here several interesting developments occur. The one certain over-all development in this phase is that the hero tends to become his own antithesis. We touched on this earlier in the case of Hamlet, in whom "the courtier's, soldier's, scholar's, eye, tongue, sword" suffer some rather savage violations before the play is done. Likewise, Othello the unshakable, whose original composure under the most trying insults and misrepresentations almost takes the breath away, breaks in this phase into furies, grovels on the floor in a trance, strikes his wife publicly. King Lear, "the great image of authority" both by temperament and position, becomes a helpless crazed old man crying in a storm, destitute of everything but one servant and his Fool. Macbeth, who would have "holily" what he would have "highly," who is too full of the milk of human kindness to catch the nearest way, whose whole being revolts with every step he takes in his own revolt— his hair standing on end, his imagination filling with angels "trumpet-tongued," his hands (after the deed) threatening to pluck out his own eyes—turns into the numbed usurper, "supped full with horrors," who is hardly capable of responding even to his wife's death. The development is equally plain in Antony and Coriolanus. "The greatest prince o' th' world, The noblest," finds his greatness slipped from him, and his nobility debased to the ignominy of having helpless emissaries whipped. The proud and upright Coriolanus, patriot soldier, truckles in the market place for votes, revolts to the enemy he has vanquished, carries war against his own flesh and blood.

This manner of delineating tragic "action," though it may be traced here and there in other drama, seems to be on the whole a property of the Elizabethans and Jacobeans. Possibly it springs from their concern with "whole" personalities on the tragic stage, rather than as so often with the ancients and Racine, just those aspects of personality that guarantee the *dénouement*. In any case, it seems to have become a consistent feature of Shakespeare's dramaturgy, and beautifully defines the sense of psychological alienation and uprootedness that tragic experience in the Elizabethan and Jacobean theater generally seems to embrace. Its distinctively tragic implications stand out the more when we reflect that psychic change in comedy (if indeed comedy can be said to concern itself with psychic change at all) consists in making—or in showing—the protagonist to be more and more what he always was.[7]

In this second phase too, either as an outward manifestation of inward change, or as a shorthand indication that such change is about to begin or end, belong the tragic journeys. Romeo is off to Mantua, Brutus to the Eastern end of the Roman world, Hamlet to England, Othello to Cyprus, Lear and Gloucester to Dover, Timon to the cave, Macbeth to the heath to revisit the witches, Antony to Rome and Athens, Coriolanus to Antium.[8] Such journeys, we rightly say, are called for by the plots. But perhaps we should not be wrong if we added that Shakespearean plotting tends to call for journeys, conceivably for discernible reasons. For one thing, journeys can enhance our impression that psychological changes are taking place, either by emphasizing a lapse of time, or by taking us to new settings, or by both. I suspect we register such effects subconsciously more often than we think.

Furthermore, though it would be foolish to assign to any of the journeys in Shakespeare's tragedies a precise symbolic meaning, several of them have vaguely symbolic overtones—serving as surrogates either for what can never be exhibited on the stage, as the mysterious processes leading to psychic change, which cannot be articulated into speech, even soliloquy, without losing their formless instinctive character; or for the processes of self-discovery, the learning processes—a function journeys fulfill in many of the world's best-known stories (the *Aeneid*, the *Divine Com-*

---

[7] I have elaborated this point in an introduction to Fielding's *Joseph Andrews* (1948).

[8] These are merely samples; other journeys occur that I have not named here.

edy, Tom Jones, etc.) and in some of Shakespeare's
comedies. Hamlet's abortive journey to England is possibly
an instance of the first category. After his return, and
particularly after what he tells us of his actions while at
sea, we are not surprised if he appears, spiritually, a
changed man. Lear's and Gloucester's journey to Dover is
perhaps an instance of the second category, leading as it
does through suffering to insight and reconciliation.

During the hero's journey, or at any rate during his
over-all progress in the second phase, he will normally pass
through a variety of mirroring situations of the sort formerly discussed (though it will be by us and not him that
the likeness in the mirror is seen). In some of these, the
hero will be confronted, so to speak, with a version of his
own situation, and his failure to recognize it may be a
measure of the nature of the disaster to ensue. Coriolanus,
revolted from Rome and now its enemy, meets himself in
Aufidius's embrace in Antium. Hamlet meets himself in
Fortinbras as the latter marches to Poland, but does not see
the likeness—only the differences. Lear goes to Goneril's
and there meets, as everyone remembers, images of his
own behavior to Cordelia. Thrust into the night, he meets
his own defenselessness in Edgar, and is impelled to pray.
Encountering in Dover fields, both Lear and Gloucester
confront in each other an extension of their own experience: blindness that sees and madness that is wise. Macbeth revisits the witches on the heath and finds there
(without recognizing them) not only the emblems of his
death and downfall to come but his speciousness and
duplicity. Antony encounters in Enobarbus's defection his
own; and possibly, in Pompey, his own later muddled inde-
cision between "honor" and *Realpolitik.* Othello hears the
innocent Cassio set upon in the dark, then goes to re-enact
that scene in a more figurative darkness in Desdemona's
bedroom. Sometimes, alternatively or additionally, the
hero's way will lie through quasi-symbolic settings or situations. The heath in both *Macbeth* and *King Lear* is infi-
nitely suggestive, even if like all good symbols it refuses to
dissipate its *Dinglichkeit* in meaning. The same is true of
the dark castle platform in Hamlet, and the graveyard; of

the cliff at Dover and Gloucester's leap; of the "monument," where both Antony and Cleopatra die; and of course, as many have pointed out, of the night scenes, the storm, the music, the changes of clothing, the banquets. So much in Shakespeare's tragedies stands on the brink of symbol that for this reason, if no other, the usual terms for describing their construction and mode of action need reinforcement.

After the hero has reached and passed through his own antithesis, there comes a third phase in his development that is extremely difficult to define. It represents a recovery of sorts; in some cases, perhaps even a species of synthesis. The once powerful, now powerless king, will have power again, but of another kind—the kind suggested in his reconciliation with Cordelia and his speech beginning "Come, let's away to prison"; and he will have sanity again, but in a mode not dreamed of at the beginning of the play. Or, to take Othello's case, it will be given the hero to recapture the faith he lost,[9] to learn that the pearl really was richer than all his tribe, and to execute quite another order of justice than the blinkered justice meted out to Cassio and the blind injustice meted out to Desdemona. Or again, to shift to Antony, the man who has so long been thrown into storms of rage and recrimination by the caprices of his unstable mistress receives the last of them without a murmur of reproach, though it has led directly to his death, and dies in greater unison with her than we have ever seen him live.

I believe that some mark of this nature is visible in all the tragedies. Coriolanus, "boy" though he is and in some ways remains, makes a triumphant choice (detract from his motives as we may), and he knows what it is likely to cost. Moreover, he refuses the way of escape that lies open if he should return now with Volumnia and Vergilia to Rome. "I'll not to Rome, I'll back with you," he tells Aufidius, "and pray you Stand to me in this cause." The young man who, after this, dies accused of treachery—by Aufidius's treachery, and the suggestibility of the crowd,

---

[9] This point is well made in Helen Gardner's *The Noble Moor* (1956).

as slippery in Corioli as Rome—cannot be thought identical in all respects with the young man who joined Menenius in the play's opening scene. He is that young man, but with the notable difference of his triumphant choice behind him; and there is bound to be more than a military association in our minds when the Second Lord of the Volscians, seeking to quell the mob, cries, "The man is noble, and his fame folds in This orb o' th' earth"; and again too when the First Lord exclaims over his body, "Let him be regarded As the most noble corse that ever herald Did follow to his urn." Even the monster Macbeth is so handled by Shakespeare, as has been often enough observed, that he seems to regain something at the close—if nothing more, at least some of that *élan* which made him the all-praised Bellona's bridegroom of the play's second scene; and everything Macbeth says, following Duncan's death, about the emptiness of the achievement, the lack of posterity, the sear, the yellow leaf, deprived of "that which should accompany old age, As honor, love, obedience, troops of friends," affords evidence that the meaning of his experience has not been lost on him.

To say this, I wish to make it clear, is not to say that the Shakespearean tragic hero undergoes an "illumination," or, to use the third term of K. Burke's sequence, a Mathema or perception.[10] This is a terminology that seems to me not very useful to the discussion of tragedy as Shakespeare presents it. It is sufficient for my purposes to say simply that the phase in which we are conscious of the hero as approaching his opposite is followed by a final phase in which we are conscious of him as exhibiting one or more aspects of his original, or—since these may not coincide—his better self: as in the case of Antony's final reunion with Cleopatra, and Coriolanus's decision not to sack Rome. Whether we then go on to give this phenomenon a specific spiritual significance, seeing in it the objective correlative of "perception" or "illumination," is a question that depends, obviously, on a great many factors, more of them perhaps situated in our own individual philos-

10 *A Grammar of Motives* (1945), pp. 38 ff.

ophies than in the text, and, so, likely to lead us away
from Shakespeare rather than towards him. Clearly if
Shakespeare wished us to engage in this activity, he was
remiss in the provision of clues. Even in *King Lear*, the one
play where some sort of regeneration or new insight in the
hero has been universally acknowledged, the man before
us in the last scene—who sweeps Kent aside, rakes all who
have helped him with grapeshot ("A plague upon you,
murderers, traitors all. I might have saved her . . ."),
exults in the revenge he has exacted for Cordelia's death,
and dies self-deceived in the thought she still lives—this
man is one of the most profoundly human figures ever
created in a play; but he is not, certainly, the Platonic idea
laid up in heaven, or in critical schemes, of regenerate man.

I have kept to the end, and out of proper order, the
most interesting of all the symbolic elements in the hero's
second phase. This is his experience of madness. One dis-
covers with some surprise, I think, how many of Shakespeare's heroes are associated with this disease. Only Titus,
Hamlet, Lear, and Timon, in various senses, actually go
mad; but Iago boasts that he will make Othello mad, and
in a way succeeds; Antony, after the second defeat at sea,
is said by Cleopatra to be

> more mad,
> Than Telamon for his shield; the boar of Thessaly
> Was never so emboss'd;   (IV.xiii.2)

Caithness in *Macbeth* tells us that some say the king is mad,
while "others, that lesser hate him, Do call it valiant fury";
Romeo, rather oddly, enjoins Paris at Juliet's tomb to

> be gone; live, and hereafter say,
> A madman's mercy bade thee run away.
>   (V.iii.66)

Even Brutus, by the Antony of *Antony and Cleopatra*, is
said to have been "mad."
What (if anything), one wonders, may this mean?

Doubtless a sort of explanation can be found in Elizabethan psychological lore, which held that the excess of any passion approached madness, and in the general prevalence, through Seneca and other sources, of the adage: *Quos vult perdere Jupiter dementat prius.*[11] Furthermore, madness, when actually exhibited, was dramatically useful, as Kyd had shown. It was arresting in itself, and it allowed the combination in a single figure of tragic hero and buffoon, to whom could be accorded the license of the allowed fool in speech and action.

Just possibly, however, there was yet more to it than this, if we may judge by Shakespeare's sketches of madness in Hamlet and King Lear. In both these, madness is to some degree a punishment or doom, corresponding to the adage. Lear prays to the heavens that he may not suffer madness, and Hamlet asks Laertes, in his apology before the duel, to overlook his conduct, since "you must needs have heard, how I am punish'd With a sore distraction." It is equally obvious, however, that in both instances the madness has a further dimension, as insight, and this is true also of Ophelia. Ophelia, mad, is able to make awards of flowers to the King and Queen which are appropriate to frailties of which she cannot be supposed to have conscious knowledge. For the same reason, I suspect we do not need Dover Wilson's radical displacement of Hamlet's entry in II. ii, so as to enable him to overhear Polonius.[12] It is enough that Hamlet wears, even if it is for the moment self-assumed, the guise of the madman. As such, he can be presumed to have intuitive unformulated awarenesses that reach the surface in free (yet relevant) associations, like those of Polonius with a fishmonger, Ophelia with carrion. Lear likewise is allowed free yet relevant associations. His great speech in Dover fields on the lust of women derives from the designs of Goneril and Regan on Edmund, of which he consciously knows nothing. Moreover, both he and Hamlet can be privileged in madness to say things—Hamlet about the corruption of human nature, and Lear

---

[11] "Those whom Jupiter wishes to destroy he first makes mad." [*Editor's note.*]

[12] *What Happens in "Hamlet"* (1935), pp. 103 ff.

about the corruption of the Jacobean social system (and by extension about all social systems whatever), which Shakespeare could hardly have risked apart from this license. Doubtless one of the anguishes of being a great artist is that you cannot tell people what they and you and your common institutions are really like—when viewed absolutely—without being dismissed as insane. To communicate at all, you must acknowledge the opposing voice; for there always is an opposing voice, and it is as deeply rooted in your own nature as in your audience's.

Just possibly, therefore, the meaning of tragic madness for Shakespeare approximated the meaning that the legendary figure of Cassandra (whom Shakespeare had in fact put briefly on his stage in the second act of *Troilus and Cressida*) has held for so many artists since his time. Cassandra's madness, like Lear's and Hamlet's—possibly, also, like the madness *verbally* assigned to other Shakespearean tragic heroes—contains both punishment and insight. She is doomed to know, by a consciousness that moves to measures outside our normal space and time; she is doomed never to be believed, because those to whom she speaks can hear only the opposing voice. With the language of the god Apollo sounding in her brain, and the incredulity of her fellow mortals ringing in her ears, she makes an ideal emblem of the predicament of the Shakespearean tragic hero, caught as he is between the absolute and the expedient. And by the same token, of the predicament of the artist—Shakespeare himself, perhaps—who, having been given the power to see the "truth," can convey it only through poetry—what we commonly call a "fiction," and dismiss.

In all these matters, let me add in parenthesis, we would do well to extend more generously our inferences about Shakespeare to the Jacobean playwrights as a group. Some of us have been overlong content with a view of Jacobean tragedy as naïve as those formerly entertained of Restoration comedy, eighteenth-century literature, and modern poetry. But a whole generation of writers does not become obsessed by the sexual feuding of cavalier and citizen, or rhetorical "rules" and social norms, or abrupt images and

catapulting rhythms, or outrageous stories of incest, madness, brutality, and lust, because the poetic imagination
has suddenly gone "frivolous," or "cold," or "eccentric,"
or "corrupt." Such concerns respond to spiritual needs,
however dimly apprehended, and one of the prime needs
of Jacobean writers, as the intelligible and on the whole
friendly universe of the Middle Ages failed around them,
was quite evidently to face up to what men are or may be
when stripped to their naked humanity and mortality, and
torn loose from accustomed moorings. Flamineo's phrase
in *The White Devil*—"this busy trade of life"—offered as
a passing summary of the play's monstrous burden of blood
and madness:

> This busy trade of life appears most vain,
> Since rest breeds rest, where all seek pain by pain—

is characteristically understated and ironic, like Iago's
"Pleasure and action make the hours seem short." The
creators of Iago and Flamineo, and all the responsible
writers of Jacobean tragedy along with them, knew perfectly well that it was not in fact the "trade," or habitude,
of life to which they held up art's mirror, but life "on the
stretch," nature at its farthest reach of possibility. They
were fascinated by violence because they were fascinated
by the potencies of the human will: its weaknesses, tri-
umphs, delusions, corruptions, its capacities for destruction
and regeneration, its residual dignity when, all else removed, man stood at his being's limit; and because they
knew that in violence lay the will's supreme test, for aggres-
sor and sufferer alike.

Whatever the themes of individual plays, therefore, the
one pervasive Jacobean theme tends to be the undertaking
and working out of acts of will, and especially (in that
strongly Calvinistic age) of acts of self-will. This is surely
the reason why, in Clifford Leech's happy phrase, these
writers know so little of heaven, so much of hell; and why,
to one conversant with their work so many products of the
century to come seem like fulfillments of ancient prophecy:
Milton's Satan and his "God"—the philosophy embodied

in *Leviathan*—even, perhaps, the clash of the Civil Wars and the cleavage in the English spirit reaching from Cavalier and Puritan to Jacobite and Whig and well beyond. At the very beginning of the century, these writers had got hold of the theme that was to exercise it in all departments, political, economic, religious, cultural, till past its close, the problem of anarchic will; and so decisive, so many-sided is their treatment of this problem that even in Milton's massive recapitulation of it in *Paradise Lost* the issue seems sometimes to be losing in vitality what it has gained in clarity, to be fossilizing and becoming formula. The utterances of *his* white devil have more resonance but less complexity and immediacy of feeling than those of Vittoria Corombona, Bosola, Macbeth, or Beatrice Vermandero; and some of them bear a perilous resemblance to the posturings of Restoration heroic tragedy, where the old agonies are heard from still, but now clogged, and put through paces like captive giants in a raree show.

However this may be, I return at the end to the proposition I set out with: there is a lot about the construction of a Shakespearean tragic "action" that we still do not know. My own attempts to get towards it in this chapter are fumbling and may be preposterous: even to myself they sound a little like Bottom's dream. But the interesting thing about Bottom's dream, from my point of view, is that, though he found he was an ass all right, the Titania he tried to tell about was real.

Robert B. Heilman

Wit and Witchcraft:

An Approach to *Othello*

The critic who proposes a reading of *Othello* may hope for it that it will appear at least to illuminate some of the parts and at most to contribute to the understanding of the sum of the parts. If *Othello* is not the most complex of the tragedies, the problem of its over-all form is still a large one, and he who aspires to a full account of the creative relationship of all the parts[1] must be content if he seems generally to be moving in the right direction. The theory of the whole that proceeds from an examination of the parts will at best be a distant cousin of the drama; such wit as the critic may have can but follow the witchcraft of the dramatist (to take Iago's words out of context) from afar. But the cousin may help identify the drama, the wit tell how the witchcraft has gone. At the same time the critic, whatever he imparts, must at many points duplicate and parallel his predecessors while essaying to be himself; so he runs the double risk of not encompassing the novelty

From *The Sewanee Review*, Vol. 64, No. 1, Winter 1956, copyright © 1956 by The University of the South, pp. 1–4, 8–10, and *Arizona Quarterly*, Spring 1956, pp. 5–16. Reprinted by permission of the author and the editors, with new transitional material supplied by the author in *Shakespeare*, ed. Leonard F. Dean. New York: Oxford University Press, Inc., 1957. Copyright © 1957 by Oxford University Press, Inc. The ideas in this essay are among those developed by Mr. Heilman in *Magic in the Web: Action and Language in* Othello, copyright 1956 by the University of Kentucky Press. Used with permission.

which will absolve him of the suspicion of merely repeating
what oft was thought, or of falling into innovations which
in other quarters will seem dubious because such things
were never thought.

The parts which make up the whole are numerous and
diverse. Othello is a part. Iago is a part. Iago's deception
of Roderigo is a part. Iago's remarks on reputation, Desdemona's incredulity at the sexual misbehavior of wives,
Emilia's revulsion against Iago, Cassio's drunken babbling
are parts. All recognitions and reversals, all thoughts and
feelings of characters are parts. The nighttime in which
most of the major actions occur is a part. Iago's use of *honesty* is a part. All the uses of *honesty* are a part. All the
metaphors of medicine and disease, the images from army
life, the language of light and dark are parts.

The point is to keep the idea of the part flexible and in-
clusive, as a step toward adequate freedom in the description of structure. A view of the parts begotten of a
preoccupation with gross anatomy will yield a coarse and
constricted account of structure. On the other hand, com-
piling an unlimited serial list of parts would be futile. The
main thing is to be aware of a part in all its relational possibilities.[2] Othello's farewell to arms (III.iii.346 ff.) is relevant to the specific situation of the moment, to Othello's
personality generally, to Shakespeare's conception of the
modes of response to disaster possible to human beings.
Emilia's picking up the handkerchief helps advance the
action by contributing to Iago's deception of Othello, but
it is also relevant to her character and to Shakespeare's
conception of the modes of wifely devotion and marital
relationship (not to mention its relations by contrast with
actions of Desdemona and Bianca and of Emilia herself
later). The theories of sex which Iago advances to Roderigo
are relevant to his purpose of controlling Roderigo, to his
modes of thought generally, and to Shakespeare's awareness of the whole realm of philosophies of love.

For working criticism, the broad categories of the parts
whose relatedness is to be observed are two: plot and
poetry. We might again borrow Iago's words for metaphor
and speak of the wit and witchcraft of the dramatist: the

conscious designing and articulating; and the mysterious endowing of many parts—especially the poetic language—with dramatic value and meaning far in excess of the minimal logical requirements of the occasion: the magic in the web. This is less a theory of composition than an effort to suggest different aspects of the play that are only theoretically separable. Let us put it another way. If love is what *Othello* is "about," *Othello* is not only a play about love but a poem about love.[8] It has parts which interact in the mode of "pure" drama—people having such and such an effect on each other, irrespective of whether they communicate in verse, prose or pantomime; it also has parts which interact in the manner of a poem. Again, this is a theoretical separation: the characters have such and such an effect by means of the words they speak; and conversely, an analysis of the words they speak involves the student regularly in a consideration of the "action" and interaction of the speakers. Yet when the dramatist has his characters speak in poetic language, he vastly complicates their communication with each other and with us. Figure, rhythm, poetic order do not merely make "more vivid" or "heighten" a literal prose statement that is otherwise unchanged; they constitute a fundamentally different statement by the introduction of the nuance, overtone, feeling, association, implication, and extension characteristic of them; in other words, by subtly carrying us beyond the finiteness, one-dimensionalism, and contextual restrictions of the pure statement determined only by the strict logical requirements of the immediate situation. When Othello summons Desdemona and dismisses Emilia, "Leave procreants alone . . . ;/Cough or cry hem if anybody come./ Your mystery, your mystery! . . ." (IV.ii.28–30), he not only dismisses Emilia, accuses Desdemona of infidelity, and betrays his own insane bitterness, but he converts the marriage into a brothel arrangement in which all three are involved, and by so doing establishes imaginative lines of connection with the role of Bianca and particularly with the Iago philosophy of sexual conduct. If we take all the lines of one character out of context and consider them as a unit, we have always a useful body of information; but if, when we study Iago's lines, we find that he consistently describes himself in images of hunting and trapping, we learn not only his plans of action but something of his attitude to occasions, to his victims, and to himself; and beyond that there is fixed for us an image of evil—one of those by which the drama interprets the human situation. When Othello says he threw away a "pearl," we recall that Brabantio, in acceding to Desdemona's departure, called her "jewel"; when Desdemona says she would rather have lost her purse than the handkerchief, we recall that Iago, who has stolen the handkerchief, has spoken of stealing a purse; we spontaneously make these connections, and, even if we go no further, our reading has brought forth linkings that cannot be expunged; but we often do go further, and seek out the formal order that is exemplified in these images that leap out of their own contexts and carry our imaginations into other parts of the play.[4] When to these we add many other instances in which poetic language, functioning doubly or triply, takes us beyond specific moments of action into others and on into general areas of character, feeling, and thought, we find that we have an immensely complicated verbal structure with which we must come to terms—the "poem about love," as I have called it. We are trying to describe what Traversi called "a new kind of dramatic unity."[5]

In pursuit of this dramatic unity we must inevitably take account of one notable characteristic of Shakespeare's verbal drama—its repetitiveness of images and likewise of abstract words. After Emilia has three times incredulously asked, "My husband?" Othello demands, "What needs this iterance, woman?" (V.ii.147). We all must play Othello to Shakespeare's Emilia: "iterance" forces itself upon us as a critical problem. The dramatist cannot conspicuously repeat words and rely upon figures of the same class (e.g., clothes, military life) without catching our eye and raising a question about what goes on. We are hardly likely to attribute this recurrency to the artist's carelessness or failing resourcefulness or to stop at description—an inert lexicon of repetitions. When editors devotedly multiply cross references to dictional or rhetorical echoes and anticipations, they act, one assumes, more from a sense of relationship than from a delight in coincidence. Speaking of *Antony and Cleopatra,* Professor Clemen uses a phrase that is valid for other plays: "this symbolical meaning of certain sequences of imagery." [6] As Paul Goodman puts it, Shakespeare's "profusion of images is so handled through a long play that it forms a systematic structure and is part of the plot." He elaborates on

> a method that is characteristically Shakespearean: this is to present a line of thought by an independent development of the system of imagery. Put formally: when several characters independently and throughout the play employ the same system of images, the diction becomes an independent part of the plot implying a thought, action, etc., whatever is the principle of the system. For it is not in character for different characters to use the same images. [7]

I suspect that it *may* be "in character for different characters to use the same images," which can be a device for suggesting similarities or even contrasts among them; or if the images belong dominantly to one character in one part of the play, and to another in another part, the change may be an important mark of dramatic progression, as when the almost pre-emptive use of animal imagery passes in mid-play from Iago to Othello. But beyond all its possible uses in characterization, recurrent diction has still other functions. Goodman's phrase "independent development" is the key. For though speeches are in one sense not separable from the characters, in another sense they do become disengaged from particular speakers and enter the general verbal fund of the play. (The more rich and profuse the language, the more this is likely to be true, just as the more rich and powerful the literary work, the more likely it is to become disengaged from its own times, however much these times may be needed for exegetic purposes, and to enter the general timeless fund of literary possessions.) Reiterative language is particularly prone to

acquire a continuity of its own and to become "an independent part of the plot" [8] whose effect we can attempt to
gauge. It may create "mood" or "atmosphere": the per-
vasiveness of images of injury, pain, and torture in *Othello*
has a very strong impact that is not wholly determined by
who uses the images. But most of all the "system of imagery" introduces thoughts, ideas, themes—elements of
the meaning that is the author's final organization of all
his materials.[9]

II

Before coming directly to the forming of the love-theme
that differentiates *Othello* from other Shakespeare plays
that utilize the same theme, I turn arbitrarily to Iago to
inspect a distinguishing mark of his of which the relevance
to thematic form in the play will appear a little later. When
Iago with unperceived scoffing reminds Roderigo, who is
drawn with merciless attraction to the unreachable Desdemona, that love effects an unwonted nobility in men, he
states a doctrine which he "knows" is true but in which he
may not "believe." Ennoblement by love is a real possibility in men, but Iago has to view it with bitterness and to
try to undermine it. With his spontaneous antipathy to
spiritual achievement, he must in principle deny the mysterious transformation of personality; instinctively he is
the observer of all these habits that suggest infinite corrupt-
ibility as the comprehensive human truth. He is the
believer in shrewd observation and in corruption in whose
credo, which is not altogether unique, man is a union of
lusting, folly, and plotting.

Good sense, hard sense, common sense, no nonsense,
rationality—all these terms, we may suppose, are ones
which Iago might consider as defining his perspective. As
he plays against Othello with his game of honest and loving
friend, he uses words that put him on that side of the
fence. First he can't tell Othello his "thoughts" (about

Cassio) because of his "manhood, honesty," or "wisdom" [10] (III.iii.153–54); a little later he finds "reason" to tell them (193). Othello considers him "wise" (IV.i.76). While privately Iago may deny his love and kid his honesty, he takes his brains seriously. "Thus do I ever make my *fool* my purse," he boasts; to spend time with Roderigo otherwise, "Mine own gain'd *knowledge* should profane" (I.iii.374–75). Othello is to be treated like an *ass* (I.iii. 393; II.i.309). Iago applies the term *fool* successively to Roderigo (II.iii.48), Cassio (II.iii.353), Desdemona (IV.i.178), and Emilia (IV.ii.147), and condescends to fools "credulous" and "gross" (IV.i.47; III.iii.401). His view of himself as the clearheaded manipulator of gulls is significantly unchallenged despite the barrage of derogatory rhetoric eventually aimed at him. He remains the "smart man," apt in "deals," scornful of "suckers."

It is more fun for the smart man if his victim thinks he is using *his* head with especial acuteness. Early in the big deception scene (III.iii.93 ff.) on which all the subsequent action turns, Iago urges Othello "that your *wisdom* yet" should "take no notice" of Iago's "unsure observance" (148–51); later he repeats, "Nay, but be *wise*" (429). The idea that he is being sharp goes to Othello's head; he resolves to be "*cunning* in my patience" (IV.i.92), and he queries erring Desdemona, "Are you *wise?*" (IV.i.234). With his new wisdom he murders his unwise wife, and Emilia tells him what he has become: "*O gull! O dolt!/ As ignorant as dirt!* . . . *O thou dull Moor,* . . . what should such a *fool/* Do with so good a wife?" (V.ii.160–231). How does Iago try to stop this confessional outburst which will ruin him? By commanding Emilia, "Be *wise,* and get you home" (220). Here he cannot induce that wisdom that serves his own end; the sharp-eyed engineer of folly in others now by necessity collapses into senseless abuse and violence. But Othello's reproach to himself, "O fool! fool! fool!" (319), inadequate a self-judgment as it is, acknowledges Emilia's indictment and, inadvertently, the success of Iago's plot to make him "egregiously an ass." After all this, Othello's "lov'd not wisely" is unconsciously an understatement.

Making a fool of someone else is an aesthetic demonstration of intellectual superiority. It is implicitly partial, temporary; a comic episode after which life goes on. Let this exploit in self-aggrandizement expand with the full pressure of passion, and the attack becomes an ultimate one against sanity: Iago's design to put Othello "into a jealousy so strong/That judgment cannot cure," driving him "even to madness" (II.i.301–02, 311). It is the extreme revenge possible to the man of "reason," a chaos that logically extends and completes the other modes of chaos which Iago instinctively seeks, in a variety of ways, at all stages of the action. Twice again he speaks of Othello's madness as a likelihood or as a formal objective (IV.i.56, 102), and his program works well enough to make Lodovico inquire about Othello's mental soundness (IV.i.269) and to make Othello express a doubt about his own sanity (V.ii.110). Madness spreads: Emilia fears lest Desdemona "run mad" (III.iii.315), Othello cries to her that he is "glad to see you mad" (IV.i.239), and she in turn fears his "fury" (IV.ii.32). But the planned madness eventually recoils upon its creator: "What, are you mad?" is Iago's response when Emilia tells the truth about what he has done (V.ii.191).

Such points in the auxiliary theme of madness (a slender anticipation of what will be done in *Lear*) mark the course of rational Iago. Insofar as he identifies rationality and wisdom with his own purposes, he is close enough to Everyman; but he is sharply individualized, and at the same time made the representative of a recognizable human class, when the drama reveals that his purposes require the irrationalizing of life for everyone else. Of the insights that create Iago, none is deeper than the recognition that a cool rationality may itself bring about or serve the irrational. Though Brabantio, awakened by the nocturnal outcries in front of his house, thinks that Iago has "lost" his "wits" and that Roderigo comes "in madness" (I.i.89–95), their universal technique of matching half-truths to latent fears makes him give up his same conclusions and accept their distorted history of what has happened to Desdemona, so much so that he then attributes "a judgment maim'd and most imperfect" (I.iii.99) i.e., failure of mind, to anyone who takes a different view of the situation. Here Iago simply has to make Brabantio as irrational as possible; shortly he has to curb Roderigo's irrationality, or rather, to convert it from a less to a more serviceable form, from suicidal despair to the sexual pursuit of Desdemona. Now for the first step in this conversion Iago utilizes the traditional argument of the "authority of . . . our wills" and of "one scale of reason to poise another of sensuality"; "But we have reason to cool our raging motions, our carnal stings, our unbitted lusts; . . ." (I.iii.321–26). If in one sense this is the devil talking Scripture, in another it is Iago paying tribute to a faculty that he values deeply. He is the self-conscious possessor of brain-power. But reason has many functions, and the critical utility of this passage is that it points to the distinction between the ostensible and the real functions that Iago assigns to reason. In no way does he press Roderigo really to apply reason to his emotional ailment, to diagnose it and moderate and perhaps cure it; on the contrary he assures him that his cause "hath . . . reason" (362–63) and encourages him to found his hopes on Desdemona's sharing in a universal unregeneracy which Iago quite evidently believes is subject to rational control by no one. But more than that we see that Iago has not the slightest thought of using reason to "cool" his own "raging motions," "carnal stings," and "unbitted lusts": reason is rather the agent of his unbitted lusts and of the raging motions of his hate. It is in their behalf that he reasons with Roderigo; his reason is instrumental, serving his own unreason by playing upon Roderigo's. When he mentions the rumor that his wife Emilia has been unfaithful with Othello, he hurries on to say, "I know not if't be true" (379); rather he intends to act on "mere suspicion," just to make sure. His mind is used not to determine the truth but to convert into action a feeling not founded in truth. This is a basic Shakespearean definition of evil: the sharp mind in the service of uncriticized passion. And the final irony, as Shakespeare sees it is that the owner of the sharp mind is eventually destroyed by the passion his mind serves.

We see the innermost mechanism of this rational instrument when the Iago-Roderigo relationship comes to its last phase. Like several of the major characters, Roderigo is able at times to assess his own headwork: once he almost resolves to give up the lecherous pursuit of Desdemona and to return to Venice with "a little more wit" (II.iii.368); he is angrily aware that he has "foolishly suffer'd" and he suspects that he is "fopp'd" (IV.ii.178, 193). Iago retorts by praising Roderigo for both his brains ("... your suspicion is not without *wit* and *judgment*") and his moral quality (210–214). The recurrent irony for Roderigo is that he cannot rely on his own good sense but falls back instead on Iago's version of what is good sense for him. Here comes the payoff. When once again Iago asserts that there is a way of sleeping with Desdemona, Roderigo's reply is, "Well, what it is? Is it within *reason* and compass?" (218–19). Is it "reasonably practical"? No other question, no other issue of sanction or value. How many philosophic frills are being got rid of, and how far down to positive bedrock this is getting, appears when Iago reveals the program: kill Cassio. Roderigo is still shockable. Iago soothes him, "Come, stand not amaz'd . . ." (239), and offers a cure for "amazement": "I will show you such a necessity in his death that you shall think yourself bound to put it on him" (240–41). To this promise of logical demonstration Roderigo responds in the same key: "I will hear further *reason* for this" (244). Iago makes good his promise, "And you shall be satisfied" (245), for when Roderigo is finally lying in wait to kill Cassio, he sums up the rationale of the project:

> I have no great devotion to the deed,
> And yet he hath given me satisfying *reasons*.
> *'Tis but a man gone.*   (V.i.8–10)

Despite his moral hesitancy, Roderigo has found "satisfying reasons" for committing murder and thinking it a way to Desdemona's bed. In this climax of persuasion to evil, Iago's "reason" mediates between his own uncontrollable irrational drives and those of Roderigo. The rational serving one irrationality and appearing to serve another while

playing selfishly upon it: this sums up, and sums up arche-
typally, the fundamental operating methods of the Iago
way of life.

" 'Tis but a man gone" is pure Iago thought. It does
away with every value or imperative or speculation that
"man" or the death of man traditionally evokes, and it
makes "a man" simply a neutral instance of a category,
a statistical item, an object that can be acted on without
moral responsibility. The philosophy " 'Tis but a man gone"
(of which there are contemporary manifestations in whole
political systems, in demagogic practices of our own, in
some methods of business and advertising and even
abstract thought, in propaganda) is consistent with Iago's
reductive contention, which he develops at length, that love
is no more than unstable sexual appetite; his declaration
that "there is more sense" in a "bodily wound" than in
"reputation," which he says is a chimera; his skepticism
about "honor," which he implies is unreal because unseen;
and even, in a slightly different way, with his contempt for
Cassio's theoretical knowledge, "Mere prattle, without
practice" (I.i.23). Theory of any kind may open the door
to values that transcend the immediately utilitarian. "Iago's
is a pragmatic world, and his imagery finds its authority in
social usage," as Arthur Sewell has said. Iago says tacitly,
"Let's get down to facts," that is, the tangible and the
visible. (Seen from a slightly different perspective, he has
affiliations with the antimetaphysical thinker, the extremist
in semantics, the constitutional debunker.)

III

Reason as an ally of evil is a subject to which Shakespeare keeps returning, as if fascinated, but in different
thematic forms as he explores different counter-forces.
In *Macbeth* the rational effort to minimize the killings
done for ambition's sake runs finally into the force of conscience. In *Lear*, rationalized self-seeking is counterbal-

anced by all the fidelities implied in *pietas*. And in *Othello*? Although Iago, as we saw, does not take seriously the ennobling power of love, he does not fail to let us know what he does take seriously. When, in his fake oath of loyalty to "wrong'd Othello," he vows "The execution of his wit, hands, heart" (III.iii.463), Iago's words give a clue to his truth: his heart is his malice, his hands literally wound Cassio and kill Roderigo, and his wit is the genius that creates all the strategy. How it enters into the dialectic of structure, or the thematic form, is made clear in one of Iago's promises to Roderigo that he shall have Desdemona: "if sanctimony and a frail vow betwixt an erring barbarian and a supersubtle Venetian be not too hard for my wits and all the tribe of hell, thou shalt enjoy her" (I.iii.350–354). "Tribe of hell" is somewhat rhetorical; the real antagonist is "my wits"—set against the rival power of love, which he cannot tolerate. But even beyond Iago's own conscious battle, his brains against a vow of love, there is a symbolic conflict in the heart of the drama. And for this symbolic conflict Iago, again assuaging the pain of Roderigo, gives us a name by the words he chooses:

Thou know'st we work by wit, and not by witchcraft;
And wit depends on dilatory time.   (II.iii.372–73)

Wit and *witchcraft:* in this antithesis is the symbolic structure, or the thematic form, of *Othello*. By *witchcraft,* of course, Iago means conjuring and spells to induce desired actions and states of being. But as a whole the play dramatically develops another meaning of *witchcraft* and forces upon us an awareness of that meaning: *witchcraft* is a metaphor for love. The "magic in the web" of the handkerchief, as Othello calls it (III.iv.69), extends into the fiber of the whole drama. Love is a magic bringer of harmony between those who are widely different (Othello and Desdemona), and it can be a magic transformer of personality; its ultimate power is fittingly marked by the miracle of Desdemona's voice speaking from beyond life, pronouncing forgiveness to the Othello who has murdered her (V.ii.123–4). Such events lie outside the realm of "wit"

—of the reason, cunning, and wisdom on which Iago rests—and this wit must be hostile to them. Wit must always strive to conquer witchcraft, and there is an obvious sense in which it should conquer; but there is another sense in which, though it try, it should not and cannot succeed; that, we may say, is what *Othello* is "about." Whatever disasters it causes, wit fails in the end: it cuts itself off in a demonic silence before death (Iago's "last words" are "I never will speak word"—(V.ii.300), while witchcraft—love—speaks after death (Desdemona's last farewell).

Between the poles of wit and witchcraft, all the major characters in the play find their orientation. Emilia looks at a good deal of life through the Iago wit, but yields to the love for Desdemona which transforms her into a sacrificial figure. Under the influence of the Iago wit, Cassio, acting through Desdemona's friendly love, tries to high-pressure Othello into a charity (a revocation of his dismissal) that could come only spontaneously. Roderigo falls under the witchcraft of love, but, instead of letting it take effect as it might, to bring him death or renunciation, chooses Iago's wit game and plays for what he cannot have. Emilia and Desdemona, dying, are not creatures of wit: what we have called witchcraft has led them to a trans-rational achievement of spirit.

The conflict of Desdemona and Iago for Othello can be called the conflict of love and hate, or the conflict of two different potentialities in the soul where both reside. It may also be called the conflict of wit and witchcraft for Othello. Though Othello seems to be all the naïveté of Everyman, and Iago to be all his calculatingness and slyness, Othello gives himself more to wit than to witchcraft because he and Iago, though in different degrees, have much in common—a histrionic bent, an inadequate selfhood that crops up in self-pity and an eye for slights and injuries, an uncriticized instinct to soothe one's own feelings by punishing others (with an air of moral propriety), the need to possess in one's own terms or destroy, an incapacity for love that is the other side of self-love. All this is in another realm from that of witchcraft. When Othello decides to follow Iago and be "wise" and "cunning," he adopts a new code: he will "see" the facts, get the "evidence," "prove" his case against Desdemona, and execute "justice" upon her. This is the program of "wit." Now this is not only utterly inappropriate to the occasion on which, under Iago's tutelage, Othello elects to use it, nor is it simply one of several possible errors; rather he adopts an attitude or belief or style which is the direct antithesis of another mode of thought and feeling which is open to him. He makes that particular wrong choice which is the logical opposite of the right choice open to him. He essays to reason when reason is not relevant: he substitutes a disastrous wit for a saving witchcraft. He could reject Iago's "proof" against Desdemona "by an affirmation of faith," as Winifred Nowottny has put it, "which is beyond reason, by the act of choosing to believe in Desdemona." Othello, the prime beneficiary of witchcraft, might win all its gifts had he the faith that would open him to its action; but he is short on faith, is seduced by wit (the two actions are simply two faces of the same experience), and ruined. He knew the first miracle of love, the thing given without claim, but cut himself off from the greater miracle, the transformation of self into a giver. His final failure is that, though he comes to recognize that he has been witless, he is never capacious enough in spirit to know how fully he has failed or how much he has thrown away. He never sees the full Desdemona witchcraft.

In the light of Desdemona's spiritual wealth—the unfailing love that continues into forgiveness of her murderer —we can understand Iago as a spiritual have-not. Like the have-not in the realm of things who in a materially oriented culture suffers from envy and malice, the spiritual have-not lives in characteristic vices that Shakespeare has analyzed with many-angled perception. The analogy between the material and the spiritual have-not is confirmed by a line in *Lear*, Edmund's "Let me . . . have lands by wit," and by Iago's own addiction to actual theft (of Roderigo's gifts meant for Desdemona). If the analogy fails at one point—that the achievement of spiritual wealth depends on the individual and cannot be essentially helped by ex-

ternal accidents or blocked by external obstacles—that
failure only underscores the failure of the spiritual have-
not. His modes of action are exhaustively canvassed in
Shakespeare's plot and in the poetry of the play. Wit is
Iago's instrument to compensate for what he does not have.
He perversely hates and yet lusts after what he does not
have (Desdemona as a person, and as a symbol of love),
and he undertakes to disparage it, minimize it, debunk it,
and destroy it. Rule-or-ruin becomes rule-by-ruining. He
must fashion the world after his own image: "And knowing what I am, I know what she shall be" (IV.i.75). So it
pleases him to trap (he repeatedly uses the language of
hunting and trapping) those who are unlike himself, by
proclaiming virtues which he does not possess ("honest
Iago," the friend of all), confusing the appearance of
things seeming to act in one way (as light-bringer and
physician during the two nocturnal brawls which he stirs
up) while acting in another (making things "dark," wounding and killing). Noisiness and vulgarity of style become
him, though as a skilled actor he can simulate the amiable,
contained, and discreet adviser and consoler. His most
far-reaching method is to seduce others philosophically—
to woo them from assumptions in which their salvation
might lie (faith in the spiritual quality of others), to baser
assumptions that will destroy them (their freedom to act
in the light of the accepted unregeneracy of all about
them). Iago the moral agent is akin to Iago the philoso-
pher: there is a common element in stealing purses, stealing
good names, and stealing ideas needed for survival.

In sociological terms we might allegorize Iago as the
criminal type, in political as the self-seeking divisive force
or the patrioteer or the power-seeker who will pay any
price, in cultural as the mass-mind, in psychological as all
the impulses that lead to despair of human possibility, in
moral as envy or hate or spiritual hardness (versions of
pride), in mythical as The Enemy—the universal destroyer
of ultimate values. Before all these, he is simply a human
being, the apparent friend and lover of everybody. We
think of these diverse tentative formulations only because
he is so variously and richly set before us as the final

outcome when certain potentialities of Everyman are
freed to develop fully. There is no single way into this
extraordinary characterization. As the spiritual have-not,
Iago is universal, that is, many things at once, and of
many times at once. He is our contemporary, and the
special instances of his temper and style—as distinct from
the Iagoism to which all men are liable—will be clear to
whoever is alert to Shakespeare's abundant formulations.
Seen in a limited and stereotyped form, he is the villain
of all melodrama. He is Elizabethan—as Envy or Machia-
vel. And to go further back still, we see in how many
parts of Dante's *Inferno* he might appear. He could be
placed among the angry and violent. But his truer place
is down among those who act in fraud and malice—the
lowest category of sinner who on earth had least of spiritual
substance and relied most on wit. Here we might put him
on a higher level with the panders, but again it is when
we reach the lower level that he is summoned more
strongly, not once but by group after group: the hypocrites,
the thieves, the evil counselors, the sowers of dissension,
and, at the very bottom of the eighth circle, the imper-
sonators and false witnesses. Finally, in the ninth and
last circle, "damn'd beneath all depth in hell," come the
treacherous. And here at last we go beyond time into
our timeless myths of evil.

By an extraordinary composition of character Shakespeare has made Iago, literally or symbolically, share in
all these modes of evil. And in Iago he has dramatized
Dante's summary analysis: "For where the instrument of
the mind is joined to evil will and potency, men can make
no defense against it." But he has also dramatized the
hidden springs of evil action, the urgency and passion and
immediacy of it. He contemplates, too, the evildoer's
"potency" and man's defenselessness: but these he interprets tragically by making them, not absolute, but
partly dependent on the flaws or desire of the victims
themselves. In the *Othello* world, Iago, seductive as he is,
is not an inevitable teacher. Whoever would, could learn
from Desdemona. He would have the choice of wit or
witchcraft.

NOTES

1. One who is committed to a detailed study of the parts might seize protectively on Edward A. Armstrong's observation, "There is a strange psychological bias which tempts those interested in large issues to belittle detailed work," in *Shakespeare's Imagination* (London, 1946), p. 125n. Cf. G. Wilson Knight's preface to the 4th edition of *The Wheel of Fire* (London: Methuen, 1949), pp. vi–vii. In *Flaming Minister* (Durham: Duke University Press, 1953), G. R. Elliott makes a detailed commentary on individual passages and on their relationships.

2. Cf. L. C. Knights, *Explorations* (New York: Stewart, 1947), p. 31.

3. Cf. E. E. Stoll's phrase, "a tragedy which is also a poem, in which the parts 'mutually support and explain each other' . . ." This is in *Shakespeare and Other Masters* (Cambridge: Harvard University Press, 1940), p. 219. In *Poetry and Drama* (Cambridge: Harvard University Press, 1951), p. 43, T. S. Eliot speaks of the "perfection of verse drama, which would be a design of human action and of words, such as to present at once the two aspects of dramatic and musical order."

4. For numerous examples of images which link separated passages, see W. H. Clemen, *The Development of Shakespeare's Imagery* (Cambridge: Harvard University Press, 1951). Clemen makes a telling comment on the general sense of the interrelatedness of all parts which is created by the imagery (p. 224).

5. D. A. Traversi, *Approach to Shakespeare* (London, 1938), p. 14; and see his whole first chapter. Of *Othello* he says, "Plot and imagery, in fact, are fused as never before" (p. 86). Cf. his "Othello," *The Wind and the Rain*, vi (1950), 268–9. On the importance of the language spoken, the "wording," there are some relevant comments

by E. E. Stoll in *Poets and Playwrights* (Minneapolis: University of Minnesota Press, 1930), pp. 5 ff., 128.

6. Page 162.

7. *The Structure of Literature* (Chicago: University of Chicago Press, 1954), pp. 17, 64.

8. One might speak of an image-system as an inner organism—a part of the whole that could not exist without the whole and yet an entity having parts that function with respect to each other. This would be "a verbal drama" as distinct from "verbal drama" generally. As a created thing it does not "just happen"; nor yet, I believe, is it deliberately blueprinted and executed. One may surmise: a certain image or kind of image "comes up" for a speaker on a certain occasion; then it is felt consciously or semiconsciously to have some relevance to the import of the whole; and it continues to be used (with the varying degrees of consciousness presumably characteristic of the creative process) as a way of exploring character or mood or theme.

9. Cf. Price, *Construction in Shakespeare* (Michigan, 1951), pp. 24 and 35 ff., and George Rylands, "Shakespeare's Poetic Energy," *Proceedings of the British Academy,* xxxvii (1951), 99–119. Note his statement that the "repetition of a word in diverse contexts throughout the play, with its correlatives and associations, often gives the clue to the poetic thought, the *dianoia,* which informs the whole" (p. 102).

10. All italics are my own.

Madelon Gohlke Sprengnether

"I wooed thee with my sword":
Shakespeare's Tragic Paradigms

Traditional textual interpretation founds itself on this
particular understanding of metaphor: a detour to
truth. Not only individual metaphors or systems of
metaphors, but fiction in general is seen as a detour
to a truth that the critic can deliver through her interpretation.

> GAYATRI CHAKRAVORTY SPIVAK,
> translator's preface, *Of Grammatology*

Much of what I have to say about Shakespeare and
about the possibility of a feminist psychoanalytic interpretation of literature, or, for that matter, of culture, depends
on a reading of metaphor. It is metaphor that allows us to
sub-read, to read on the margins of discourse, to analyze
what is latent or implicit in the structures of consciousness
or of a text. A serious feminist critic, moreover, cannot
proceed very far without becoming paranoid, unless she
abandons a strictly intentionalist position. To argue sexism
as a conscious conspiracy becomes both foolish and absurd.
To pursue the implications of metaphor, on the other hand,
in terms of plot, character, and possibly even genre, is to

Madelon Gohlke, "'I wooed thee with my sword': Shakespeare's
Tragic Paradigms," in *The Woman's Part: Feminist Criticism of Shake-
speare*, ed. Carolyn Ruth Swift Lenz, Gayle Greene, and Carol Thomas
Neely (Urbana, Ill.: University of Illinois, 1980), pp. 150–70.

adopt a psychoanalytic strategy that deepens the context of feminist interpretation and reveals the possibility at least of a feminist psychohistory.

Metaphor provides a convenient entrance into a text, as it provides a point of departure for psychoanalytic interpretation because of the way in which vehicle consistently outdistances tenor. The following two lines, from *A Midsummer Night's Dream,* for instance, "Hippolyta, I wooed thee with my sword, / And won thy love, doing thee injuries" (I.i.16–17), convey far more than the simple prose explanation offered in my text: "Theseus had captured Hippolyta when he conquered the Amazons." [1] These lines, in which the sword may be the metaphoric equivalent of the phallus, in which love may be either generated or secured by hostility, and in which the two partners take up sadistic and masochistic postures in relation to one another, are not irrelevant to the concerns of the play. They may be seen to reverberate in the exaggerated submission of Helena to Demetrius, in the humiliation of Titania by Oberon, in the penetration by violence of the language of love. They even bear an oblique relation to the "lamentable comedy" of *Pyramis and Thisbe,* the failed marriage plot contained within the larger structure of successful heterosexual union celebrated at the end of the play.

Metaphor may also elucidate character, as in the case of *Much Ado about Nothing*'s Claudio, whose speech is relatively poor in imagery until it erupts into his condemnation of Hero in the middle of the play, where among other things he claims "But you are more intemperate in your blood / Than Venus, or those pamp'red animals / That rage in savage sensuality" (IV.i.58–60). It is Claudio's suspicious predisposition which composes this violent and disproportioned outburst. It is no accident that the "solution" to this conflict hinges on the fiction that Claudio has killed Hero through his slander. In this sense the conventional marriage plot of Shakespeare's comedy may also be read metaphorically. The prospect of heterosexual union arouses emotional conflicts which give shape to the plot, unleashing a kind of violence which in the comedies remains symbolic, imagined rather than enacted.

I shall, in the following pages, be considering the uses of metaphor in several related ways. In some instances, I will refer to the function of metaphor in individual discourse, assuming that it is this kind of highly charged imagistic expression that offers the most immediate clues to unconscious awareness. I am assuming furthermore that metaphor may be seen to structure action, so that some features of plot may be regarded as expanded metaphors. Moving outward from this premise, I then want to consider the possibility that certain cultural fictions may be read metaphorically, that is, as expressions of unconsciously held cultural beliefs. I am particularly interested in Shakespeare's tragedies, in what seem to me to be shared fictions on the part of the heroes about femininity and about their own vulnerability in relation to women, fictions interweaving women with violence, generating a particular kind of heterosexual dilemma.

The primacy of metaphor in the structures of individual consciousness, as in the collective fiction of the plot, appears in an early tragedy, *Romeo and Juliet*, where the failure of the play to achieve the generic status of comedy may be read as the result of the way in which heterosexual relations are imagined. In the conversation between the servants Sampson and Gregory, sexual intercourse, through a punning reference to the word "maidenhead," comes to be described as a kind of murder.[2]

> *Sampson.* 'Tis all one. I will show myself a tyrant. When I have fought with the men, I will be civil with the maids—I will cut off their heads.
> *Gregory.* The heads of the maids?
> *Sampson.* Ay, the heads of the maids or their maidenheads. Take it in what sense thou wilt. (I.i.23–28)

To participate in the masculine ethic of this play is to participate in the feud, which defines relations among men as intensely competitive, and relations with women as controlling and violent, so that women in Sampson's language "being the weaker vessels, are ever thrust to the wall" (I.i.

17–18). That Romeo initially rejects this ethic would seem to redefine the nature and structure of male/female relationships. What is striking about the relationship between Romeo and Juliet, however, is the extent to which it anticipates and ultimately incorporates violence.

Both lovers have a lively imagination of disaster. While Romeo ponders "some vile forfeit of untimely death" (I.iv.111), Juliet speculates "If he is marrièd, / My grave is like to be my wedding bed" (I.v.136–37). Premonition, for both, has the force of self-fulfilling prophecy. While Romeo seeks danger by courting Juliet, and death by threatening suicide in the wake of Tybalt's death, Juliet, under pressure, exclaims: "I'll to my wedding bed; / And death, not Romeo, take my maidenhead!" (III.ii.136–37). Read metaphorically, the plot validates the perception expressed variously in the play that love kills.

The paradigm offered by *Romeo and Juliet*, with some modifications, may be read in the major tragedies as well. Here, the structures of male dominance, involving various strategies of control, expressed in the language of prostitution, rape, and murder, conceal deeper structures of fear, in which women are perceived as powerful, and the heterosexual relation one which is either mutually violent or at least deeply threatening to the man.

Murder in the Bedroom: *Hamlet* and *Othello*

Hamlet's violent behavior in his mother's bedroom expresses some of the violence of his impulses toward her. Obsessed as he is with sexual betrayal, the problem of revenge for him is less a matter of killing Claudius than one of not killing his mother.[3] Hamlet's anger against women, based on his perception of his mother's conduct, finds expression in the language of prostitution in his violent outburst against Ophelia: "I have heard of your paintings, well enough. God hath given you one face, and you make yourselves another. You jig and amble, and you lisp; you nickname God's creatures and make your wantonness your ignorance. Go to, I'll no more on't; it hath made me mad" (III.i.143–48). It is painting which makes women two-faced, which allows them to deceive, to wear the mask of chastity, while lust "Will sate itself in a celestial bed / And prey on garbage" (I.v.56–57). Like whores, all women cannot be trusted.

The paradox of prostitution in the tragedies is based on the masculine perception of the prostitute as not so much the victim as the agent of exploitation. If women are classed as prostitutes and treated as sexual objects, it is because they are deeply feared as sexually untrustworthy, as creatures whose intentions and desires are fundamentally unreadable. Thus, while Helen in *Troilus and Cressida* is verbally degraded, as the Trojans discuss her in terms of soiled goods and contaminated meat, she is, through her infidelity to Menelaus, the source of the sexual pride and humiliation that animate the entire conflict between the two warring nations. Honor among men in this play, though it takes the form of combat, is ultimately a sexual matter, depending largely on the fidelity or infidelity of women. For a man to be betrayed by a woman is to be humiliated or dishonored. To recover his honor he must destroy the man or woman who is responsible for his humiliation, for placing him in a position of vulnerability.

In *Hamlet,* it is the player queen who most clearly articulates the significance attributed to feminine betrayal. "A second time I kill my husband dead / When second husband kisses me in bed" (III.ii.188–89). It hardly matters whether Gertrude was implicated in the actual death of the elder Hamlet. Adultery is itself a form of violence and as great a crime. Hamlet, who reacts as an injured husband in seeking revenge against Claudius, also seeks retribution against his mother. Not having any sanction to kill his mother, however, he must remind himself to "speak daggers to her, but use none" (404). That his manner suggests physical violence is confirmed by Gertrude's response: "What wilt thou do? Thou wilt not murder me? / Help, ho!" (III.iv.22–23). It is at this point that the violence that Hamlet seeks to contain in his attitude toward his mother is deflected onto another object presumed to be appropriate.

This single act of displaced violence, moreover, has

further ramifications in terms of Hamlet's relation to
Ophelia, whose conflicted responses to the killing of her
father by her lover increase the burden of double messages
she has already received from the men in the play and
culminate in her madness and death. It is not his mother
whom Hamlet kills (Claudius takes care of that) but
Ophelia. Only when she is dead, moreover, is he clearly
free to say that he loved her. Othello, in whom are more
specifically and vividly portrayed the pathology of jealousy,
the humiliation and rage that plague a man supposedly
dishonored by the woman he loves, will say of Desdemona
late in the play "I will kill thee, / And love thee after"
(V.ii.18–19).

If I seem to be arguing that the tragedies are largely
about the degeneration of heterosexual relationships, or
marriages that fail, it is because I am reading the development from the comedies through the problem plays and
the major tragedies in terms of an explosion of the sexual
tensions that threaten without rupturing the surface of the
earlier plays. Throughout, a woman's power is less social
or political (though it may have social and political ramifications) than emotional, expressed in her capacity to give
or to withhold love. In a figure like Isabella the capacity to
withhold arouses lust and a will to power in someone like
Angelo, whose enforcing tactics amount to rape. In Portia,
the threat of infidelity, however jokingly presented, is a
weapon in her struggle with Antonio for Bassanio's alle-
giance. Male resistance, comic and exaggerated in Bene-
dick, sullen and resentful in Bertram, stems from fears of
occupying a position of weakness, taking in essence a
"feminine" posture in relation to a powerful woman.

The feminine posture for a male character is that of the
betrayed, and it is the man in this position who portrays
women as whores. Since Iago occupies this position in relation to Othello, it makes sense that he seeks to destroy him,
in the same way that Othello seeks to destroy the agent of
his imagined betrayal, Desdemona. There is no reason to
suppose, moreover, that Iago's consistently degraded view
of women conceals any less hostile attitude in his actual
relations with women. He, after all, like Othello, kills his

wife. The difference between the two men lies not in their fear and mistrust of women but in the degree to which they are able to accept an emotional involvement. It is Othello, not Iago, who wears his heart on his sleeve, "for daws to peck at" (I.i.62). Were it not for Othello's initial vulnerability to Desdemona he would not be susceptible to Iago's machinations. Having made himself vulnerable, moreover, he attaches an extraordinary significance to the relation. "And when I love thee not, / Chaos is come again" (III.iii.91–92). "But there where I have garnered up my heart, / Where either I must live or bear no life, / The fountain from the which my current runs / Or else dries up" (IV.ii.56–59).

Once Othello is convinced of Desdemona's infidelity (much like Claudio, on the flimsiest of evidence), he regards her, not as a woman who has committed a single transgression, but as a whore, one whose entire behavior may be explained in terms of lust. As such, he may humiliate her in public, offer her services to the Venetian ambassadors, pass judgment on her, and condemn her to death. Murder, in this light, is a desperate attempt to control. It is Desdemona's power to hurt which Othello seeks to eliminate by ending her life. While legal and social sanctions may be invoked against the prostitute, the seemingly virtuous woman suspected of adultery may be punished by death. In either case it is the fear or pain of victimization on the part of the man that leads to his victimization of women. It is those who perceive themselves to be powerless who may be incited to the acts of greatest violence.

The paradox of violence in *Othello*, not unlike that in *Macbeth*, is that the exercise of power turns against the hero. In this case the murder of a woman leads to self-murder, and the hero dies attesting to the erotic destructiveness at the heart of his relation with Desdemona. "I kissed thee ere I killed thee. No way but this, / Killing myself, to die upon a kiss" (V.ii.357–58). If murder may be a loving act, love may be a murdering act, and consummation of such a love possible only through the death of both parties.

"Of Woman Born": *Lear* and *Macbeth*

The fantasy of feminine betrayal that animates the drama of *Othello* may be seen to conceal or to be coordinate with deep fantasies of maternal betrayal in *Macbeth* and *Lear*.[4] Here the emphasis falls not so much on the adult heterosexual relation (though there are such relations) as on the mother/son or the fantasy of the mother/son relation. In these plays, the perception of the masculine consciousness is that to be feminine is to be powerless, specifically in relation to a controlling or powerful woman. For Lear, rage as an expression of power acts as a defense against this awareness, while tears threaten not only the dreaded perception of himself as feminine and hence weak but also the breakdown of his psychic order.

> Life and death, I am ashamed
> That thou hast power to shake my manhood thus!
> That these hot tears, which break from me perforce,
> Should make thee worth them. Blasts and fogs upon thee!
> (I.iv.298–301)

> You think I'll weep.
> No, I'll not weep.
> I have full cause of weeping, but this heart
> Shall break into a hundred thousand flaws
> Or ere I'll weep. O Fool, I shall go mad! (II.iv.279–83)

> O, let me not be mad, not mad, sweet heaven!
> Keep me in temper, I would not be mad! (I.v.45–46)

It is not Lear who annihilates his enemies, calling down curses on the reproductive organs of Goneril and Regan, but rather Lear who is being banished by the women on whom he had depended for nurturance. It is they who are the agents of power and destruction, allied with the storm, and he like Edgar, who is "unaccommodated man," a "poor, bare, forked animal" (III.iv.105–7), naked and vulnerable. That the condition of powerlessness gives rise to compassion in Lear is part of his dignity as a tragic hero. It does not, however, alter his perceptions of women as

either good or bad mothers. If the banishment of Cordelia
initiates a process by which Lear becomes psychotic, moreover, it may be argued that her return is essential to the
restoration of his sanity. The presence or absence of
Cordelia, like Othello's faith in Desdemona's fidelity,
orders the hero's psychic universe. When Cordelia dies,
Lear must either believe that she is not dead or die with
her, being unable to withstand the condition of radical
separation imposed by death.

The most powerful image of separation in *King Lear*,
that of the child who is banished by his mother, is that of
birth. "We came crying hither: / Thou know'st, the first
time that we smell the air / We wawl and cry" (IV.vi.
178–80). In this sense, the mother's first act of betrayal
may be that of giving birth, the violent expulsion of her
infant into a hostile environment. In other passages, a
woman's body itself is perceived as a hostile environment.

But to the girdle do the gods inherit,
Beneath is all the fiend's.
There's hell, there's darkness, there is the sulphurous pit.
                                            (IV.vi.126–29)

The dark and vicious place where thee he got
Cost him his eyes.   (V.iii.173–74)

Intercourse imaged as violent intrusion into a woman's
body may be designed to minimize the cost.

If it is birth itself, the condition of owing one's life to a
woman and the ambivalence attending an awareness of
dependence on women in general, which structures much
of Lear's relations to his daughters, *Macbeth* may be read
in terms of a systematic attempt on the part of the hero to
deny such an awareness. The world constructed by Macbeth attempts to deny not only the values of trust and
hospitality, perceived as essentially feminine, but to eradi-
cate femininity itself.[5] Macbeth reads power in terms of a
masculine mystique that has no room for maternal values,
as if the conscious exclusion of these values would elimi-

nate all conditions of dependence, making him in effect invulnerable. To be born of woman, as he reads the witches' prophecy, is to be mortal. Macbeth's program of violence, involving murder and pillage in his kingdom and the repression of anything resembling compassion or remorse within, is designed, like Coriolanus's desperate militarism, to make him author of himself.

The irony of *Macbeth,* of course, is that in his attempt to make himself wholly "masculine," uncontaminated, so to speak, by the womb, he destroys all source of value: honor, trust, and, to his dismay, fertility itself. It is his deep personal anguish that he is childless. The values associated with women and children, which he considers unmanly, come to be perceived as the source of greatest strength. It is procreation, in this play, rather than violence, which confers power. "The seeds of Banquo kings!" (III.i.70). To kill a child or to imagine such an act, as Lady Macbeth does in expressing contempt for her husband's vacillations, is to betray not only the bonds of human society, but to betray one's deepest self. To reject the conditions of weakness and the dependence is to make oneself weak and dependent. Macbeth's relentless pursuit of power masks his insecurities, his anxieties, and ultimately his impotence. *Macbeth,* more clearly than any of the other tragedies, with the possible exception of *Coriolanus,* enacts the paradox of power in which the hero's equation of masculinity with violence as a denial or defense against femininity leads to his destruction.

Macbeth's attempt to avoid the perception of Lear that "we cry that we are come / To this great stage of fools" (IV.vi.182–83), that the human infant is radically defenseless and dependent on the nurturance of a woman, gradually empties his life of meaning, leading to his perception of it as "a tale / Told by an idiot . . . / Signifying nothing" (V.v.26–28). Of all the tragic heroes, moreover, Macbeth is the most isolated in his death, alienated from himself, his countrymen, his queen. He has become what he most feared, the plaything of powerful feminine forces, betrayed by the "instruments of darkness," the three witches.

"The Heart of Loss:" *Antony and Cleopatra*

Interwoven into the patriarchal structure of Shakespeare's tragedies is an equally powerful matriarchal vision. The two are even, I would argue, aspects of one another, both proceeding from the masculine consciousness of feminine betrayal. Both inspire a violence of response on the part of the hero against individual women, but more important, against the hero's ultimately damaging perception of himself as womanish. The concurrence of these themes is particularly evident in *Antony and Cleopatra,* a play that recalls the ritual marriage conclusion of the comedies as it deepens the sexual dilemma of the tragic hero.

Antony's relation both to Cleopatra and to Caesar may be read in terms of his anxieties about dominance, his fear of self-loss in any intimate encounter. Early in the play, Cleopatra uses this perception to her advantage by suggesting that for Antony to respond to the Roman messengers is to acknowledge his submission either to Caesar or to Fulvia. Her own tactics, of course, are manipulative and a form of dominance that Antony himself recognizes. "These strong Egyptian fetters I must break / Or lose myself in dotage" (I.ii.117–18). The advice of the soothsayer to Antony concerning his proximity to Caesar is similar in structure if not in content: "near him thy angel / Becomes afeard, as being o'erpow'red" (II.iii.20–21). When Antony returns to Egypt, he is in effect "o'er pow'red" by Cleopatra. "O'er my spirit / Thy full supremacy thou knew'st" (III.xi.58–59). "You did know / How much you were my conqueror, and that / My sword, made weak by my affection, would / Obey it on all cause" (65–68). Antony, like Romeo earlier, perceives himself as having been feminized by love. "O sweet Juliet, / Thy beauty hath made me effeminate / And in my temper soft'ned valor's steel!" (III.i.115–17). "O, thy vile lady! / She has robbed me of my sword" (IV.xiv.22–23).

If affection makes Antony weak, it also makes him suspicious of Cleopatra's fidelity. "For I am sure, / Though you can guess what temperance should be, / You know not what it is" (III.xiii.120–22). He falls easy prey to the con-

viction that Cleopatra has betrayed him to Caesar, making
him the subject of sexual as well as political humiliation.
"O, that I were / Upon the hill of Basan to outroar / The
hornèd herd!" (126–28). In this light, Cleopatra becomes
a "witch," a "spell," a "triple-turned whore."

> O this false soul of Egypt! This grave charm,
> Whose eye becked forth my wars, and called them home,
> Whose bosom was my crownet, my chief end,
> Like a right gypsy hath at fast and loose
> Beguiled me, to the very heart of loss.
> What, Eros, Eros!   (IV.xii.25–30)

Antony, under the power of erotic attachment, like Othello
feels himself to have been utterly betrayed. Under the impact of this loss, moreover, his sense of psychic integrity
begins to disintegrate. "Here I am Antony, / Yet cannot
hold this visible shape, my knave" (IV.xiv.13–14). Chaos
is come again.

While the fiction of Cleopatra's death restores Antony's
faith in her love, it does not restore his energy for life.
Rather, the withdrawal of her presence destroys any vestige
of interest he has in the world of the living. "Now all
labor / Mars what it does; yea, very force entangles / Itself with strength" (IV.xiv.47–49). It is Cleopatra who not
only dominates Antony's emotional life, but who invests
his world with meaning. The fact that she, unlike Juliet,
Ophelia, Desdemona, Cordelia, and Lady Macbeth, dies
so long after her lover, not only reveals her as a complex
figure in her own right, but also attests to her power to
give imaginative shape to the hero's reality.

Cleopatra in many ways is the epitome of what is hated,
loved, and feared in a woman by Shakespeare's tragic
heroes. She is, on the one hand, the woman who betrays, a
Circe, an Acrasia, an Eve, the Venus of *Venus and Adonis*.
To submit to her, or to be seduced by her, is to die. She is
the player queen, for whom adultery is also murder. She
is a Goneril, a Lady Macbeth, a non-nurturing mother.
What she takes, on the other hand, she also has the power
to give. She is imaginative, fertile, identified with the pro-

creative processes of the Nile. If Antony lives in our imagination, it is because of her "conception" of him. In this sense, she, like Desdemona and Cordelia, is the hero's point of orientation, his source of signification in the world. Union with her is both celebrated, as a curious comic counterpoint to the tragic structure of double suicide, and portrayed as a literal impossibility. Moreover, for this sexually powerful woman to escape censure, the fate of a Cressida or a Helen, she must negate her own strength, she must die. While Theseus's phallic sword, in Antony's hands, turns against himself, Cleopatra, like Juliet, will accept death "as a lover's pinch, / Which hurts, and is desired" (V.ii.295–96). Throughout Shakespeare's tragedies the imagery of heterosexual union involves the threat of mutual or self-inflicted violence.

Looked at from one angle, what Shakespeare's tragedies portray is the anguish and destruction attendant on a fairly conventional and culturally supported set of fictions regarding heterosexual encounter. The tragedies, as I read them, do not themselves support these fictions except to the extent that they examine them with such acute attention. The values that emerge from these plays are, if anything, "feminine," values dissociated from the traditional masculine categories of force and politics, focused instead on the significance of personal relationships, or the fact of human relatedness: the values of feeling, of kinship, of loyalty, friendship, and even romantic love. That the recognition of these values entails the destruction of the hero and everyone who matters to him attests perhaps to a kind of cultural determinism, or at least to the very great difficulty of re-imagining habitual modes of behavior. It is the basis in cultural fictions of certain kinds of heterosexual attitudes to which I now wish to turn.

On the Margins of Patriarchal Discourse

Shakespeare's tragic paradigms offer the possibility of a deconstructive reading of the rape metaphor that informs Theseus's words to his captured queen.[6] Violence against women as an aspect of the structure of male dominance in

Shakespeare's plays may be seen to obscure deeper patterns of conflict in which women as lovers, and perhaps more important as mothers, are perceived as radically untrustworthy. In this structure of relation, it is women who are regarded as powerful and men who strive to avoid an awareness of their vulnerability in relation to women, a vulnerability in which they regard themselves as "feminine." It is in this sense that one may speak of a matriarchal substratum or subtext within the patriarchal text. The matriarchal substratum itself, however, is not feminist. What it does in Shakespeare's tragedies is provide a rationale for the manifest text of male dominance while constituting an avenue of continuity between these plays and the comedies in which women more obviously wield power.

The preceding analysis may be seen, moreover, to parallel the movement of psychoanalytic theory from an emphasis on oedipal to pre-oedipal stages of development. Roughly speaking, the shift has occurred in terms of a decrease of concern with father/son relations and a corresponding increase of concern with mother/son relations. (Although the shift from father to mother is clear in the work of such theorists as John Bowlby, Melanie Klein, Margaret Mahler, and D. W. Winnicott, the child or infant, partly for grammatical reasons, tends to be regarded as male.)[7] Certainly it may be said that the theories of object-relations, narcissism, schizophrenia, and separation-individuation have more to do with the child's early relations with his mother than with his father. Whether or not these theories are read in consonance with Freud's formulation of the Oedipus complex, the shift in focus relocates the discussion of certain issues. This relocation, in turn, reveals new interpretive possibilities. Specifically, it reopens the question of femininity.

A deconstructive reading of the rape metaphor in Shakespeare's tragedies leads directly or indirectly to a discussion of the masculine perception of femininity as weakness. The macho mystique thus becomes a form of "masculine protest," or a demonstration of phallic power in the face of a threatened castration. It is for the male hero, however, that femininity signifies weakness, while actual women are perceived by him as enormously powerful, specifically in their maternal functions. It is not the female herself who is perceived as weak, but rather the feminized male. To project this problem back onto women, as Freud does when in his discussions of femininity he portrays the little girl as perceiving herself castrated, is to present it as incapable of resolution.[8] If femininity itself is defined as the condition of lack, of castration, then there is no way around the masculine equation that to be feminine is to be castrated, or as Antony puts it, to be robbed of one's sword.

It is the masculine consciousness, therefore, that defines femininity as weakness and institutes the structures of male dominance designed to defend against such an awareness. Shakespeare's tragedies, as I read them, may be viewed as a vast commentary on the absurdity and destructiveness of this defensive posture. While Shakespeare may be said to affirm the values of feeling and vulnerability associated with femininity, however, he does not in dramatic terms dispel the anxiety surrounding the figure of the feminized male. At this point, dramatic metaphors, I would say, intersect with cultural metaphors.[9]

Freud's views of femininity may be useful to the extent to which they articulate some deeply held cultural convictions. In one sense, what they do is reveal the basis of some powerful cultural metaphors, so powerful in fact that they continue to find formulation in the midst of our vastly different social and intellectual context. In the midst of profound structural changes in habits of philosophic and scientific thinking, as a culture we cling to the language of presence and absence, language and silence, art and nature, reason and madness to describe the relations between the terms masculine and feminine. It is as though the breakdown of hierarchical modes of thought, of vertical ways of imagining experience, finds its deepest resistance in our habits of imagining the relations between the sexes. Some, like the Jungian James Hillman, would even argue that in order to effect real changes in our intellectual formulations of reality, we must find ways of reimagining femininity.[10] Sexual politics may lie at the heart of human culture, of our constantly shifting and evolving world views.

The preceding discussion, of course, rests on assumptions to which Freud would not have subscribed, chief among which is a hypothesis concerning the relation between cultural metaphors and the concept of a cultural unconscious. What I would like to propose is that the notion of the unconscious may be culture specific, that is to say, that the guiding metaphors of a given society or culture may legitimately be seen to express the structure of its unconscious assumptions, in the same way that the metaphoric structure of individual discourse may be seen to convey some of the unconscious freight of a given life. If Thomas Kuhn is correct in assuming that scientific revolutions are the result of paradigm shifts, or profound changes in our habits of imagining the world, then it may also be possible to consider the unconscious implications of certain habits of imagining.[11] Literary conventions may then be viewed as aspects of these imaginative habits, as codifications of a certain spectrum of unconscious attitudes, at the same time that they change and evolve, live and die according to their relation to the society out of which they arise and to which they respond. Cultural changes, to pursue the implications of Kuhn's argument, are in effect profound metaphoric changes which in turn involve changes in the structuring of the unconscious.

Literary history, may, in this light, be read psychologically. The questions one might ask then would concern the spectrum of psychic needs served by specific conventions and genres. Tracing the uses of a convention would then also yield a literary version of psychohistory. To offer an example close to the subject of this essay, I would like to pursue briefly some of the ramifications of the rhetoric of courtly love.

It is interesting to observe the language of de Rougement, who is so careful to situate the courtly love phenomenon in a historical sense, when he refers to the rhetorical trope of love as war. "There is no need, for example, to invoke Freudian theories in order to see that the war instinct and eroticism are fundamentally allied: it is so perfectly *obvious* from the common figurative use of language." [12] Obvious to whom? Is the war instinct, for instance, perceived as an aspect of the feminine psyche? Here the common (and to many readers unquestioned) assumption that reference to the male of the species includes women may be seen to obscure a process by which a fundamentally "masculine" attitude is proposed as a universal norm. More important, however, is the interpretive process by which de Rougemont reads a metaphor specific to a certain set of conventions, albeit powerful ones, as an inalterable aspect of the unconscious life of the species. "All this confirms the natural—that is to say, the physiological —connexion between the sexual and fighting instincts." [13]

It is this supposedly natural "connexion between the sexual and fighting instincts" that structures the language of the courtly love lyric, as it structures the language of sexual encounter in Shakespeare. To term this rhetoric "conventional" is not to demean it but rather to call attention to its psychological power (which de Rougemont himself agrees exists) at the same time that one recognizes its mutability, its historicity. Images of sexual intercourse as an act of violence committed against women run deep in our culture. The depth and persistence of these images, however, may tell us more about the anxieties of a culture in which femininity is conceived as castration and in which women are perceived paradoxically as a source of maternal power than it does about the actual or possible relations between the sexes.

Toward a Feminist Discourse

And, as I have hinted before, deconstruction must also take into account the lack of sovereignty of the critic himself. Perhaps this "will to ignorance" is simply a matter of attitude, a realization that one's choice of evidence is provisional, a self-distrust, a distrust of one's own power, the control of one's vocabulary, a shift from the phallocentric to the hymeneal.

GAYATRI CHAKRAVORTY SPIVAK,
translator's preface, *Of Grammatology*

Literary history, finally, is an aspect of cultural history. Both attest to changing patterns of awareness, to the constant refiguring of our relation to our specific location in time and space, to our own historicity. If individual history, as Ortega y Gasset writes, may be conceived as a process of casting and living out or living through metaphors of the self, is it not possible to imagine cultural history in similar terms?[14] To interpret these metaphors, to read on the margins of discourse, is not only to engage in a process characteristic of psychoanalytic interpretation but also to become engaged in a fundamentally historical process, that of making what is unconscious conscious and thus altering and displacing the location of the unconscious. This process, obviously akin to that of psychotherapy, is not to be perceived statically as an attempt to eliminate the unconscious but rather as one to dislodge it, to transform its metaphoric base.

Psychoanalytic theory in this sense may also be read in the historical dimension, as a means of reading the unconscious figurings of a given life within a specific cultural moment. As such, it will of course be subject to change and will of course to some extent serve the interests of the society that supports it. I am not arguing here against psychoanalytic theory in any sense but rather *for* a recognition of its historicity.[15] While Freud's elaboration of the Oedipus complex may have served to assuage the neurotic dilemmas of his society, it does not serve the needs of contemporary feminism. In a society like ours in which most women can expect to work outside the home for a significant part of their lives, and to bear fewer than three children, the interpretive myths offered by Freud for women are increasingly pathological. In order to be useful, the theory must bear a demonstrable relation to perceived reality. To argue that the social reality of women should be altered in order to fit the theory is not only reactionary, but naïve. It would make more sense to pursue the directions of contemporary psychoanalytic theory toward a redefinition of femininity, assuming as I do that implicit within the current focus on the mother/child relation is a reawakening of interest in the question of femininity. There are even some theorists, like Dorothy Dinnerstein, who would argue that such a reformulation is necessary for cultural survival, given the destructiveness in political terms of the masculine mystique.[16]

What then, in psychoanalytic terms, would constitute the beginnings of feminist discourse? How is a woman, according to the painful elaborations of Julia Kristeva and others, to avoid the Scylla of silence or madness and the Charybdis of alienated or masculine discourse?[17] Gayatri Spivak has lately been suggesting that what we need is something like a Copernican revolution from the phallocentric formulation of femininity as absence to a gynocentric language of presence.[18] If it makes sense that the male child should perceive his own sex as primary and difference as an inferior version of himself, then it makes as much sense that the little girl should also initially perceive her sex as primary. That each sex should take itself as the norm is perhaps part of the Ptolemaic universe of children which must undergo several stages of decentering before maturity. Not to undergo this process of decentering is to elaborate structures of dominance and submission in which dominance becomes the mask of weakness and submission a subversive strategy in the mutual struggle for power. For a woman to read herself obliquely through the patriarchal discourse as "other" is to assent to this structure. For a critic, male or female, to read this discourse as representative of the true nature of masculinity or femininity is to accept this structure. For a femininist critic to deconstruct this discourse is simultaneously to recognize her own historicity and to engage in the process of dislocation of the unconscious by which she begins to affirm her own reality.

NOTES

1. *A Midsummer Night's Dream, The Complete Signet Classic Shakespeare,* ed. Sylvan Barnet (New York: Harcourt Brace Jovanovich, 1963, 1972), p. 530. Quotations from Shakespeare in this essay refer to this edition.

2. Two critics have dealt specifically with the relation between sex and violence in this play. A. K. Nardo notes that "To the youths who rekindle the feud on a point of honor, sex, aggression, and violence are inextricably united." While Juliet undergoes an extraordinary process of development, Nardo argues, she is ultimately unable to survive in this hostile atmosphere and is finally "thrust to the wall by the phallic sword her society has exalted." "Romeo and Juliet Up Against the Wall," *Paunch*, 48–49 (1977), 127–31. Coppélia Kahn in a more extensive consideration of this subject relates the ethic of the feud, in which sex and violence are linked, to the patriarchal structure of the society, commenting on the extent to which the conclusion of the play, associating death with sexual consummation, is also contained within this structure. Fate is thus not only a result of powerful social forces, but also of the individual subjective responses to these forces. "Coming of Age in Verona," *Modern Language Studies*, 8 (1977–78), 5–22, reprinted in this anthology.

3. Theodore Lidz represents Hamlet as torn between the impulse to kill his mother for having betrayed his father and the desire to win her to a state of repentence and renewed chastity. My reading of Hamlet is very much indebted to his analysis in *Hamlet's Enemy: Madness and Myth in Hamlet* (New York: Basic Books, 1975).

4. Murray Schwartz discusses the difficulty of the hero's recognition of his relation to a nurturing woman in "Shakespeare through Contemporary Psychoanalysis," *Hebrew University Studies in Literature*, 5 (1977), 182–98. While Lear's dilemma, according to Schwartz, results from a "refusal to mourn the loss of maternal provision" (p. 192), Macbeth's difficulty may be seen as the result of an attempt to usurp maternal functions and to control the means of nurturance himself.

5. My discussion of the ways in which masculinity and femininity are perceived in this play is indebted to Cleanth Brooks's classic essay on *Macbeth*, "The Naked Babe and the Cloak of Manliness," in *The Well Wrought Urn* (1947; rpt. London: Dobson Books, 1968), pp. 17–39. For

Brooks, it is Macbeth's war on children which reveals most clearly his own weakness and desperation. In Brooks's view, the issue of manliness is related ultimately to the theme of humanity or lack of it, but he does not raise questions about masculine and feminine stereotypes.

6. I would assent to the following description by Gayatri Spivak of the task of deconstruction: "To locate the promising marginal text, to disclose the undecidable moment, to pry it loose, with the positive lever of the signifier, to reverse the resident hierarchy, only to displace it; to dismantle in order to reconstitute what is always already inscribed. Deconstruction in a nutshell." Jacques Derrida, *Of Grammatology,* translator's preface (Baltimore: Johns Hopkins University Press, 1976), p. lxxvii. While Spivak points out that there is no end to this process in that the work of deconstruction is itself subject to deconstruction, she also notes that "as she deconstructs, all protestations to the contrary, the critic necessarily assumes that she at least, and for the time being, means what she says," p. lxxvii. While it may not be strictly necessary to borrow this terminology for the reading I am proposing, it may be useful to observe that any large-scale reinterpretation, from a minority position, of a majority view of reality must appear at least in the eyes of some as a "deconstruction."

7. Here, the problem inherent in the use of the masculine pronoun to refer to both sexes emerges. Textually speaking, the construction often obscures a shift of consideration from the development of the infant, male or female, to the exclusive development of the male infant. This convention is related to the cultural assumption by which the male of the species is taken as a norm, of which the female then becomes a variant. To remove this convention would not merely introduce a stylistic awkwardness (for some people at least), it would also reveal a fundamental awkwardness in the structure of an author's argument. While the male pronoun often *is* used generically to indicate both men and women, its use frequently serves to exclude consideration of the female without calling attention to the process by which she has been removed from the discussion.

8. Although Freud approaches the subject of femininity from different angles in his three major discussions of it, there is no question that he links the process of feminine development indissolubly to the recognition on the part of the little girl that she is castrated. It would seem at least reasonable to argue, however, that the presence or absence of a penis is of far greater significance to the boy or man, who feels himself subject to the threat of its removal, than it could ever be to the girl or woman, for whom such a threat can have little anatomical meaning. I wonder too, why, in Freud's argument, a little girl would be inspired to give up the manifestly satisfying activity of masturbation on the basis of the illusion of a loss—the assumption perhaps that she might have had more pleasure if she had once had a penis, of which she seems mysteriously to have been deprived? The problem which gives rise to these baroque speculations is, of course, Freud's assumption that there must be some reason why the little girl would withdraw her love from her mother in order to bestow it upon her father. Freud can imagine no other reason than the little girl's recognition of her own inferiority and thus "penis envy," and her resentment of her mother, equally deprived, for not having provided her with the desired organ. There can be no heterosexual love, in this account, without the theory of feminine castration. One can understand, from this vantage point, why Freud was reluctant to give it up. See "Some Psychical Consequences of the Anatomical Distinction between the Sexes" (1925), "Female Sexuality" (1931), and "Femininity" (1933), *Standard Edition*, trans. and ed. James Strachey (London: Hogarth Press, 1961, 1964), XIX, 241–60; XXI, 221–46; XXII, 112–35. For various critiques of Freud, see also Roy Shafer, "Problems in Freud's Psychology of Women," *Journal of the American Psychoanalytic Association*, 22 (1974), 459–85; *Women and Analysis*, ed. Jean Strouse (New York: Grossman, 1974); *Psychoanalysis and Women*, ed. Jean Baker Miller (Baltimore: Penguin Books, 1973).

9. One might wish to argue that social, psychic, and literary structures are so intimately interwoven that the rela-

tion between plot and culture is like that between Hamlet and his fate, between a text which is given and that which is generated, enacted, in part, chosen. With this in mind, one might begin to speak of "patriarchal plots," the complex set of figures by which Western culture has elaborated its relation to the structures by which it lives. The question then becomes the extent to which a powerful social movement warps, flexes, alters, reimagines these essential structures, how genres are born, how transformed.

10. James Hillman, *The Myth of Analysis: Three Essays in Archetypal Psychology* (Evanston: Northwestern University Press, 1972), pp. 215–98.

11. Thomas Kuhn, *The Structure of Scientific Revolutions* (Chicago: University of Chicago Press, 1966).

12. Denis de Rougemont, *Love in the Western World,* trans. Montgomery Belgion (New York: Harcourt Brace, 1940, 1956), p. 243. I have chosen the passages from de Rougemont because they are central to the elucidation of the courtly love tradition and because they are so clearly, though unintentionally, biased. A more contemporary (and more complex) example of the same kind of bias might be found in the concluding chapters of Leo Bersani's *A Future for Astyanax: Character and Desire in Literature* (Boston: Little, Brown, 1976).

13. De Rougemont, *Love in the Western World,* p. 244.

14. Ortega y Gasset, *History as a System, and Other Essays Toward a Philosophy of History* (New York: Norton, 1941, 1961), pp. 165–233.

15. The following articles make a case for the relevance of Freud's personal history to the structure of his thought: Arthur Efron, "Freud's Self-Analysis and the Nature of Psychoanalytic Criticism," *The International Review of Psychoanalysis,* 4 (1977), 253–80; Jim Swan, "*Mater* and Nannie: Freud's Two Mothers and the Discovery of the Oedipus Complex," *American Imago,* 31 (1974), 1–64; Patrick Mahony, "Friendship and Its Discontents," paper presented to the Canadian Psychoanalytic Society, Montreal, May 19, 1977. Freud's instrument of self-analysis, from the point of view of these critics, becomes a double-

edged sword, a manifestation of his genius for the articula-
tion of the structural principles of his own psyche, as well
as a measure of the necessary limitation of his method.
Murray Schwartz elucidates this point further in "Shakespeare through Contemporary Psychoanalysis." Juliet
Mitchell might be seen to treat this subject on a large scale
in *Psychoanalysis and Feminism* (New York: Pantheon,
1974), when she argues that the Oedipus complex acts as
a structural representation of the psychic organization of
patriarchal society.

16. Dorothy Dinnerstein, *The Mermaid and the Minotaur:
Sexual Arrangements and Human Malaise* (New York:
Harper & Row, 1976).

17. Julia Kristeva, who seems to accept the Lacanian explanation of the process of the child's induction into the
symbolic order in Western culture, presents the position
of women within this construct as one of agonized conflict
in the opening chapters of *About Chinese Women*, trans.
Anita Barrows (New York: Urizen Books, 1977). Sho-
shona Felman states the problem of defining a feminist
discourse within a masculinist ethic as follows: "If, in our
culture, the woman is by definition associated with madness, her problem is how to break out of this (cultural)
imposition of madness *without* taking up the critical and
therapeutic positions of reason: how to avoid speaking
both as *mad* and as *not mad*. The challenge facing the
woman today is nothing less than to 're-invent' language,
to *re-learn how to speak:* to speak not only against, but
outside of the specular phallocentric structure, to establish
a discourse the status of which would no longer be defined
by the phallacy of masculine meaning. An old saying would
thereby be given new life: today more than ever, changing
our minds—changing the mind—is a woman's preroga-
tive." "Women and Madness: The Critical Phallacy,"
Diacritics, 5, No. 4 (1975), 2–10.

18. This statement derives from remarks made by Gavatri
Spivak toward the end of a session at the 1977 MMLA
convention in Chicago in which she spoke of "the womb
as a tangible place of production," as the point of departure for a new discourse on femininity. She has suggested

that since the work on which this comment is based is not yet in print, I refer to my memory of her statements. I wish to apologize in advance for any error of understanding on my part of her position.

Sylvan Barnet

Othello on Stage and Screen

The earliest mention of a performance of *Othello*, in an account of 1604, reports only that the play was acted before James I at Whitehall Palace. Next come two references to performances in 1610, one telling us that it was acted at the Globe in April, the other telling us that it was acted in September at Oxford. The reference to the Oxford production is especially valuable, since it provides one of the very few glimpses we have of early seventeenth-century acting and of an audience's response to a performance. The relevant passage, in Latin, may be translated thus:

> In their tragedies they acted with appropriate decorum; in these they caused tears not only by their speaking, but also by their action. Indeed Desdemona, although greatly successful throughout, moved us especially when at last, lying on her bed, killed by her husband, she implored the pity of the spectators in her death with her face alone.

This may not seem like much, but it is more than we have for all but a few of Shakespeare's other plays, and it is especially valuable as a reminder that the Renaissance boy actors—a boy played Desdemona—were highly skilled performers.

There are only a few additional references to performances in the first half of the seventeenth century, but a very large number of rather general references to the play (as opposed to specific performances) allows us to conclude that the play must have been popular on the stage. From 1642 to 1660 the theaters were closed by act of Parliment, but when the theaters reopened in 1660, *Othello* was staged almost immediately. Samuel Pepys saw it in 1660:

> To the Cockpit to see *The Moor of Venice,* which was well done. [Nathaniel] Burt acted the Moor: by the same token, a very pretty lady that sat by me called out, to see Desdemona smothered.

He saw it again in 1669, this time with less pleasure:

> To the King's playhouse, and there in an upper box . . . did see *The Moor of Venice*: but ill acted in most parts; [Michael] Mohun which did a little surprise me not acting Iago's part by much so well as [Walter] Clun used to do . . . nor, indeed, Burt doing the Moor's so well as I once thought he did.

During this period, the great interpreter of the title role was Thomas Betterton, who performed it from 1684 to 1709. Although he was the leading Othello of the period and was much praised, the only informative contemporary account of his performance in the role tells us little more than that his

> aspect was serious, venerable, and majestic. . . . His voice was low and grumbling, though he could time it by an artful climax, which enforced attention. . . . He kept this passion under, and showed it most.

Betterton's successor as Othello was James Quin, who played the part from 1722 to 1751. Wearing a white wig and the white uniform (including white gloves) of a British officer, he was said to have presented an impressive appearance, but his acting was characterized as statuesque,

even stiff, lacking in tenderness, pathos, fire, and any
suggestion of inner pain. Quin was eclipsed in 1745 by
David Garrick, whose Othello was quite different: the
complaint now was that this Othello lacked dignity. The
accusation was not merely a glance at Garrick's relatively
short stature (he sought to compensate for his height by
adding a turban to the costume of an officer in the British
army), or even at his bold restoration of the fainting episode (IV.i.45), which had been cut by his predecessors.
Rather, it was directed at Garrick's violent gestures, which
suggested to one critic that Othello seemed afflicted with
St. Vitus dance. Garrick defended his interpretation by
arguing that Shakespeare

> had shown us white men jealous in other pieces, but
> that their jealousy had limits, and was not so terri-
> ble. . . . [In] Othello he had wished to paint that passion
> in all its violence, and that is why he chose an African
> in whose being circulated fire instead of blood, and
> whose true or imaginary character could excuse all
> boldness of expression and all exaggerations of passion.

Garrick's rival, Quin, was not convinced. Of Garrick's
Othello, Quin said: "Othello! . . . psha! no such thing.
There was a little black boy . . . fretting and fuming about
the stage; but I saw no Othello."

A reader can scarcely overlook the racism in these remarks, and something should be said about attitudes
toward Moors. There is no doubt that most Elizabethans
regarded Moors as vengeful—largely because they were
not Christians. That Moors were black—the color of the
devil—was thought to be a visible sign of their capacity
for endless evil. (In fact, Shakespeare specifies that Othello is a Christian, and this is only one of several ways in
which Othello departs from the stereotype.) Othello's
physical blackness, by the way, seems not to have been
doubted until the early nineteenth century. Certainly Quin
and Garrick played him in blackface, and presumably so
did their predecessor Betterton. And there is no doubt that

on the Elizabethan stage Othello was very black. The only contemporary illustration of a scene from Shakespeare shows another of Shakespeare's Moors, Aaron in *Titus Andronicus*, as having an inky complexion. But in the early nineteenth century one finds expressions of distinct discomfort at the thought that Othello is black rather than, say, bronzed, or (to use an even loftier metaphor) golden. Even the best critics were not exempt from the racist thinking of their times. Thus, in 1808 Charles Lamb, picking up Desdemona's assertion that she judged Othello by his mind rather than by his color, argued that although we can share her view when we read the play, we cannot do so when we see a black Othello on the stage:

> She sees Othello's color in his mind. But upon the stage, when the imagination is no longer the ruling faculty, but we are left to our poor unassisted senses, I appeal to every one that has seen Othello played, whether he did not, on the contrary, sink Othello's mind in his color; whether he did not find something extremely revolting in the courtship and wedded caresses of Othello and Desdemona, and whether the actual sight of the thing did not over-weigh all that beautiful compromise which we make in reading. . . .

At about the time that Lamb offered his comment on Othello, Lamb's friend Coleridge made some notes to the effect that Shakespeare could not possibly have thought of Othello as a black:

> Can we suppose [Shakespeare] so utterly ignorant as to make a barbarous *negro* plead royal birth? Were negroes then known but as slaves; on the contrary, were not the Moors the warriors? . . . No doubt Desdemona saw Othello's visage in his mind; yet, as we are constituted, and most surely as an English audience was disposed in the beginning of the seventeenth century, it would be something monstrous to conceive this beautiful Venetian girl falling in love with a veritable negro. It would argue a disproportionateness, a want of bal-

ance in Desdemona, which Shakespeare does not appear
to have in the least contemplated.

Given Coleridge's certainty that Othello could not possibly
have been black, it is well to reiterate that the Elizabethans
thought of Moors as black. True, there are a few references in Elizabethan literature to "tawny" Moors, but
there is no evidence that the Elizabethans distinguished
between tawny and black Moors, and in any case, if they
did, various passages in *Othello* indicate that the protagonist is surely a black Moor. Admittedly, most of the
references to Othello's Negroid features are made by
persons hostile to him—Roderigo calls him "the thick-
lips," for instance, and Iago speaks of him as "an old
black ram"—but Othello himself says that his name "is
now begrimed and black / As mine own face." Of course
"black" is sometimes used in the sense of brunette, but
there really cannot be any doubt that Othello is black in
the most obvious modern sense, and to call him tawny or
golden or bronzed, or to conceive of him as something of
an Arab chieftan, is to go against the text of the play.

When Spranger Barry, the actor who displaced Garrick
as Othello in the middle of the eighteenth century (he was
said to have not only the passion of Garrick but also the
majesty that in Quin was merely stiffness), the question
of color seems not to have come up, nor did it come up
when the role in effect belonged to John Philip Kemble,
the chief Othello at the turn of the eighteenth century (he
played his first Othello in 1785, his last in 1805). Kemble,
tall and stately, acted in what can be called a classic rather
than romantic manner, a style suited more to, say, Brutus
than to Othello. His interpretation of the role was criti-
cized for its superabundance of dignity and for its lack of
variety and fire, but not for its blackness. But when Edmund Kean played the role in 1814 he is said to have
used a light brown makeup in place of the usual burnt
cork. Oddly, there is some uncertainty about this—most
critics of the period did not comment on the novelty—but
putting aside the question of who made the change, and

exactly when, about this time the color changed. By 1827 Leman Thomas Rede's *The Road to the Stage* (a book on makeup) could report that "A tawny tinge is now the color used for the gallant Moor." Here it is evident that the makeup no longer uses burnt cork. Most of the Othellos of the rest of the century were tawny, their bronze skin suggesting that they were sons of the desert, but Henry Irving's Othello of 1881 was conspicuously dark (darker than his "bronze" Othello of 1876), and, as we shall see, in the twentieth century dark Othellos have been dominant, especially in our own generation, when American blacks have often played the part.

Putting aside the point that Kean's Othello was lighter than usual, it was exceptional for its power and its pathos. If Kemble is the paradigm of classical acting, Kean—passionate, even spasmodic—is the paradigm of romantic acting. Coleridge wrote: "Seeing [Kean] act was like reading Shakespeare by flashes of lightning." Another great romantic writer, William Hazlitt, at first found Kean too passionate. In the following passage Hazlitt complains that the fault in the performance is not in the color of Kean's face, or in Kean's relatively short stature:

> Othello was tall, but that is nothing; he was black, but that is nothing. But he was not fierce, and that is everything. It is only in the last agony of human suffering that he gives way to his rage and despair. . . . Mr. Kean is in general all passion, all energy, all relentless will. . . . He is too often in the highest key of passion, too uniformly on the verge of extravagance, too constantly on the rack.

Kean later moderated the passion, perhaps under Hazlitt's influence, but, curiously, Hazlitt regretted the change, remarking: "There is but one perfect way of playing Othello, and that was the way . . . he used to play it." Equally compelling is the tribute to Kean offered by the American actor Junius Brutus Booth, who in England in 1817–18 played Iago to Kean's Othello. Booth said that "Kean's

Othello smothered Desdemona and my Iago too." Kean's triumph in the role was undoubted, but in 1825, two weeks after he had been proved guilty of adultery, public opinion turned against him, denouncing the hypocrisy of an adulterer who dared to play the outraged husband lamenting his wife's infidelity. Still, he continued in the role, playing Othello almost to the day of his death. His last performance was in this role, in 1833, when he collapsed on the stage and died a few weeks later.

Other nineteenth-century actors have made their mark in the role—for instance William Macready (he sometimes played Iago against Kean's Othello) and Samuel Phelps—but here there is space to mention only four, Ira Aldridge, Edwin Booth, Tommaso Salvini, and Henry Irving. Aldridge, a black, was born in New York in 1807. As a very young man he determined to be an actor, but seeing no possibility of a career as an actor in America, he went to London in 1824 and never returned to the United States. At least one black actor, James Hewlett, had already played Othello in America, but that was with the all-black African Company, and Aldridge's ambition was to be accepted as an actor, not as a black actor, an ambition impossible to fulfill in the United States, where there were no interracial companies. He performed throughout the British Isles and also on the Continent, playing not only Othello but also (with white makeup) such roles as Richard III, Shylock, Hamlet, Macbeth, and Lear.

In America, Edwin Booth (son of Junius Brutus Booth) acted Othello almost annually from 1826 to 1871. From time to time he changed his performance, sometimes working in the violent style associated with Tommaso Salvini, hurling his Iago to the ground, but sometimes he played with restraint—occasionally he even omitted striking Desdemona at IV.i.240—and he was especially praised for his tender passion. Most critics, however, preferred his Iago, which seemed genial, sincere, and terrifyingly evil; he was widely regarded as the greatest Iago of the later nineteenth century. (Among the performers with

whom he alternated the roles of Othello and Iago were
Henry Irving and James O'Neill, Eugene O'Neill's father;
and he played Iago to Salvini's Othello.) Here is his advice on how to play Iago:

> Don't *act* the villain, don't *look* it or *speak* it (by
> scowling and growling, I mean), but *think* it all the
> time. Be genial, sometimes jovial, always gentlemanly.
> Quick in motion as in thought; lithe and sinuous as a
> snake. A certain bluffness (which my temperament does
> not afford) should be added to preserve the military
> flavor of the character; in this particular I fail utterly,
> my Iago lacks the soldierly quality.

Henry Irving played Othello only in 1876 and 1881.
Although he had already achieved success in the roles of
Hamlet, Macbeth, and Lear, his Othello did not find equal
favor. It was not especially violent, but it was said to lack
dignity (apparently there was much lifting up of hands
and shuffling of feet), and after the attempt in 1881 Irving
decided to drop the role. Still, some things about the 1881
performance should be mentioned. The makeup was very
black, the costume exotic (a white jeweled turban, an
amber robe), and the killing of Desdemona very solemn—
until Desdemona tried to escape, at which point he flung
her on the bed. The play ended with Othello's suicide, the
curtain descending as he fell at Gratiano's feet. Iago
(played by Booth) stood by, smiling malignantly.

By common consent the greatest Othello of the later
nineteenth century was Tommaso Salvini, who acted in
Italian—even when in England or the United States, with
the rest of the company speaking English. Some Victorians
regarded Salvini as too savage, too volcanic, too terrifying
to arouse pity—he seized Iago by the throat and hurled
him to the floor, and put his foot on Iago's neck, and of
course he did not hesitate to strike Desdemona—but most
audiences were deeply moved as well as terrified by his
performance. We are told that especially in the first three
acts, where some of the love play seemed almost to be

high comedy, his Othello was "delightful" and "delicate."
Still, the overall effect was that of enormous energy,
though not of mere barbarism. Henry James was among
Salvini's greatest admirers:

> It is impossible to imagine anything more living, more
> tragic, more suggestive of a tortured soul and of gener-
> ous, beneficent strength changed to a purpose of de-
> struction. With its tremendous force, it is magnificently
> quiet, and from beginning to end has not a touch of
> rant or crudity.

Actors of note who played Othello or Iago in the early
twentieth century include Johnston Forbes-Robertson,
Oscar Asche, and Beerbohm Tree, but none of these was
widely regarded as great. Indeed, the standard opinion is
that the twentieth century did not have a great Othello
until Paul Robeson's in 1943 or possibly even until
Olivier's in 1964. But Paul Robeson was not primarily an
actor. As a college student at Rutgers he distinguished
himself not in theatrics but in athletics (all-American end
in football in 1918, and letters in several varsity sports)
and in scholarship (Phi Beta Kappa). He next prepared
for a career in the law, taking a law degree at Columbia
University, but while at Columbia in 1921 he performed
in his first amateur production. He soon began to appear
in some professional productions, including *Showboat*,
where his singing of "Ol' Man River" led to a career as a
concert singer, especially of spirituals and work songs,
though he returned to the stage to play Othello in 1930
in England, in 1942 in Cambridge, Boston, and Princeton,
in 1943 in New York, and in 1959 at Stratford-upon-
Avon. Observers agree that the 1959 performance was
poor; Robeson had been weakened by an attack of bron-
chitis, his political beliefs had been shaken (earlier he had
praised Stalin, but now the crimes of the Stalin era were
evident), and, perhaps worst of all, the director's presence
was too strongly felt, for instance in a distracting fog that
supposedly was the result of the storm at Cyprus. Many

scenes were so dark that spectators could not see the actors' faces, and there seems no reason to doubt the accuracy of those reviewers who accused the director of obliterating the principal actors.

Robeson's first Othello—indeed, his first performance in a play by Shakespeare, in 1930—was much more enthusiastically received. The London *Morning Post* said: "There has been no Othello on our stage for forty years to compare with his dignity, simplicity, and true passion." But not all of the reviewers were entirely pleased. James Agate, the leading theater critic of the period, said that Robeson lacked the majesty that Shakespeare insists on early in the play, for instance in such lines as

> I fetch my life and being
> From men of royal siege, (I.ii.20–21)

and

> Were it my cue to fight, I should have known it
> Without a prompter, (I.ii.82–83)

and

> Keep up your bright swords, for the dew will
> rust them. (I.ii.58)

The majesty displayed in such passages, Agate said, tells us how Othello must behave when he puts down Cassio's drunken brawl, but according to Agate, Robeson (despite his height—six feet, three inches) lacked this majesty. Thus, when Robeson's Othello said "Silence that dreadful bell! It frights the isle / From her propriety" (II.iii.174–75), he showed personal annoyance rather than the "passion for decorum" (Agates' words) that the line reveals. Agate found Robeson best in the third and fourth acts, where he captured the jealousy of the part, but weak (lacking in dignity) in the last act, where he failed to perform the murder with a solemn sense of sacrifice.

Despite the reservations of Agate and others, there was

some talk of bringing the production to the United States,
but nothing came of it, doubtless because of uncertainty
about how American audiences (and perhaps performers?) would respond to a company that mixed whites and
blacks. In 1938 Margaret Webster again raised the topic,
but she was discouraged by the Americans with whom she
talked. It was acceptable for a black actor to kiss—and
later to smother—a white girl in England, but not in the
United States. Fortunately, however, Webster later persuaded the Theatre Guild to invite Robeson to do *Othello*
in the United States in 1942, if not on Broadway at least
as summer stock, with José Ferrer as Iago and Uta Hagen
as Desdemona. The production was enthusiastically received, but Robeson's concert commitments prevented it
from going to New York until the fall of 1943. When it
did open in New York, the reviews were highly favorable,
but some of them contained reservations about Robeson's
ability to speak blank verse and to catch the grandeur of
the role. In any case, the production was an enormous
success, running for 296 continuous performances. The
previous record for a New York *Othello* had been 57.

Robeson inevitably was asked to discuss his conception
of the role; equally inevitably, he said different things at
different times, and perhaps sometimes said what reporters
wanted to hear—or perhaps the reporters heard only what
they wanted to hear. Sometimes he was reported as saying
that the matter of color is secondary, but on other occasions he is reported as saying: "The problem [of *Othello*]
is the problem of my own people. It is a tragedy of racial
conflict, a tragedy of honor, rather than of jealousy."

Until Robeson, black actors in the United States were
in effect limited to performing in all-black companies.
With Robeson, a black actor played Othello with an otherwise white company. His appearance as Othello in 1943
was an important anticipation of the gains black actors
were to make in later decades. Earle Hyman, Moses Gunn,
Paul Winfield, William Marshall, and James Earl Jones
are among the black actors who have played impressive
Othellos in mixed-race companies. More important, how-

ever, as the careers of these actors show, a black may now also play a role other than Othello, as Ira Aldridge did a hundred and fifty years ago, though he had to cross the Atlantic to do it.

Before looking at Laurence Olivier's Othello in 1964, mention should be made of Olivier's Iago in a production of 1937, directed by Tyrone Guthhrie at the Old Vic. Olivier and Guthrie talked to Ernest Jones, friend of Sigmund Freud, and came away with the idea that Iago's hatred for Othello was in fact based on a subconscious love for Othello. That Iago protests "I hate the Moor" means nothing, for he is unaware of his true emotions. Ralph Richardson was Othello in this production, but Guthrie and Olivier decided not to shock him (remember, this was 1937) by any such unconventional idea, and so, the story goes, Richardson could never quite understand what Olivier was making out of the role. (What Olivier apparently made out of it was something like this: Iago is manic because he cannot face his true feelings.) The critics, like Richardson and the general public, were in the dark, and the production was poorly reviewed. Guthrie himself later called the production "a ghastly, boring hash," and Olivier has said that he no longer subscribes to Jones's interpretation.

In 1964 Olivier played Othello, with Frank Finlay as Iago, and Maggie Smith as Desdemona, in a production directed by John Dexter. (This production was later filmed, and most of what is true of the stage production is true also of the film.) Far from suggesting that Othello was some sort of desert chief, Olivier emphasized the Negroid aspects, or at least the white man's stock ideas of Negroid aspects. Thus, Othello's skin was very dark, his lips were red and sensuous, and his lilting voice had something of a West Indian accent. He rolled his eyes a good deal, and he walked (bare-footed and adorned with ankle bracelets) with a sensuous sway. More important (worse, some viewers felt), was the idea behind this Othello, which was indebted to some thoughts by T. S. Eliot and F. R. Leavis. For Eliot (in an essay called "Shakespeare and the Stoicism of Seneca," first published in 1927) and for Leavis (in an essay first published in a journal in 1937 but more readily available, in reprinted form, in Leavis's *The Common Pursuit*), Othello is not so much a heroic figure —the noble Moor who gains our sympathy despite the terrible deed he performs—as a fatuous simpleton, a man given to egotistical self-dramatizing. The playbill included some passages from Leavis's essay, which the director in effect summarized when he told the cast that

> Othello is a pompous, word-spinning, arrogant black general. . . . The important thing is not to accept him at his own valuation. . . . He isn't just a righteous man who's been wronged. He's a man too proud to think he could ever be capable of anything as base as jealousy. When he learns he *can* be jealous, his character changes. The knowledge destroys him, and he goes beserk.

Thus, Olivier delivered "Farewell the tranquil mind" (III.iii.345)—a speech customarily delivered reflectively —in a frenzy. It's probably fair to say that the gist of the idea underlying this production is fairly old: Othello is a barbarian with a thin veneer of civilization. Thus, the early speeches were delivered with easy confidence because Othello had no understanding of how simple and how volatile he really was. The change from civilized man to barbarian was marked by Othello tearing off a crucifix he wore, an effective enough bit of business but one at odds with two aspects of the end of Shakespeare's play: Othello (who just before he kills Desdemona is careful to urge her to make her peace with God; "I would not kill thy soul") murders Desdemona partly because he believes she has been false to the highest ideals. Second, when he comes to understand the horror of his action he executes justice upon himself. Still, although much in the conception could be faulted, it was widely agreed that Olivier's acting was a triumph—a triumph won, among other things, at the expense of an unprepossessing Iago and a negligible Desdemona.

The film with Olivier (1965), directed by Stuart Burge, was made in a sound studio, using sets that were essentially those of the stage production—even for scenes set out-of-doors—but it was not simply a filmed version of what a spectator sitting in the third row center would have seen. For instance, because close-ups are used for all of Iago's soliloquies, Iago becomes considerably more prominent in the film than he was on the stage.

Olivier said that the backgrounds in the film were minimal because he was concerned with "offering as little visual distraction as possible from the intentions of Shakespeare—or our performance of them." For a film of the opposite sort, a film that does not hesitate to introduce impressive visual effects not specified in the text, one should look at Orson Welles's *Othello*, a black and white film begun in 1951 and completed and released in 1955, with Welles in the title role. The film was shot on location, chiefly in Morocco and Venice, but what especially strikes a viewer is not that the camera gives us a strong sense of the real world, but that the camera leads us into a strange, shadowy world of unfamiliar and puzzling appearance. The film begins with Welles reading a passage from Shakespeare's source while we see a shot of the face of the dead Othello. The camera rises above the bier, which is carried by pallbearers, and we then see Desdemona's body, also being borne to the grave. We see the two funeral processions converge, and then we see Iago, in chains, thrust into a cage and hoisted above the crowd. From above—Iago's viewpoint—we look down on the bodies of Othello and Desdemona. All of this is presented before we see the credits for the film. The film ends with a dissolve from the dying Othello to a shot of the funeral procession and then to shots of the fortress at Cyprus, the cage, and Venetian buildings and ships. Between this highly cinematic beginning and ending, other liberties are taken with the text. The murder of Roderigo, for instance, is set in a steamy bathhouse. Welles had intended to shoot the scene in a street, but because he had run out of money and didn't have costumes, he set it in a steam bath, where a few towels were all the clothing that was needed. In short, Welles's *Othello* is not for the Shakespeare purist (too much is cut and too much is added), but it is imaginative and it often works. Admirers will want to see also *Filming "Othello,"* a film memoir (1978) in which Welles and others discuss the work.

The BBC television version of *Othello,* directed by Jonathan Miller and released in 1981, is, like Olivier's film, somewhat in the Eliot-Leavis tradition. In the introduction to the printed text of the BBC version, Miller says that the play does not set forth "the spectacle of a person of grandeur falling." Rather,

> what's interesting is that it's not the fall of the great but the disintegration of the ordinary, of the representative character. It's the very ordinariness of Othello that makes the story intolerable.

Miller is insistent, too, that the play is not about race. "I do not see the play as being about color but as being about jealousy—which is something we are all vulnerable to." In line with this emphasis on the ordinary, Othello (Anthony Hopkins) is relatively unheroic, though he is scarcely as commonplace as Miller suggests, since he is full of energy and rage. More successful is Iago (Bob Hoskins), a bulletheaded hood who delights in Othello's anguish. The sets, in order to reduce any sense of heroism or romance, are emphatically domestic; no effort was made to take advantage of the camera's ability to record expansive space. Interestingly, however, the domestic images on the screen are by no means ordinary; notably beautiful, they often remind us of Vermeer.

During the course of this survey it has been easy to notice racist implications in the remarks of certain actors and critics. And it was racism, of course, that kept blacks from acting in *Othello* (and in other plays) along with whites. One point that has not been raised till now is this: Does it matter if a black plays Othello? When Robeson played the part, some theatergoers found that the play made more sense than ever before, partly because Robeson (whatever his limitations as an actor) was a black. Others found that it was distracting for a black to play the part; it brought into the world of *Othello* irrelevant issues of twentieth-century America. Jonathan Miller, holding the second position, puts it thus:

> When a black actor does the part, it offsets the play, puts it out of balance. It makes it a play about blackness, which it is not. . . . The trouble is, the play was hijacked for political purposes.

Many things can be said against this view, for instance that when the white actor Olivier played Othello he expended so much energy impersonating a black that a spectator was far more conscious of the performer's blackness than one is of, say, James Earl Jones's. In any case, Miller has not said the last word on this topic, which will continue to be debated.

Bibliographic note: A list of all of the sources used in preparing this essay would almost equal the length of the essay, but readers who wish to study the stage history of *Othello* further may want some suggestions. Obviously newspapers and weekly news magazines are good sources for recent productions; *Shakespeare Quarterly* covers productions throughout the world, and *Shakespeare Survey* includes an annual essay on some English productions. Biographies of actors and directors are also obvious places to begin.

For a survey of *Othello* on the stage, see Marvin Rosenberg, *The Masks of "Othello"* (1961); for a brief study of five recent productions (including Robeson in 1943, Olivier in 1964, and the BBC television version of 1981), see Martin L. Wine, *"Othello": Text and Performance* (1984). Errol Hill's *Shakespeare in Sable* (1984), a history of black actors of Shakespeare, contains much information about *Othello*. Other items especially relevant to the productions discussed above include: Arthur Colby Sprague, *Shakespearian Players and Performances* (1953), for Kean's Othello and Edwin Booth's Iago; Daniel J. Watermeier, "Edwin Booth's Iago," *Theatre History Studies* 6 (1986), 32–55; Kenneth Tynan, ed., *"Othello" by William Shakespeare: The National Theatre Production* (1966), on Olivier; *The BBC TV Shakespeare: "Othello"* (1981), on the version directed by Jonathan Miller. On Robeson, see Susan Spector, "Margaret Webster's *Othello*," *Theatre History Studies* 6 (1986), 93–108. For film versions, see Jack J. Jorgens, *Shakespeare on Film* (1977), and, for Welles's film only, see Micheal MacLiammoir, *Put Money in Thy Purse* (1952).

Suggested References

The number of possible references is vast and grows alarmingly. (The *Shakespeare Quarterly* devotes one issue each year to a list of the previous year's work, and *Shakespeare Survey*—an annual publication—includes a substantial review of recent scholarship, as well as an occasional essay surveying a few decades of scholarship on a chosen topic.) Though no works are indispensable, those listed below have been found especially helpful.

1. SHAKESPEARE'S TIMES

Byrne, M. St. Clare. *Elizabethan Life in Town and Country.* Rev. ed. New York: Barnes & Noble, 1961. Chapters on manners, beliefs, education, etc., with illustrations.

Joseph, B. L. *Shakespeare's Eden: The Commonwealth of England, 1558–1629.* New York: Barnes & Noble, 1971. An account of the social, political, economic, and cultural life of England.

Schoenbaum, S. *Shakespeare: The Globe and the World.* New York: Oxford University Press, 1979. A readable, handsomely illustrated book on the world of Elizabethans.

Shakespeare's England. 2 vols. London: Oxford University Press, 1916. A large collection of scholarly essays on a wide variety of topics (e.g., astrology, costume, gardening, horsemanship), with special attention to Shakespeare's references to these topics.

Stone, Lawrence. *The Crisis of the Aristocracy, 1558–1641,* abridged edition. London: Oxford University Press, 1967.

2. SHAKESPEARE

Barnet, Sylvan. *A Short Guide to Shakespeare.* New York: Harcourt Brace Jovanovich, 1974. An introduction to all of the works and to the dramatic traditions behind them.

Bentley, Gerald E. *Shakespeare: A Biographical Handbook.* New Haven, Conn.: Yale University Press, 1961. The facts about Shakespeare, with virtually no conjecture intermingled.

Bush, Geoffrey. *Shakespeare and the Natural Condition.* Cambridge, Mass.: Harvard University Press, 1956. A short, sensitive account of Shakespeare's view of "Nature," touching most of the works.

Chambers, E. K. *William Shakespeare: A Study of Facts and Problems.* 2 vols. London: Oxford University Press, 1930. An invaluable, detailed reference work; not for the casual reader.

Chute, Marchette. *Shakespeare of London.* New York: Dutton, 1949. A readable biography fused with portraits of Stratford and London life.

Clemen, Wolfgang H. *The Development of Shakespeare's Imagery.* Cambridge, Mass.: Harvard University Press, 1951. (Originally published in German, 1936.) A temperate account of a subject often abused.

Granville-Barker, Harley. *Prefaces to Shakespeare.* 2 vols. Princeton, N.J.: Princeton University Press, 1946–47. Essays on ten plays by a scholarly man of the theater.

Harbage, Alfred. *As They Liked it.* New York: Macmillan, 1947. A long, sensitive essay on Shakespeare, morality, and the audience's expectations.

Kernan, Alvin B., ed. *Modern Shakespearean Criticism: Essays on Style, Dramaturgy, and the Major Plays.* New York: Harcourt Brace Jovanovich, 1970. A collection of major formalist criticism.

——. "The Plays and the Playwrights." In *The Revels*

History of Drama in English, general editors Clifford Leech and T. W. Craik. Vol. III. London: Methuen, 1975. A book-length essay surveying Elizabethan drama with substantial discussions of Shakespeare's plays.

Schoenbaum, S. *Shakespeare's Lives.* Oxford: Clarendon Press, 1970. A review of the evidence, and an examination of many biographies, including those by Baconians and other heretics.

————. *William Shakespeare: A Compact Documentary Life.* New York: Oxford University Press, 1977. A readable presentation of all that the documents tell us about Shakespeare.

Traversi, D. A. *An Approach to Shakespeare.* 3rd rev. ed. 2 vols. New York: Doubleday, 1968–69. An analysis of the plays beginning with words, images, and themes, rather than with characters.

Van Doren, Mark. *Shakespeare.* New York: Holt, 1939. Brief, perceptive readings of all of the plays.

3. SHAKESPEARE'S THEATER

Beckerman, Bernard. *Shakespeare at the Globe, 1599–1609.* New York: Macmillan, 1962. On the playhouse and on Elizabethan dramaturgy, acting, and staging.

Chambers, E. K. *The Elizabethan Stage.* 4 vols. New York: Oxford University Press, 1945. A major reference work on theaters, theatrical companies, and staging at court.

Cook, Ann Jennalie. *The Privileged Playgoers of Shakespeare's London, 1576–1642.* Princeton, N.J.: Princeton University Press, 1981. Sees Shakespeare's audience as more middle-class and more intellectual than Harbage (below) does.

Gurr, Andrew. *The Shakespearean Stage: 1574–1642.* 2d edition. Cambridge: Cambridge University Press, 1981. On the acting companies, the actors, the playhouses, the stages, and the audiences.

Harbage, Alfred. *Shakespeare's Audience*. New York: Columbia University Press, 1941. A study of the size and nature of the theatrical public, emphasizing its representativeness.

Hodges, C. Walter. *The Globe Restored*. London: Ernest Benn, 1953. A well-illustrated and readable attempt to reconstruct the Globe Theatre.

Hosley, Richard. "The Playhouses." In *The Revels History of Drama in English,* general editors Clifford Leech and T. W. Craik. Vol. III. London: Methuen, 1975. An essay of one hundred pages on the physical aspects of the playhouses.

Kernodle, George R. *From Art to Theatre: Form and Convention in the Renaissance*. Chicago: University of Chicago Press, 1944. Pioneering and stimulating work on the symbolic and cultural meanings of theater construction.

Nagler, A. M. *Shakespeare's Stage*. Trans. Ralph Manheim. New Haven, Conn.: Yale University Press, 1958. A very brief introduction to the physical aspects of the playhouse.

Slater, Ann Pasternak. *Shakespeare the Director*. Totowa, N.J.: Barnes & Noble, 1982. An analysis of theatrical effects (e.g., kissing, kneeling) in stage directions and dialogue.

Thomson, Peter. *Shakespeare's Theatre*. London: Routledge and Kegan Paul, 1983. A discussion of how plays were staged in Shakespeare's time.

4. MISCELLANEOUS REFERENCE WORKS

Abbott, E. A. *A Shakespearean Grammar*. New Edition. New York: Macmillan, 1877. An examination of differences between Elizabethan and modern grammar.

Bevington, David. *Shakespeare*. Arlington Heights, Ill.: A. H. M. Publishing, 1978. A short guide to hundreds of important writings on the works.